JCMS Annual Review
of the European Union
in 2019

T0340617

Edited by

Theofanis Exadaktylos,
Roberta Guerrina
and
Emanuele Massetti

General Editors: Toni Haastrup and Richard Whitman

WILEY

CONTENTS

JCMS 2020 Volume 58. Annual Review pp. 5–12   DOI: 10.1111/jcms.13105

Calm before the Storm? 2019 in Perspective

THEOFANIS EXADAKTYLOS,[1] ROBERTA GUERRINA[2] and EMANUELE MASSETTI[3]
[1]University of Surrey, Guildford [2]University of Bristol, Bristol [3]University of Trento, Trento

At the end of our 2018 Annual Review editorial we reflected on a tough year for the EU, arguing that it was sailing through troubled waters into an unknown direction (Exadaktylos *et al.,* 2019). The waves of populism and right-wing extremism were sweeping across Europe, the negotiations around Brexit were a political drama not only at the European but also at the British level, and EU leaders were looking to re-infuse trust in the euro, EU institutions and community processes and breathe new life into the vision of integration.

It now feels as if 2019 was a fairly calm and stable year, given that we are reflecting on it in the middle of 2020 and in the context of a global pandemic. This is an interesting observation, as it was not the overwhelming sense we had as we lived through the events or even looked back on some of the challenges facing the EU and its Member States at the end of 2019. The appointment of a new European Commission, following the election of a new European Parliament (EP) presented themselves as opportunities for institutional renewal. However, even though political, social and economic turbulence endured in some Member States, the EP elections seemed to put a break on what had previously felt like an inevitable populist and eurosceptic advance. The return to relevance of the European Greens is also reflected in a shift in the priorities of the European public towards substantial issues, namely, climate change. Even this turn was not enough to block or reverse the nationalist and ethnocentric tendencies emerging in 2018. The tensions between parties pushing for European reform and those seeking to dismantle the European project has become a marker for a deeper culture war between progressive and conservative forces. At the time, this conflict felt it was simply entrenching trends we have covered in previous issues of the Annual Review, especially in the past two years, not least the fact that Brexit had normalized the rhetoric of disintegration. Looking at 2019 from the vantage point of 2020, we know now that 2019 was the year in which the EU was actually able to take a breath before the large storm on the horizon arrived. As EU institutions looked at 2020 with some optimism about the potential for a renewed Union a public health crisis was looming. The question is whether 2019 provided sufficient breathing space to tackle head on the economic and societal challenges brought about by Covid-19. In this context, had the foundations of integration and cooperation been sufficiently strengthened last year to allow the EU to endure the new crisis emerging in the horizon already by January 2020, and therefore safeguard the future of European integration?

In 2019 the EU was afforded a year of reflection and coming together in search for its unitary voice and sufficient time (much needed, as it turns out) to consider its position, identity and vision not only among its own citizens and member state governments but also internationally. We did not know in 2019 how important these reflections were going to be, given the health, social, political and economic challenges that would be facing the

Union and is Member States in 2020. This issue of the Annual Review assesses and critically reflects on how effective the EU was in using the breathing space it had been afforded in 2019.

It is tempting just to look forward to what we know now was on the horizon. However, it is equally important to understand the impact of historical trends and trajectories. It is worth remembering a number of key anniversaries of events that shaped the outlook of the EU and its Member States. In 2019 we marked 30 years from the end of the Cold War and the fall of the Berlin Wall in 1989. This critical moment was not just geo-strategically significant in tearing down artificial barriers to European cooperation, it also marked the beginning of the Eastern Enlargement of the EU. It was the beginning of a process through which the Eastern Bloc reconnected with its Western counterparts away from the Russian sphere of influence. In addition, this last year also marked 20 years of the euro (1999) and 15 years of the largest enlargement in the history of the EU (2004) with ten new Member States, the majority of them from Eastern Europe. Each of these anniversaries provides scholars, politicians and practitioners an opportunity to reflect on how the EU faced those challenges and, in so doing, reshaped and reaffirmed the direction of European integration.

It is worth starting our review of 2019 by revisiting some of the key developments at the European level. The influx of new personalities in the European Commission and EP is probably one of the defining institutional moments of the year. A pragmatic and identity-focused European Commission was faced with a EP that was politically more fragmented than before with an increased presence of populist anti-European political formations. This juxtaposition between and demographic composition of two of the pivotal EU decision-making bodies thus set up a new set of dynamics that will unfold in future years. The appointment of the first woman as President of the European Commission is symbolically important, as the EU has historically sought to position itself as a gender actor in internal and external affairs. Perhaps more significantly, Ursula von der Leyen came in with a vision to revive the Commission, put European identity at its core, create an environment of inclusion, and a common direction.

It is against the backdrop of institutional renewal that in June 2019 the European Council adopted the new Strategic Agenda 2019–24 (Blockmans et al., 2019). The focus of the agenda is on future-proofing the Union by addressing some of its most urgent priorities: (1) closing the gap between European institutions and the citizens of Europe; (2) building economic resilience; (3) taking action on climate change; (4) redefining the role and position of the EU in world (European Council, 2019). In a note of optimism, Maurice and Menneteau (2019) see this as the moment in which the EU moved from crisis management to addressing key challenges. More cautiously, Thieme and Galariotis (2020) do not see this strategy as providing the necessary foundations for the EU and its Member States to confront the many crises it continues to face.

This new strategy seeks to mitigate citizens' concerns about the migration crisis. Strengthening external borders and Schengen thus take priority, and are positioned alongside protection of democratic systems, EU values and the rule of law. Migration policy thus becomes a vehicle for centring discussions about European identity. This has significant implications in relation to social inclusion and social justice that are discussed in some detail by Solanke's contribution to this issue. The second priority is securing the position of the European economy, in which 'economic and social convergence between

Member States is underlined, no longer as a means by which to get lastingly out of the crisis, but as an instrument to ensure Europe's in the global stage' (Maurice and Menneteau, 2019, p. 3). These are also some of the issues touched on by Crespy and, Katsanidou and Lefkofridi in their contributions in this issue. What is now clear is just how important this work was going to be for preparing the EU for the storm of 2020.

The third priority focuses on climate change and action. Linking the impact of climate change to socioeconomic inequalities, the strategy sets out an ambition for a socially and economic inclusive model. Perhaps what is missing from the strategy is a detailed plan of action. Allwood's contribution in this issue examines the EU's approach to climate change and social justice as a platform for both gender and climate mainstreaming. Finally, the strategy document reasserts the EU's ambition to be a world leader. In a way this document seeks to confirm the EU's role in the global politics, thus preparing to be a strong bloc without the UK. This is something to which we will return, thanks to the analysis by Schumacher reflecting on the European Neighbourhood in the context of EU external affairs.

Reflecting on the impact of 2019 on the EU's future, the Annual Review lecture by Thomas Christiansen (2020) examines the ability of the EU to manage the various crises it has had to face over the last ten years. For Christiansen the ability of European institutions to adapt has been the key to their success in managing the various crises. Beyond the rise of euroscepticism and the challenge posed by populism, Christiansen urges us to think about shifting from the pursuit of a liberal approach to trade to one that favours geo-strategic considerations. Europe's economic power thus becomes more important than ever, particularly as von der Leyen is looking to develop the Commission's geopolitical role.

Looking at the defining topics for 2019, we identify three broad themes. The first, as noted earlier, is the change in institutional politics initiated by the appointment of a new European Commission and the outcome of the EP elections. The second is the political trends and trajectories, including the continued challenge posed by the ascendency of populist parties following austerity policies in Member States and the return of nationalism. Finally, the third theme encompasses Europe's place in the world: 2019 is the year when Europe started to face up to some of the challenges arising from climate change and social inequalities, as well as the model it provided to the near abroad for democracy.

Looking at the renewal of European institutions, the contribution by Abels and Mushaben examines the appointment of the first woman President of the European Commission as a potentially key moment for the development of a more inclusive Europe. Their analysis points to ongoing discussions about leadership at the European and member-state level as a way to bridge the gap between citizens and institutions. Gattermann's analysis of the media coverage of the EP election also notes the absence of a European public sphere. The introduction of the *Spitzenkandidaten* procedure in 2014 was supposed to herald a new era in which the Commission would become more closely connected to citizens. Its suspension for the election of Ursula von der Leyen is thus significant. Gattermann points to the failure of the media to engage with the candidates and thus 'bring the election' closer to the citizens of Europe. The continued focus on domestic issues in media coverage of EU news further undermined the development of a European public sphere and concentrated political identities at the national level. Moreover, we could also add that failing to underscore the importance of von den Leyen's election in terms of symbolic representation also serves to downplay her focus on gender-sensitive representation in her new Commission.

The restructuring of the Commission's portfolio that von der Leyen undertook points to an increased awareness of the need to acknowledge the limitations of European integration to capture the citizens' imagination and speak to the politics of identity (Duff, 2019; von der Leyen, 2019). This gap is all the more evident in the results of the EP election. Gattermann's analysis of the personalization of European politics in the EP election over the last 20 years is particularly important in this context. Her analysis finds that this process has not successfully created a European imaginary or augmented the development of a European public sphere. Rather, it is interesting that where there has been coverage of European-level issues, it has focused on anti-European and anti-establishment parties and candidates. This analysis thus raises important questions for how pathways for the activation and mobilization of the European polity, which will have increasing resonance for the future of the Union in years to come. The 2019 EP elections thus take on a significance that perhaps no observer could have been entirely aware of at the time.

Ahead of the May 2019 EP elections, many pundits predicted that right-wing populist parties would come to dominate the EP with significant repercussions for inter- and intra-institutional politics. It is this challenge from the right, and where the results matched the predictions, that Stockemer and Amengay's contribution focuses on. Their detailed overview of the rise of right-wing populism from the fringes into mainstream political movements provides important insights about the consolidation of nationalism across Europe. The absence of a meaningful European public sphere allows national populists to frame key messages on the relationship between Member States and the EU, and in so doing they can undermine what is already a thin identity (Medrano, 2009).

In a nutshell, the 2019 EP election demonstrated the reach of anti-establishment parties across Europe. The results also highlighted the crystallization of socio-political cleavages among the European electorate. The 2019 Annual Review examines in detail three stories of the European elections in key Member States, each with its own set of peculiarities and dynamics, showing the diverse and fractured nature of the European electorate. In the case of Italy the story of the European elections revolves around the almost inevitable rise of populist right-wing parties. Jones and Matthijs examine Lega's recipe for success in this election and the impact of the results on national politics. Although Italy's trajectory towards euroscepticism has been widely noted (Maggini and Chiaramonte, 2019), the results of this election demonstrates the Italian electorate's lack of trust in traditional political institutions and its shift to the radical right. Jones and Matthijs examine the tenor and focus of the campaign. Primarily concerned with national issues, it essentially provided a platform for Lega to channel growing dissatisfaction amongst the electorate.

Conversely, in France the prospect of significant populist gains led to a public discussion about the very nature of European integration as a political and economic project. Looking at the EP elections from a French perspective, Goodliffe's contribution finds that although this opened up a space for public debate, it also polarized the polity. The 2019 EP elections are therefore likely to have a significant impact at both the national and European level, particularly in relation to Macron's ambition for a renewed European agreement on the future of the Union.

Finally, the story in Germany is interesting as it stands apart from France and Italy in so far as the EP elections resulted in the return to relevance of the Green party and the displacement of traditional support for both the Christian Democratic Party (CDU/CSU) and the Social Democratic Party (SPD). Berning and Ziller in their contribution examine the social and political implications of this result for Germany. Specifically, 2019 marked a shift in political salience from issues relating to migration and security to that of climate change. Their analysis, however, points to a divided electorate in Germany where gains were recorded at the polar opposites of the political spectrum. What is clear from this brief overview is that despite the rise of the Greens in Germany, the defining trend of this election comes from the radical right.

Many of the right-wing populist and nativist parties have been emboldened by the 2019 EP election, becoming a sizeable bloc within the EP. Therefore, the likelihood of the Parliament becoming a theatre for political posturing is high. Given the economic and social crisis emerging from the current pandemic, European institutions and Member States cannot predict the impact of political populism coming from the populist right. Nonetheless, we should note that so far, the pandemic has favoured mainstream political parties across Europe and has uncovered the emptiness of populist promises as people look up to the EU for solutions (also in the form of the EU recovery fund from the impact of the pandemic) (see for example, comments by Exadaktylos [2020] and De Vries [2020]).

Finally, we should note that the 2019 EP elections were the last ones for British Members of the European Parliament. The UK had to postpone its departure from the EU, and as still a Member State, it had to hold an EP election by default. In her contribution, Vasilopoulou notes that this unexpected election was the result of a stalemate over the EU Withdrawal Bill in the UK parliament. The 2019 EP election in Britain was largely focused on British issues and residual fault-lines from unresolved Brexit debates. Hence, unsurprisingly Brexit dominated public discourse. Leading the Leave campaign, Nigel Farage created a new short-lived political group, the Brexit Party, which took the largest share of seats by a single party in the EP, although the pro-European parties in Britain achieved the largest combined share of the votes by a small margin. Vasilopoulou suggests that this EP election in Britain showed the impact of ongoing cleavages in the country and the growing dissatisfaction with traditional parties (namely, Labour and the Conservatives).

It therefore seems an opportune moment to reflect on the EU's handling of some the key political trends and challenges that it faced during 2019. As outlined above, the broad trends we identify highlight some of the challenges faced by the Union and its Members into 2020. They point to the undercurrent of 'crisis management' that has defined European politics for the last decade. What we know now is that 2019 was not going to resolve these crises, but instead it was going to lay the foundations for the EU to be able to handle its biggest crisis yet; a crisis which will come to define every aspect of social, political and economic relations in 2020: the impact of the global pandemic.

Understanding the steady advance of right-wing populism evident in the EP elections, although it was less offensive than predicted, requires a holistic assessment of the relationship between the EU and its Member States, as well as its citizens. The first port of call must be the impact of the financial crisis on the European psyche. As Crespy and, Katsanidou and Lefkofridi remind us in their contributions to the Annual Review, 2019 marks ten years of the onset of Greek crisis, which threatened to destabilise the whole of the European monetary and financial architecture. The causes and effects of this crisis have also been widely discussed in previous annual reviews (De Grauwe and Ji, 2019; Verdun, 2018). Much of this body of work has centred on the functioning of economic and monetary union and the political economy of the euro (Hodson and Quaglia, 2009). The introduction of the troika and the imposition of the austerity measures on Greece highlighted some of the rising tensions in European institutions. Reflecting on these issues in the Annual Review of 2015, Featherstone (2016) pointed out that the European financial crisis exposed the tension between conditionality, instrumentalism and legitimacy. It is this tension between European institutions and public opinion, particularly in the worst affected by austerity countries, that has been seen as the trigger for a rise in populism across Europe (Vasilopoulou *et al.,* 2014; Halikiopoulou, 2018).

On the basis of these observations, Crespy's article this year outlines the impact of the EU's austeritarianism on socioeconomic cleavages in Europe. She explains the link between growing inequalities and the EU's slow response in moving away from the recipe of austerity and mitigating the mounting polarization of European politics. Mostly importantly, she discusses the longer term legacies of Europe's great recession in conjunction with the challenges poses towards the new European Commission. On a similar trajectory, but looking specifically at the evolution of the Greek crisis, Katsanidou and Lefkofridi in their contribution draw lessons from the ten years since the Greek crisis began, in terms of political tensions, the economic and social erosion and the overhauling of the Greek political system on the road to recovery. Given that the existing literature on the Greek crisis focuses on 2009 as a critical juncture for the rise of populism and far-right nationalism beyond Greece and across Europe, they ask if Greece has finally found a new balance and a new role to play in the EU. Their analysis follows an argument similar to that of Cavaghan and O'Dwyer (2018), whose contribution in the 2017 Annual Review provided a critical assessment of the EU's pathway out of the crisis and the way the EU ignored the deeply gendered and racialized effects of the austerity politics.

The contributions by Crespy and, Katsanidou and Lefkofridi remind us of the centrality of citizens in the process of integration. Failing to engage with the electorate had deep implications for European democracy, as is evident in the downgrading of the quality of democracy in central and eastern Europe. In her contribution in this year's Annual Review Solska investigates the claims that Poland and Hungary are undergoing a process of democratic backsliding and assesses the processes that have led to the consolidation of authoritarian-leaning regimes. This piece not only points to their difficult relationship with the EU institutions, namely the European Commission, but also the inability of the opposition to launch a sustained counter-argument against the ruling parties in Poland and Hungary in conjunction with tension regarding the lack of a common understanding of European values. The processes of inclusion and belonging within a common idea of Europe are significant in so far as they define the boundaries of the 'other' both within and on Europe's external borders. In her contribution, Solanke makes detailed assessment of the Zambrano case in the context of Brexit, driving home the issue of the racialized nature of European citizenship and its impact on minority ethnic groups across Europe. What is clear is that European institutions have yet to develop a European ideal that bridges socioeconomic cleavages. This contribution is an important prelude to understanding the European reaction to current transnational social movements, such as Black Lives Matter, and how the European public absorbs debates that originate abroad within their domestic contexts.

The question is thus starting to emerge is whether it is in its external affairs that the EU has been projecting a more cohesive than before identity. The two contributions to this year's Annual Review by Schumacher and Allwood, respectively, examine the EU's role as a global leader. In his overview of EU external relations however, Schumacher finds little optimism for the EU's relationship with its eastern and southern neighbours or for the coherence of the EU's approach towards the near abroad. Pointing to the new European strategy mentioned earlier in this editorial, Schumacher finds that the EU has yet to become effective in promoting norm diffusion across the European Neighbourhood. Similarly, in her analysis of EU climate action, Allwood identifies a number of missed opportunities amidst growing political pressure to deal with the challenge of climate change. Just as in the context of the European Neighbourhood, on the issue of climate change the EU seeks to project an image as a global actor and norm entrepreneur. However, these efforts are undermined by creating silos around European values and by the pursuit of economic priorities over social justice and inclusion.

The key question for us now is whether 2019 prepared the EU for 2020. In his Annual Review lecture, Christiansen (2020) reflects on the resilience of European institutions. The project of European integration will undoubtedly have to find new ways to deal with the challenges posed by populist parties and the growth in citizens' satisfaction or disengagement with the project. Christiansen finds optimism in EU institutions' response to the key trends and challenges of 2019. For him, what is clear is that, rather than being displaced, the EU is becoming more relevant than ever.

Looking back at our analysis of 2019 it is clear that the EU and its Members are preparing themselves for a potential no-deal Brexit. Positioning the EU as a global leader is intended to maximize the political and economic reach of the bloc, possibly at the expense of a newly 'independent' UK. It may well be the case that by keeping the EU's preparations for crisis response on the agenda, Brexit has provided a platform for the bloc to deal with the much bigger crisis that was looming at the end of 2019. We will be able to assess the true impact of this year only when we can look back at the achievements and missed opportunities of the EU through the lenses of the coronavirus pandemic.

References

Blockmans, S., Lannoo, K., Gros, D., Russack, S., Egenhofer, C., De Groen, W.P. *et al.* (2019) 'What Comes after the Last Chance Commission? Policy Priorities for 2019–2024'. Brussels: CEPS.

Cavaghan, R. and O'Dwyer, M. (2018) 'European Economic Governance in 2017: A Recovery for Whom?' *Journal of Common Market Studies*, Vol. 56, No. S1, pp. 96–108.

Christiansen, T. (2020) 'The EU in an Era of Crises – European Integration in the Context of Populism, Geo-economics and Institutional Resilience'. *Journal of Common Market Studies*, Vol. 58, No. S1.

De Grauwe, P. and Ji, Y. (2019) 'Making the Eurozone Sustainable by Financial Engineering or Political Union?' *Journal of Common Market Studies*, Vol. 57, No. S1, pp. 40–8.

De Vries, C. (2020) 'Why the EU struggles to agree on anything'. Available online at: https://www.politico.eu/article/why-the-eu-cant-agree-on-anything-coronavirus-budget-mff-recovery-fund/. Last accessed 5 August 2020.

Duff, A. (2019) 'The Political Reform Agenda of Ursula von der Leyen'. EPC Discussion Paper 30 August 2019. Available online at: http://aei.pitt.edu/100410/1/pub_9311_political_reform_agenda.pdf. Last accessed 14 August 2020.

European Council (2019) 'A New Strategic Agenda 2019–2024'. Brussels June 2019. Available online at: https://www.consilium.europa.eu/media/39914/a-new-strategic-agenda-2019-2024.pdf. Last accessed 3 August 2020.

Exadaktylos, T. (2020) *The State of the Union – Or, where the EU was in January 2020'*. European Community Studies Association Canada, (ECSA-C) commentary. Available online at: https://www.ecsa-c.ca/post/the-state-of-the-union-or-where-the-eu-was-in-january-2020. Last accessed 5 August 2020.

Exadaktylos, T., Guerrina, R. and Massetti, E. (2019) 'Sailing through Troubled Waters and towards "Someplace ...."'. *Journal of Common Market Studies*, Vol. 57, No. S1, pp. 5–12.

Featherstone, K. (2016) 'Conditionality, Democracy and Institutional Weakness: The Euro-Crisis Trilemma'. *Journal of Common Market Studies*, Vol. 54, No. S1, pp. 48–64.

Halikiopoulou, D. (2018) 'A Right-wing Populist Momentum? A Review of 2017 Elections across Europe'. *Journal of Common Market Studies*, Vol. 56, No. S1, pp. 63–73.

Hodson, D. and Quaglia, L. (2009) 'European Perspectives on the Global Financial Crisis: Introduction'. *Journal of Common Market Studies*, Vol. 47, No. 5, pp. 939–53.

Maggini, N. and Chiaramonte, A. (2019) 'Euroscepticism behind the Victory of Eurosceptic Parties in the 2018 Italian General Election? Not Exactly'. *Journal of Common Market Studies*, Vol. 57, No. S1, pp. 77–89.

Maurice, E. and Menneteau, M. (2019) 'From Crisis Exit to World Challenges: The EU's Strategic Agenda 2019–2014'. No. 521, Foundation Robert Schuman Policy Paper. Available online at: https://www.robert-schuman.eu/en/doc/questions-d-europe/qe-521-en.pdf. Last accessed 14 August 2020.

Medrano, J. (2009) 'The Public Sphere and the European Union's Political Identity'. In Checkel, J. and Katzenstein, P. (eds) *European Identity* (Cambridge: Cambridge University Press), pp. 81–108.

Thieme, A. and Galariotis, I. (2020) *The European Council's Strategic Agenda 2019–2024*. European University Institute Policy Brief'. Available online at: https://cadmus.eui.eu/bitstream/handle/1814/67068/STG_PB_2020_03-EN.pdf?sequence=3&isAllowed=y. Last accessed 14 August 2020.

Vasilopoulou, S., Halikiopoulou, D. and Exadaktylos, T. (2014) 'Greece in Crisis: Austerity, Populism and the Politics of Blame'. *Journal of Common Market Studies*, Vol. 52, No. 2, pp. 388–402.

Verdun, A. (2018) 'Institutional Architecture of the Euro Area'. *Journal of Common Market Studies*, Vol. 56, No. S1, pp. 74–84.

von der Leyen, U. (2019) A Union that Strives for More, *My Agenda for Europe*. Available online at: https://austria-forum.org/attach/Europa/political-guidelines-next-commission_en.pdf. Last accessed 14 August 2020.

JCMS 2020 Volume 58. Annual Review pp. 13–27   DOI: 10.1111/jcms.13106

The EU's New Normal: Consolidating European Integration in an Era of Populism and Geo-Economics*

THOMAS CHRISTIANSEN
Luiss University, Rome

Introduction

May 2020: the world is in the grips of the Covid-19 pandemic, and Europe has become the epicentre of this global crisis – a crisis which quickly escalates from the devastating impact it has on public health to wider concerns about the economic, financial and fiscal impact that lockdowns, closed borders and other mitigation measures are having on the EU and its Member States. An economic depression (Strauss *et al.*, 2020) of historical proportion is on the cards. For the European Union (EU), the pandemic almost instantly also turns into a political crisis, indeed it appears to constitute – yet again – an existential threat (Rankin, 2020) to a potentially fragile construction.

In an alternate universe, free from the disruption of a global pandemic, May 2020 would have provided an occasion for EU observers to mark the 20th anniversary of former German foreign minister Joschka Fischer's speech at the Humboldt University in Berlin (Fischer, 2000). This speech, calling for a *finalité politique* for the European Union, generated a widespread response in politics, the media, academia and among the wider public about the future of Europe (Joerges et al., 2020). As such, it is generally seen as the starting point for a decade-long process of constitutional debate and treaty reform that culminated in the coming into force of the Lisbon Treaty almost ten years later. Fischer's call for a constitutional settlement was ambitious and far-reaching in its consequences (and hence worthy of recognition on the occasion of a special anniversary). Yet the process that followed was also noteworthy for the limitations about the integration project it revealed: the popular opposition to the creation of a state-like polity, this risk of elevating the EU, however symbolically, to a higher level above that of the nation-states, and the opportunities it offered for Eurosceptics and populists to use such fears in order to mobilize public opinion (Fieschi, 2020) against the European project.

Atmospherically, the contrast between *May 2000* – the hopeful launch of a process of constitutionalizing the EU – and *May 2020* – the EU facing the onslaught of the pandemic in a fragmented and weakened state after a decade of crises – could hardly be starker. By early 2020 the enthusiasm and ambition of the early 2000s had given way to a sense of fatigue, foreboding and dissatisfaction about the integration project. An EU, seen to be incapable to successfully address the multiple crises it had faced during the past decade, was regarded with growing scepticism by elites and wider public alike.

*The author gratefully acknowledges valuable feedback received from the editors and the research assistance provided by Isabel Hernandez Pepe.

Increasingly, the EU found itself trapped (in public opinion terms) between two camps: on the one side, those that want to see less interference (Schlipphak, 2016) from Brussels in the domestic affairs of the Member States, greater respect for national identity and state sovereignty and a more limited approach to further integration, and, on the other side, those that lament the inability of the EU to deliver on its promise, the lack of solidarity across EU Member States and the resultant loss of faith in the European project.

This article assesses the state of European integration in this era of crises. Having examined in the following sections the EU's the response to the challenges it had to address over the past decade, the article considers the impact of two broader developments on the integration process: on the one hand, the rise of populism and the contestation of expertise that comes with it, and, on the other hand, the shift from a regulated system of liberal world trade to one of geo-economic rivalry between the major global powers. Both of these developments constitute grave threats to the foundations of the European integration project: liberalism, multilateralism and the rule of law. Considering in this context also the EU's response to the global pandemic, the article concludes that the EU's institutional structure has demonstrated a remarkable degree of resilience in the era of crises. As European nations are forced to confront far-reaching structural changes, the EU constitutes an essential element in meeting these challenges.

I. The EU in an Era of Crises

When Europe was struck by threat of Covid-19 in early 2020, with both national governments and EU institutions scrambling for an adequate response, the EU had already experienced a number of body blows over the previous years (Caporaso, 2018). Over the previous decade the EU had to respond to global financial crisis, which in turn led to a sovereign debt crisis in the Eurozone as well as the migration and refugee crisis, and in each case managed to keep the Union together even if none of these challenges was fundamentally resolved. Brexit – the fractious withdrawal of one of the larger member states, albeit a long-standing 'awkward partner' (George, 1990) – had added further to the sense of impending doom for the EU, even if the initial expectation of other member states following the UK out of the door did not materialize.

The emergence of an 'arc of instability' (Dijkstra et al., 2019) around the EU's eastern and southern borders, the US administration's systematic weakening of the structures of global governance (the support of which the EU had nailed to its mast), and the continuing confrontation with Putin's Russia (Barigazzi, 2020) over its disrespect for international law, the worsening relations with China (Le Corre, 2020) – these and other external developments constitute a hostile environment for a regional integration project committed to multilateralism and liberal trade. A multipolar world was never a place in which the European Union would be fully at home, but by 2020, with the trade war between the US and China, the two leading economies in the world, escalating into a new 'Cold War', it had become an extraordinary challenging place in which to protect the values and interests embodied in the EU.

It has been against the backdrop of previous, unresolved crises, creating a latency of internal divisions, and an extremely unhelpful external environment, that Europe was forced to confront the unique challenge of Covid-19. For a number of reasons, the pandemic constituted – more so than even the earlier challenges – an existential threat to the very idea of integration in Europe: it presented – inevitably – an asymmetrical shock, with some Member States much harder hit than others; it instantly questioned the idea of open borders and free movement, one of the cornerstones of the integration project; as a matter of life and death, it instinctively led publics and decision-makers alike to search for solutions in the national context; and it saw EU institutions unprepared for the kind of immediate responses that were required and that only national (or regional and local) authorities were able to deliver. In other words, even though the pandemic constituted a common problem threatening the foundations and the fruits of European cooperation, it put national governments in the driving seat of searching for solutions. EU institutions initially appeared marginal and ineffective in their attempts to protect the Single Market or to offer pan-European response to the pandemic.

While it is too early at the time of writing to make any statements about the long-term consequences the pandemic, and the response of the EU and its Member States might have had, it only took a couple of months for the above picture to alter rather fundamentally. The existential threat of Covid-19 had not dealt a death blow to the project of European integration. Instead, by July 2020 EU leaders had agreed on a historic 'deal' (Strupczewski *et al.*, 2020) creating a recovery fund that promised hitherto unimaginable amounts of EU support to address the economic and fiscal fallout of the crisis. Probably even more important in the long run, the agreement on the 'Next Generation EU' fund included, for the first time ever, the authorization for the European Commission to borrow money to finance spending programmes, overcoming the previously iron-clad prohibition against mutualized debt. For these reasons, observers have likened the developments in June and July 2020 to a 'Hamiltonian Moment' (Calhoun, 2020; Kaletsky, 2020) for the EU, comparing the new spirit (if not the actual agreement) to the decision in the United States of America in 1790 for the federal government to bail out individual states.

This recovery of the EU's political fortunes – from staring at the abyss of an existentialist threat to passing a critical juncture on the road to fiscal federalism – in the space of a few months is remarkable, even if the long-term consequences of both the crisis and its response are not foreseeable at this time. However, when seen in the context of the manner in which the EU has dealt with and 'survived' previous crises, it does not come as too much of a surprise. The EU may not have fundamentally resolved the earlier problems, and indeed has not exhibited a capability to respond swiftly and resolutely to crises more generally. Yet, it did nevertheless demonstrate a capacity to alleviate even major problems to such a degree that, in the short term, centrifugal tendencies among the member states were counteracted, partial solutions could be developed and implemented, and the immediate threat could thus be averted.

This tendency of 'muddling through' appears at one level to be unsustainable – a series of short-term fixes papering over the limitations of the EU's institutional and legal framework and the lack of political will among national governments to go further. Yet, as a decade of crisis-management has shown, 'muddling through' has proven to be a surprisingly successful approach. It turns out that the time bought with such short-term fixes has helped to create spaces in which more complex and long-term arrangements to overcome problems could be designed. This has been critical not merely to 'keep things going' but indeed to design new institutional arrangements which ultimately served to deepen the level of integration further.

Consequently, the 2010s were not only an era of near-continuous crisis-response for the European Union. They also constituted a period of remarkable institutional growth, involving the creation or strengthening of EU agencies (European Union, 2010a, 2010b, 2017a), the design of novel regulatory frameworks (European Union, 2011a, 2011b, 2013a, 2013b, 2014), the agreement on new intergovernmental treaties (European Union, 2011c; European Commission, 2017), the building-up of additional institutional capacity in a variety of areas (European Union, 2013c, 2013d), new forms of cooperation among member states (European Union, 2017b), the setting up of new financial instruments (European Commission, 2018), and the transfer of new competences to the European Commission (European Union, 2013e). On their own, these various reforms and innovations are not game-changing, and some were indeed still 'left-overs' arising from the Lisbon Treaty. Taken together, however, they amount to a period of remarkable institutional development having occurred against the background of the EU supposedly being 'in crisis' during much of this period.

The various instances of institutional reform undertaken during the era of crises did not follow a strategic plan or grand design. Instead, they have been necessarily piecemeal and ad hoc measures to address particular problems. This puts the crisis-driven wave of reforms undertaken during the 2010s in contrast to the constitutional treaty project of the previous decade. In the era of crises there has been neither the time nor the political will to conduct major institutional reform in a strategic manner, as envisaged by the Lisbon Treaty. The expectation of the treaty's drafters that reform proposals would be subject to extensive public debate and thorough deliberation in a 'Convention on the Future of Europe', before being negotiated in an Intergovernmental Conference and adopted through a lengthy process of ratification in the Member States was an impossible idea in the context of constant crisis-management.

The institutional reforms of the 2010s therefore lacked the transparency, public scrutiny and democratic legitimacy that formal treaty change would have involved. Yet the absence of formal treaty change did not mean that the process of constitutionalizing the EU ended, but rather that it continued through other, less formal, channels (Christiansen and Reh, 2009). In the context of crisis-management, EU decision-makers merely avoided the uncertainty and the extended planning horizon implied by formal treaty revision, and instead reverted to the earlier logic of relying chiefly on output legitimacy to justify institutional reforms: the need of finding solutions to particular problems at hand, of delivering suitable policies to address these, and of achieving satisficing outcomes. Scholars have referred to this manner of proceeding as 'failing forward' (Jones et al., 2015) – the EU, stumbling in the face of a crisis that prevents the continuation of the status quo, agreeing (eventually) short-term and/or partial solutions to address the in-built limitations of the original design. Ultimately, further action would be required in the future to address the problem, creating a dynamic that actually serves to deepen the integration process further.

With 'muddling through' and 'failing forward' as the hallmarks of EU decision-making in the era of crises, the integration process did not take a major leap forward. But all throughout this period the EU continued to function, produced results, however sub-optimal, and remained central to addressing the public policy needs of the member states. This in turn meant that also in the face of the Covid-19 pandemic, national governments eventually accepted that a response required EU-level cooperation, paving the way for the agreement on the recovery fund and other measures in July 2020.

This necessarily brief overview of the EU's response to a series of crises cannot do justice to either the complexity of the many challenges or the effectiveness of the crisis-management, not least because all of these issues – sovereign debt, migration, instability in the neighbourhood, post-Brexit arrangements, Covid-19 – still require attention and remain fundamentally unresolved. Indeed, the effects of the *interaction* between these various developments – for example, how the pandemic recovery might aggravate pre-existing fiscal imbalances and intra-EU inequality, or whether the spread of Covid-19 might generate new patterns of migration – are impossible to anticipate at the time of writing in mid-2020. Beyond the immediate response to the pandemic, there is also the contingent development of the launch of the "Conference on the Future of Europe" in 2020 (Fabbrini, 2019). Depending on the outcome of this (already delayed) project, it may even signal - against the odds - a return to a more formal and explicit process of constitutional reform in the EU.

Notwithstanding the prospects for further constitutionalization in the 2020s, the examination of the EU's performance after a decade of crisis-response permits the observation that none of these 'existential threats' ultimately turned out to be that. No matter the fractious debates, lengthy negotiations, sub-optimal solutions or substantively unresolved problems – the era of crises re-confirmed rather than diminished the EU's role as *the* forum for decision-making. There are arguments to be had about whether or not during this period the centre of gravity has shifted from supranational governance to intergovernmental arrangements (Bickerton *et al.,* 2014; Dehousse, 2015) or whether the increasing trend towards differentiated integration is at odds with principles of democratic accountability (Fossum, 2019). The observation here is simply that the EU as a political system has managed not only to withstand a series of severe challenges, but actually emerged strengthened from this period, with its centrality to political processes on the European continent confirmed.

II. The Populist Challenge to European Integration

As well as being crisis-ridden, the 2010s already were also marked by a deterioration in public support for European integration. Indeed, the constitutional project of the 2000s had been stopped in its tracks by the electorates in France and the Netherlands voting against the Constitutional Treaty in 2005. The Irish electorate later also voted against the revised Lisbon Treaty, further delaying the reform project. These experiences demonstrated the growing gulf between European elites and the wider public, and the end of the permissive consensus which had hitherto facilitated the integration process. The more technocratic manner in which the Lisbon Treaty was negotiated, and the avoidance of public debate about its substance, foreshadowed the manner in which institutional reforms would be handled in the 2010s.

Abandoning the idea of large-scale constitutional reform did not, however, silence the EU's critics. Opposition to the EU and the idea of an 'ever-closer union' had become entrenched in many member states, and a growing number of political parties across the political spectrum succeeded on the basis of an anti-European discourse. While political mobilization against (further) regional integration has constituted a pan-European phenomenon, it nevertheless has taken different shapes among member states (Foster and Frieden, 2017). At one end of the spectrum it involves far-right parties that pursue a nationalist discourse and oppose EU policy-making as an interference in a country's 'own affairs' and ultimately as a threat to national identity. In this incarnation, anti-European populism goes hand in hand with opposition to immigration, welfare chauvinism and anti-elitism.

At the other end of the spectrum, parties of the radical left have objected to the EU as a neoliberal project that furthers economic and social inequality. In particular in Mediterranean Europe, the EU has been criticized not only for not acting in solidarity with people in Southern member states during the economic and financial crisis, but in particular for imposing structural reforms, fiscal surveillance and austerity policies on them in return for bail-outs.

These and other shades of anti-European sentiment have become increasingly well established in the various national political systems, and indeed in the European Parliament which after the 2014 elections included three separate Eurosceptic groups. In the course of the 2010s, successive crises interacted with these pre-existing and underlying sentiments, providing further opportunities for mobilization and growth. As already mentioned, the EU's response to the sovereign debt crisis in the Eurozone, affecting in particular member states in the South, provided fuel for anti-globalists opposing the interference by the Troika and the imposition of austerity policies. The 2016 migration crisis, on the other hand, created anti-European sentiment on both sides of the political divide: in Southern states such as Greece, Malta and Italy, the absence of an effective EU policy to address the arrival of large numbers of migrants across the Mediterranean appeared to confirm previous assumptions about the lack of solidarity. In Northern and in particular Eastern Europe, the EU's attempts to create a system of burden-sharing and 'redistribution' helped to reinforce earlier discourses about the EU being a 'threat' to territorial integrity, national identity and Christian values.

Both the sovereign debt crisis and the migration crisis hit the EU in an asymmetrical manner: not only were member states unevenly affected by them, but they ended up in both cases on opposite sides of the ensuing debate. In both cases, the 'problem' appeared to be in the South, and the 'solution' required the support from the North – a configuration that provided ample opportunity for populists on either side to mobilize against the allegedly unsatisfactory intervention by the EU.

Throughout this period, growing Euroscepticism went hand in hand with a wider phenomenon of populism and anti-system politics (Hopkin, 2020). Tapping into latent dissatisfaction with the political process and the increasingly complex nature of decision-making, populists successfully mobilized against 'the elites' and 'the establishment', not only in Europe but also in the United States and elsewhere. Globalization in this perspective is regarded as a 'foreign takeover' that benefits cosmopolitan 'elites' and multinational corporations at the cost of 'ordinary people', permits the influx of migrants and foreign cultural influences, and removes the capacity of communities to take independent decisions. In the populist discourse, the EU was a prime expression of such alleged developments, given the legal requirements it imposes on member states with regard to free movement, non-discrimination and the rule of law.

Another target of populist mobilization has been the reliance of governments, EU institutions and international organizations on technocracy and scientific expertise. The exclamation by Michael Gove, one of the leading Brexit campaigners, when confronted with expert opinion about the cost of leaving the EU, that 'people in this country have had enough of experts' (Staples, 2020), perfectly illustrated the discursive amalgamation of anti-European sentiment, populism and contestation of expertise. Populist challenges to science and expertise are not specific to Euroscepticism, as climate change denial, anti-vax movements and the expansive world of conspiracy theories demonstrate. But the greater contestation of expertise that has come with the rise of populist mobilization is a particular challenge for a European Union that has long based its legitimacy on technocratic expertise and evidence-based policy-making (Abazi et al., 2020).

In the UK, where expert opinion about the economic damage that leaving the EU would inflict on the UK was denounced as 'Project Fear', populist mobilization succeeded (at least during the crucial period of campaigning) to turn public opinion against the EU, leading to the UK's withdrawal. Initial assumptions that Brexit might trigger a wave of other countries following suit did not materialize, however. Populist parties, espousing hostile views vis-à-vis the EU, have made inroads in most member states, and their discourses and electoral successes have impacted on mainstream politics, creating an increasingly hostile environment for EU decision-making. Yet, they have, by and large, remained minority voices in opposition to mainstream parties, with the notable exception of *PiS* in Poland and *Fidesz* in Hungary. The formation, in 2018, of a populist government in Italy, bringing Matteo Salvini's *La Lega* into office, was a comparatively short-lived experience, and one that arguably failed precisely because of its inability to engage constructively in EU-level politics.

In any case, Brexit has not been a model that anti-European populists have wanted to follow. Indeed, the reverse has been the case: the political turmoil, economic disruption and societal upheaval experienced by the UK following its 2016 vote have acted – in the words of former European Council President Tusk – as a 'vaccine' against the desire of other nations to leave the Union (Randerson, 2019). Instead of advocating the departure from the EU, the populist challenge to European integration is precisely the one that comes from the inside: populist-led governments, such as in those in Hungary and Poland, maintaining a consistently anti-European discourse while seeking to change the direction of the integration process and utilizing the financial resources that come with EU membership.

The populist challenge to European integration then is not the break-up of the Union, nor the obstruction to decision-making (even if on particular issues matters did become problematical), but rather the normative erosion that populism has brought into the EU. Populism resulting in democratic backsliding in multiple member states constitutes a fundamental problem for the EU as a whole, given the hybrid nature of a Union composed of peoples and states (Fabbrini, 2019). Violations by national governments against essential liberal democratic norms such as the freedom of the press, the independence of the judiciary or the protection of fair and free elections are in conflict with the EU's own constitutional order. Yet, in the non-sovereign context of European governance, the ability of the EU to impose such norms on obstinate governments are limited, as the inconclusive attempts to adopt a rule of law mechanism on Hungary and Poland have demonstrated. The expectation that, in the context of negotiations over the new Multiannual Financial Framework it would be possible to introduce a mechanism that would link disbursements from the EU budget to compliance with EU norms has faltered as the urgency of finding an agreement on the recovery fund took precedence (Kelemen, 2020).

It remains to be seen how the EU navigates these precarious currents. The EU's apparent inability to protect basic liberal norms – with national governments in the EU openly revelling in their practice of 'illiberal democracy' – not only compromises the Union's capacity to uphold the law in other areas of policy-making. It also severely undermines its ability to promote such norms externally. The latter is highly problematic (to say the least) considering that much of EU external action is built around the principle of conditionality, obliging trade partners, recipients of development assistance or accession countries to abide by EU norms. And it is precisely in the international realm that the EU has to confront another momentous transformation that also threatens its fundamental norms, as discussed in the following section.

III. The Global Retreat from Liberal Trade: Towards Geo-Economics

A remarkable shift has occurred over the past decade: the rules-based global trading system, which had been a pillar of the international liberal order and a key driving force behind the process of globalization, has been in retreat for a number of years. Following the initial failure of finding a global agreement in the context of the Doha Round, the main trading powers engaged in negotiations about regional and bilateral free trade agreements (FTA). This has been a process in which also the EU has been very active, pursuing comprehensive FTAs with a range of partners in Asia and the Americas. In the absence of a revision of global trading rules, it served the EU to leverage its 'market power' in order to negotiate bilateral access to important markets such as South Korea, Japan, Singapore, Canada or MERCOSUR in Latin America.

The other leading economies pursued their own agendas with regard to trade: the United States under President Obama initiated ambitious multilateral trade negotiations with partners around the Atlantic (TTIP) and the Pacific (TPP), while China launched the Belt and Road Initiative (BRI) to facilitate greater trade and investment opportunities in Central Asia, Africa and Europe. Both the US and Chinese initiatives combined the promotion of trade with power politics: in the case of the US, the strategic goal was the capacity to set the standards for the majority of global trade without the involvement of China, and more specifically to contain China's growing economic dominance in Asia with a trading regime under US leadership. For China, the BRI (and new multilateral development banks that were founded alongside it) has been a vehicle to channel infrastructure investment to developing and emerging countries, and thereby also enhance the influence that it could wield in those countries, regions and globally.

While these developments already pointed to a fragmentation of the global trading regime, they nevertheless were still in line with the underlying assumption that the promotion of international trade and investment is desirable and mutually beneficial. Yet, the faltering TTIP negotiations between the US and the EU, the problems in getting internal EU approval for the CETA agreement with Canada, and question-marks over the ratification of the FTA between the EU and MERCOSUR have all been indications that the climate for liberal trade was deteriorating rapidly. To some extent this trend is related to the previous argument about populist challenges: anti-globalists have been at the forefront of campaigns against the major FTAs pursued by the EU, and Brexit itself constitutes the most significant retreat from free trade that any country has pursued in the post-WWII era.

Despite these difficulties, there remained underlying support for liberal trade among governments of the main trading powers, and mainstream opinion in these countries. However, with the election of Donald Trump to the US Presidency the balance tipped markedly, from qualified support for liberal trade to mistrust and outright hostility towards major trading partners of the US. With the US administration viewing trade not as being mutually beneficial, but instead in zero-sum terms, long-standing US allies such as the EU, Germany, Japan or South Korea were all regarded as rivals, and whole sectors of their economies targeted by tariffs that were justified on national security grounds. Negotiations with the EU on TTIP were discontinued, and the US withdrew from the TPP agreement that had already been completed.

Trade disputes frequently occur, also among allies. However, what aggravated the situation at this time has been the parallel strategy by the United States to incapacitate the dispute-settlement system of the World Trade Organization (WTO) – the institution that would ordinarily adjudicate on such disputes. By refusing to appoint new judges to the appellate body, the US effectively rendered the WTO's DSM inoperative. This sabotage was accompanied by the threat to withdraw the US completely from the WTO 'unless the US keeps winning cases' (Feinberg, 2020). These actions raise the spectre of an end to the rules-based system of world trade that US leadership had helped to create in the late 1940s.

The main target of the trade wars being waged by the Trump administration has been China. The imposition of punitive tariffs on Chinese imports, the spiral of tit-for-tat tariffs that either side would impose on the other, the ban (or threat thereof) of leading Chinese firms such as Huawei, Bytedance (TikTok) or Tencent (WeChat) from operating in the United States, and the threat of penalising US firms with outsourced manufacturing in China – relations between the world's two largest economies have deteriorated markedly and rapidly during the Trump Presidency. Beyond trade, the level of hostility and mistrust between the US and China has reached a point at which the spectre of a new Cold War is being discussed (Wintour, 2020).

The aggressive posture of the United States towards China also implied the expectation that allies follow the same line. In its logical conclusion, this policy leads to European states having to choose between the continued benefits of the transatlantic alliance, and the deepening of economic ties with China. The American threat that European governments who award contracts to Huawei in the construction of their 5G telecommunications infrastructure would risk limits to the intelligence sharing with the US is a prime example.

The future of these will depend on the outcome of the US elections in November 2020, but the emerging confrontation between the two global powers was already present under President Obama, and is bound to continue under a President Biden. The rise of China, and the threat it constitutes to the US' position in the world, is a long-term structural change in international relations whose impact goes deeper than domestic party politics in the US.

In any case, notwithstanding the policies of the Trump administration, European attitudes towards China had already markedly cooled in recent years. China's uncompromising stance with regard to the territorial disputes in the South China Sea, its increasing presence – and competition with the EU – as a provider of development assistance in Africa, and the clamp-down on pro-democracy protesters in Hong Kong are all evidence of the growing conflict between China's pursuit of its interests and the EU's pursuit of its norms (Christiansen et al., 2018).

The adoption of a new 'EU Strategy on China' in 2016 and the publication of a Joint Communication of European Commission and the High Representative on

'EU–China Strategic Outlook' reaffirmed the EU's commitment to engaging with China, while hinting at a tougher stance with regard to issues of economic security, industrial strategy and investment protection. However, the EU's balancing act between drawing the benefits from economic relations with China and protecting its interests and values has become ever more difficult. Not least in view of pressure from the US, the EU finds itself confronted with the hard choice of whether to continue the path of deeper economic cooperation, and risk serious repercussions for the transatlantic alliance, greater interference of China in its internal affairs and further compromises in its normative agenda, or whether to join the US in a more adversarial posture towards China and incur the economic cost of the loss of Chinese trade and investment.

This dilemma is amplified by the Covid-19 crisis. On the one hand, China is seen by some as being responsible for the pandemic, having sought to cover up the initial outbreak in Wuhan. The crisis also served as a reminder that Europe's dependence on supplies from China, in particular with regard to medical gear and protective equipment, has potentially serious effects on its security. On the other hand, the pandemic also provided opportunities for China, once it had overcome the peak of infections domestically, to mount an effective public diplomacy campaign in assisting European countries with medical personnel and supplies – an effort that has proven effective in countries such as Italy that were already favourably predisposed towards China. More broadly, China – having managed the pandemic better than Western powers – is expected to emerge strengthened from the crisis (*The Economist*, 2020).

The global retreat from liberal trade, and the emergence of spatially distinct arenas for trade, infrastructure investment and development finance has given prominence to the concept of geo-economics. Geo-economics emphasizes the interaction between geographical location, economic interaction and political power (Baru, 2012). Trade, FDI and economic interdependence more generally, rather than being unifying forces as per the liberal internationalist understanding, instead become tools of power politics. Interdependence, indeed, can be 'weaponized' when powers leverage the presence of infrastructure connections or transnational supply chains for political advantage (Farrell and Newman, 2019). Developments in East Asia, and China's BRI strategy in particular, have been viewed by Western observers in terms of geo-economics (Beeson, 2018), but the manner in which Russia has used its oil and gas exports, or the United States utilized its privileged access to nodal points in global telecommunications networks for intelligence gathering are other prominent examples of economic interconnections being used as instruments of power.

The logic of geo-economics threatens to undermine the EU's long-standing commitment to multilateralism, global governance and international law, while the prospect of a Cold War between the US and China makes it increasingly unlikely that a functioning transatlantic alliance can be balanced with deepening trade and investment relations with China. How will the EU manage to protect European interests and promote its values in a world in which trade, economic interdependence and globalization have become tools of power politics? A world governed by geo-economic considerations will require a fundamental re-think from the EU with regard to its reliance on, and promotion of, a rules-based system of economic interaction with the major powers in the world.

Conclusion: The EU's New Normal beyond 2020

It follows from the above discussion that after muddling through an era of crises, and even after emerging strengthened from the political, economic and fiscal threats of the Covid-19 pandemic, the EU is facing more fundamental challenges in the coming decade. The rise of populism in Europe (and elsewhere), the growing contestation of expertise and the demise of liberal trade all imply that the EU has to adapt to a new normal. These developments are linked, and they have in common the erosion of the system of rules and norms on which the EU has based not only its actions, but indeed its legitimacy.

2019 saw the comprehensive change in the leadership at the European level, with new presidents appointed or elected to the European Commission, the European Parliament, the European Council and the European Central Bank, alongside the appointment of a new High Representative. This offered the opportunity for the new leadership to further reform the institutions and enhance the capacity of the EU to confront these challenges. For Commission President Ursula von der Leyen and European Council President Charles Michel, the success in achieving agreement on the recovery fund and the Multiannual Financial Framework was an early boost for their credibility, providing the political capital to take more ambitious steps in the future.

However, greater credit for this achievement needs to go to Emmanuel Macron and Angela Merkel who had jointly initiated the proposal that led to the subsequent agreement. After many years of dissonance in relations between the EU's largest member states, the budget negotiations in the summer of 2020 provided strong evidence that the Franco-German 'engine' was working again, and that it has the capacity to deliver transformative outcomes even in the face of significant opposition. In the hybrid polity that the EU is, this combination – the presence of capable institutional leadership in Brussels, and the willingness of national leaders to push for collective solutions – is what will be required in order for Europe to weather the storms ahead.

The demands that the future challenges discussed above make on the EU's leadership are indeed formidable, given the contradictory demands that anti-European populism and geo-economic statecraft make on European leaders: on the one hand, populists are pushing for the re-nationalization of EU competences, the return of national borders (controls) and the reimaging of national sovereignty. The logic of geo-economics, on the other hand, requires a further strengthening of the European level, more capable European institutions and more robust defence of European interests. In other words, the tension between centrifugal and centripetal forces pulling the process of European integration in opposite directions is only bound to intensify.

As it happens, the EU does actually possess an impressive arsenal of geo-economic instruments, given the size of the Single Market (and the 'market power' that comes with it (Damro, 2012)), its status as a global leader in providing development assistance, and the expertise that EU institutions have acquired in designing incentive, sanction and conditionality regimes to manage relations with countries around the world. Consequently, the EU, having demonstrated its institutional resilience during an era of extraordinary crises, is rather well positioned to engage in geo-economic statecraft (especially if compared to its capacity to manage traditional military conflicts). From a geo-economic perspective, the EU is in principle a capable global actor notwithstanding its reluctance to enter into hostile confrontations with other powers.

What has largely been lacking, however, has been the unity among Member States and the political will among the EU leadership to apply these tools in a systematic and sustained manner. The ability of the European Commission to respond robustly and skilfully to the imposition US tariffs, the steadfastness of maintaining sanctions against Russia following the illegal annexation of the Crimea, and the cohesion maintained by the EU27 in the Brexit negotiations with the UK, have all been indications that in the face of external threats EU institutions and member-state governments are able to defend common interests. By contrast, the rather fragmented manner in which member states maintain relations with China, creating frequent opportunities for 'divide-and-rule' tactics by Beijing, demonstrate that the picture remains mixed.

When at the beginning of 2020 von der Leyen took over as Commission President, her self-declared aim was to lead 'a geopolitical Commission', and her first 'foreign' visit was not to Washington or Beijing, but to the African Union headquarters in Addis Ababa, Ethiopia. While a more systematic and meaningful engagement with Africa is certainly overdue, the wider question is whether the EU's new leadership is capable of managing the game of geo-economic statecraft also vis-à-vis major global powers, and whether national governments are consistently and genuinely supportive of the required policies and actions. This will be a serious and demanding test not only because the engagement in geo-economic statecraft will need to go beyond the liberal and multilateral commitments the EU has long espoused and promoted, but also because the costs of such a strategy will likely impact the member states unevenly, and hence – in interaction with populist and opportunist forces – make it difficult to maintain a common front in any prolonged geo-economic dispute.

References

Abazi, V., Adriaensen, J. and Christiansen, T. (eds) (2020) *The Contestation of Expertise in the European Union* (London: Palgrave Macmillan).

Barigazzi, J (2020) 'EU Criticizes Russia Vote that Could Extend Putin's Rule until 2036', *Politico*, 7 February 2020, available online at: https://www.politico.eu/article/the-eu-criticises-vote-that-extends-putin-rule-until-2036/

Baru, S. (2012) 'Geo-economics and Strategy'. *Survival*, Vol. 54, No. 3, pp. 47–58.

Beeson, M. (2018) 'Geoeconomics with Chinese Characteristics: The BRI and China's Evolving Grand Strategy'. *Economic and Political Studies*, Vol. 6, No. 3, pp. 240–56.

Bickerton, C., Hodson, D. and Puetter, U. (2014) 'The New Intergovernmentalism: European Integration in the Post-Maastricht Era'. *JCMS: Journal of Common Market Studies*, Vol. 53, No. 4), pp. 703–22.

Calhoun, G (2020) 'Europe's Hamiltonian Moment: What Is It Really?' Forbes, 26 May, available online at: https://www.forbes.com/sites/georgecalhoun/2020/05/26/europes-hamiltonian-moment–what-is-it-really/#2f523e7e1e1a

Caporaso, J. (2018) 'Europe's Triple Crisis and the Uneven Role of Institutions: The Euro, Refugees and Brexit'. *Journal of Common Market Studies*, Vol. 56, pp. 1345–1361.

Christiansen, T., Kirchner, E. and Wissenbach, U. (2018) *The European Union and China* (London: Palgrave Macmillan).

Christiansen, T. and Reh, C. (2009) *Constitutionalizing the European Union* (London: Palgrave Macmillan).

Damro, C. (2012) 'Market Power Europe'. *Journal of European Public Policy*, Vol. 19, No. 5, pp. 682–

Dehousse, R. (2015) 'The New Supranationalism'. Paper prepared for presentation at the 2015 ECPR General Conference, Montreal, 26-29 August. Available online at https://ecpr.eu/Filestore/PaperProposal/281383a5-0285-4417-a613-eed8cd5d36bd.pdf/ (last accessed 3 September 2021)

Dijkstra, L., Poelman, H. and Rodriguez-Pose, A. (2019) 'The Geography of EU Discontent'. VoxEU.org, Centre for Economic Policy Research, https://voxeu.org/article/geography-eu-discontent

European Commission (2017) The Fiscal Compact – Taking Stock, EC Publications, 22 February 2017, https://ec.europa.eu/info/publications/fiscal-compact-taking-stock_en

European Commission (2018) 'Proposal for a Regulation of the European Parliament and of The Council Establishing the European Defence Fund', COM(2018) 476 final, 13 June 2018.

European Union (2010a) 'Regulation (EU) No 439/2010 of the European Parliament and of the Council Establishing a European Asylum Support Office'. *Official Journal*, Vol. L132, p. 11.

European Union (2010b) 'Regulation (EU) No 1092/2010 of the European Parliament and of the Council of 24 November 2010 on European Union Macro-prudential Oversight of the Financial System and Establishing a European Systemic Risk Board'. *Official Journal*, Vol. L331.

European Union (2011a) 'Council Regulation (EU) No 1177/2011 of 8 November 2011 Amending Regulation (EC) No 1467/97 on Speeding Up and Clarifying the Implementation of the Excessive Deficit Procedure'. *Official Journal*, Vol. L306, pp. 33–40.

European Union (2011b) 'Regulation (EU) No 1175/2011 of the European Parliament and of the Council of 16 November 2011 Amending Council Regulation (EC) No 1466/97 on the Strengthening of the Surveillance of Budgetary Positions and the Surveillance and Coordination of Economic Policies'. *Official Journal*, Vol. L306, pp. 12–24.

European Union (2011c) 'Treaty Establishing the European Stability Mechanism (ESM)'. *Official Journal*, Vol. L91, p. 1.

European Union (2013a) 'Council Regulation (EU) No 1024/2013 Conferring Specific Tasks on the ECB Concerning Policies Relating to the Prudential Supervision of Credit Institutions'. *Official Journal*. Vol. L287, pp. 63–89.

European Union (2013b) 'Regulation (EU) No 472/2013 of the European Parliament and of the Council of 21 May 2013 on the Strengthening of Economic and Budgetary Surveillance of Member States in the Euro Area Experiencing or Threatened with Serious Difficulties with Respect to their Financial Stability'. *Official Journal*, Vol. L140, pp. 1–10.

European Union (2013c) 'Regulation (EU) No 1052/2013 of the European Parliament and of the Council of 22 October 2013 Establishing the European Border Surveillance System (Eurosur)'. *Official Journal*, Vol. L 295, pp. 11–26.

European Union (2013d) 'Directive 2013/33/EU of the European Parliament and of the Council of 26 June 2013 Laying Down Standards for the Reception of Applicants for International Protection'. *Official Journal*.

European Union (2013e) 'Regulation (EU) No 473/2013 of 21 May 2013 on Common Provisions for Monitoring and Assessing Draft Budgetary Plans and Ensuring the Correction of Excessive Deficit of the Member States in the Euro Area'. *Official Journal*.

European Union (2014) 'Regulation (EU) No 468/2014 of the European Central Bank Establishing the Framework for Cooperation within the Single Supervisory Mechanism between the European Central Bank and National Competent Authorities and with National Designated Authorities (SSM Framework Regulation) (ECB/2014/17)'. *Official Journal*.

European Union (2017a) 'Council Regulation (EU) 2017/1939 of 12 October 2017 Implementing Enhanced Cooperation on the Establishment of the European Public Prosecutor's Office ("the EPPO")'. *Official Journal*, Vol. L283, pp. 1–71.

European Union (2017b) 'Council Decision (CFSP) 2017/2315 of 11 December 2017 Establishing Permanent Structured Cooperation (PESCO) and Determining the List of Participating Member States'. *Official Journal*, Vol. L 331, pp. 57–77.

Fabbrini, F. (2019) 'The Conference on the Future of Europe A New Model to Reform the EU?' *DCU Brexit Institute Working Paper N. 12*.

Fabbrini, S. (2019) *Europe's Future* (Cambridge: Cambridge University Press).

Farrell, H. and Newman, A.L. (2019) 'Weaponized Interdependence'. *International Security*, Vol. 44, No. 1, pp. 42–79.

Fieschi, C. (2020) Europe's Populists Will Try to Exploit Coronavirus. We Can Stop Them, *The Guardian*, 17 March, available online at: https://www.theguardian.com/world/commentisfree/2020/mar/17/europe-populists-coronavirus-salvini, last accessed 4 August 2020.

Fischer, J. (2000) 'From Confederacy to Federation – Thoughts on the Finality of European Integration'. Speech at the Humboldt University in Berlin, European Commission Files, available online at: https://ec.europa.eu/dorie/fileDownload.do?docId=192161&cardId=192161, last accessed 4 August 2020.

Fossum, J.E. (2019) 'Europe's triangular challenge: Differentiation, dominance and democracy'. *EU3D Research Papers No. 1*.

Foster, C. and Frieden, J. (2017) 'Crisis of Trust: Socio-economic Determinants of Europeans' Confidence in Government'. *European Union Politics*, Vol. 18, No. 4, pp. 511–35.

George, S. (1990) *An Awkward Partner: Britain in the European Community* (New York: Oxford University Press).

Hopkin, J. (2020) *Anti-System Politics: The Crisis of Market Liberalism in Rich Democracies* (Oxford: Oxford University Press).

Joerges, C., Mény, Y. and Weiler, J.H.H. (2020) *What Kind of Constitution for What Kind of Polity? Responses to Joschka Fischer* (Florence: Robert Schuman Centre for Advanced Studies at the European University Institute).

Jones, E., Kelemen, D. and Meunier, S. (2015) 'Failing Forward? The Euro Crisis and the Incomplete Nature of European Integration'. *Comparative Political Studies*, Vol. 49, No. 7, doi 10.1177/0010414015617966.

Kaletsky, A. (2020) 'Europe's Hamiltonian Moment'. *Project Syndicate*, 21 May, available online at: https://www.project-syndicate.org/commentary/french-german-european-recovery-plan-proposal-by-anatole-kaletsky-2020-05?barrier=accesspaylog, last accessed 4 August 2020.

Kelemen, D. (2020), 'Europe's Faustian Union'. *Foreign Policy*, 30 July 2020. Available online at https://foreignpolicy.com/2020/07/30/europes-faustian-union/. Last accessed 7 August 2020.

Le Corre, P. (2020) 'The EU's New Defensive Approach to a Rising China', *ISPI Online*, 29 June 2020, available online at:https://www.ispionline.it/it/pubblicazione/eus-new-defensive-approach-rising-china-26760

Randerson, J. (2019) 'Brexit Is "Vaccine" Against Euroskepticism, Says Tusk', *Politico Europe*, 28 August 2019, available online at: https://www.politico.eu/article/brexit-is-vaccine-against-euroskepticism-says-tusk/, last accessed 4 August 2020.

Rankin, J. (2020) 'EU Faces "Existential Threat" if Coronavirus Recovery Is Uneven'. *The Guardian*, 13 May, available online at: https://www.theguardian.com/world/2020/may/13/eu-faces-existential-threat-if-coronavirus-recovery-uneven-paolo-gentiloni, last accessed 4 August 2020.

Schlipphak, B. (2016) 'Playing the Blame Game on Brussels: The Domestic Political Effects of EU Interventions against Democratic Backsliding'. *Journal of European Public Policy*, Vol 24, No. 3, pp. 352–365.

Staples, L. (2020) 'Tories Want Us to Trust Experts on Coronavirus. Too Bad They Spent Years Turning Us Against Them', *Indy100*, 16 March 2020, available online at: https://www.indy100.com/article/coronavirus-advice-experts-michael-gove-tories-boris-johnson-9390216, last accessed 4 August 2020.

Strauss, D., Cocco, F. and Bruce-Lockhard, C. (2020) 'Coronavirus plunges eurozone economy into historic recession', *The Financial Times*, July 31 2020, available online at: https://www.ft.com/content/c45cf867-2821-4d3a-ab48-0bc809f8cf26, last accessed 4 August 2020.

Strupczewski, J., Chalmers, J. and Emmott, R. (2020) 'EU Reaches Historic Deal on Pandemic Recovery after Fractious Summit'. *Reuters*, 21 July, available online at: https://www.reuters.com/article/us-eu-summit/eu-reaches-historic-deal-on-pandemic-recovery-after-fractious-summit-idUSKCN24M0DF, last accessed 4 August 2020.

The Economist (2020), 'Leader: Is China Winning?', 18 April 2020, available online at: https://www.economist.com/leaders/2020/04/16/is-china-winning

Wintour, P. (2020) 'US v China: Is This the Start of a New Cold War?' *The Guardian*, 22 June 2020, available online at https://www.theguardian.com/world/2020/jun/22/us-v-china-is-this-the-start-of-a-new-cold-war. Last accessed on 4 August 2020.

JCMS 2020 Volume 58. Annual Review pp. 28–42   DOI: 10.1111/jcms.13077

The 2019 Elections to the European Parliament: The Continuation of a Populist Wave but Not a Populist Tsunami

DANIEL STOCKEMER[1] and ABDELKARIM AMENGAY[2]
[1]School of Political Studies, University of Ottawa, Ottawa, Canada [2]Department of Political Science and International Relations, Doha Institute for Graduate Studies, Doha, Qatar

Introduction

Between 23 and 26 May 2019, eligible citizens from 28 EU countries voted to choose their representatives in the 8th European Parliament (EP). In the months preceding the elections many commentators expected that there would be an opportunity to gauge the power of populism in Europe (Erlanger, 2019) and that European populist parties would 'more than likely [...] reinforce their position in the European Parliament' (RTE, 2019). Such predictions reflected the specific context in which the 2019 European elections took place. Among others, the continuing Brexit debates in the UK, the growing citizen disaffection with EU institutions and the highly mediatized electoral alliance that united some of the most vocal populist parties in the EU a few weeks before the elections (Walker, 2019) were signs that a right-wing populist (RWP) tsunami would strike Brussels. The idea was not far-fetched, given that RWP parties have generally performed well in the European elections, and that the structural conditions seemed favourable for such a landslide. Nevertheless, these fears were exaggerated. With approximately 26 per cent of seats (EP, 2019), RWP parties had their best showing ever in any European elections. However, their gains (less than 5 per cent) from the 2014 elections were moderate and in line with the gains these parties had made in every EP election since 1999.

In this short overview we present a descriptive analysis of the electoral performance of populist parties in the 2019 European parliament elections. We do not restrict our analysis to the right-wing variant, but also include left-wing populist (LWP) parties in our discussion. In identifying populist parties that are pertinent for this overview we employed two inclusion criteria. First, we used Boros *et al.*'s (2016) list of European populist parties. The classification is one of the most recent lists of European populist parties and covers the 28 EU member states. Boros *et al.* (2016) mobilize Cas Mudde's definition of populism that currently appears to be a generally accepted and practical characterization.[1] Second, we restricted ourselves to populist parties that matter at the European level. In other words, we included only those parties that had had at least one MEP elected in each election covered by this article (i.e. the 2014 and 2019 elections to the EP).[2]

---

[1]Mudde defines populism as a thin-centred 'ideology that considers society to be ultimately separated into two homogeneous and antagonistic groups, "the pure people" versus "the corrupt elite," and which argues that politics should be an expression of the *volonté générale* of the people' (Mudde, 2004, p. 543).

[2]We do not count as LWP most 'communist parties' in Western European countries (such as the Greek communist KKE) as populist parties, unless they have gone through substantive organizational and ideological changes (like merging with other political organizations) that make these parties clearly populist. However, we do consider the German Party of Democratic Socialism (PDS) and later Die Linke as populist, even if the party's populist nature is subject to academic debate.

Figure 1: Number of Seats Held by Populist Parties in the European Parliament. Legend: RWP, right-wing populist parties, LWP, left-wing populist parties, CP, populist centre parties. [Colour figure can be viewed at wileyonlinelibrary.com]

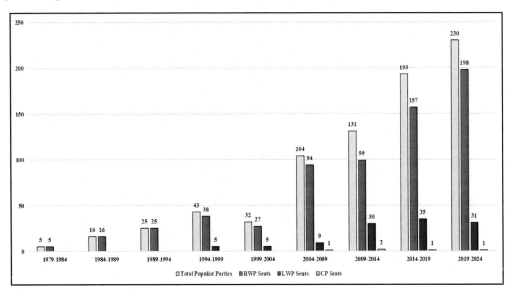

Source: Boissieu (2019), EP (2014, 2019), Cyprus Ministry of the Interior (2014), Norsk Senter for Forskningdata (2019), Pew Research Center (2014).

We organized this short article as follows. The first section retraces the evolution of the representation of populist parties in the EP from 1979 to 2019. In the next section, we compare RWP and LWP electoral performances. This comparison confirms that RWP parties continue to drive the current populist wave. The third section summarizes the 2019 European election results. In particular, we show that the pre-election predictions of an unprecedented upsurge of populism in Europe turned out to be exaggerated. Nevertheless, we show that RWP parties effectively succeeded in consolidating their presence in the EP in 2019.

I. Populist Parties in the European Elections: From Marginality to the Centre Stage

The evolution in terms of the seat and vote share of populist parties in the EP is one of constant expansion. Figures 1 and 2 show that, except for the 1999 European elections, the progression of the electoral performances of populist parties has followed a rising trend from election to election; more than doubling during the last 15 years from 14.2 per cent in 2004 to 30.6 per cent in 2019. Since the first European elections in 1979, no less than 71 populist parties have found their way into the EP (see Annex 1). Populist parties elected 779 populist members of the European Parliament (MEPs) from 1979 to 2019. Among them, 659 (84.6 per cent) belong to RWP

Figure 2: Percentage of Populist MEPs in the European Parliament. [Colour figure can be viewed at wileyonlinelibrary.com]

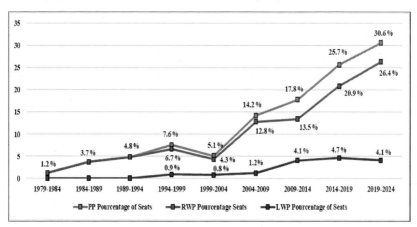

Sources: Boissieu (2019), EP (2014; 2019), Cyprus Ministry of the Interior (2014), Norsk Senter for Forskningdata (2019), Pew Research Center (2014). LWP, left-wing populist; PP, populist parties; RWP, right-wing populist.

parties,[3] 115 (14.8 per cent) to LWP parties and five (0.6 per cent) to centrist populist parties.[4] This represents 14.1 per cent of the 5,525 MEPs elected during the last 40 years. These numbers also show that populism 'at least in the Western European context, has more often than not been associated with the radical right and xenophobic politics' (van Kessel, 2013, p.4). This implies that, despite some stunning successes by LWP actors in Greece, Spain, Germany and France, in particular, in the aftermath of the 2007–2008 economic crisis, LWP parties have remained a rather fringe phenomenon, at least at the European level.

The two first populist parties to enter the EP in the 1979 European elections were the Dansk Folkeparti (Danish Progress Party) and the Italian Movimento Sociale Italiano (MSI); two parties that had gained less than 6 per cent share of the vote in their respective countries and sent one and four MEPs to Brussels, respectively. Subsequently, in the 1984 elections, RWP parties tripled their representation when the French National Front (NF) elected ten MEPs in addition to the five seats won by the MSI and one won by a coalition

---

[3]The classification of the Italian Five Star Movement (Movimento 5 Stelle, M5S) is particularly challenging. During the party's electoral breakthrough in the aftermath of the economic crisis of 2007–2008 the M5S attracted mostly left and centre-left voters (Bordignon and Ceccarini, 2013, p. 444). Yet, it 'does not fit in the pattern of left-wing populism' (Hooghe and Oser, 2016, p. 33) and it does not belong to the same radical left family as the Greek Syriza or the Spanish Podemos (Segatti and Capuzzi, 2016, p. 54). Rather 'Grillo's proposals concerning immigration control, and an anti-European attitude that let him to call a referendum for a possible exit of the country from the monetary union seem to be in line with the positions of the Italian right wing' (Bordignon and Ceccarini, 2015, p. 460). In addition, between 2014 and 2019 M5S MEPs sat in the Europe of Freedom and Direct Democracy Group, which is widely recognized as a collection of RWP parties. Therefore, we decided to count the party's MEPs together with those of RWP parties.

[4]There is a consensus in the literature that the Estonia Centre Party (Eesti Keskerakond) is one of the rare parties that can be classified as a centrist populist party in Europe, as 'populist discourse is evident in the rhetoric of Centre Party (KE)' (Jakobson *et al.*, 2012, p. 59). According to Havlík and Voda (2018), the centrist populist party that emerged 'in post-communist Europe [...] does not present a radical ideology [...] it tries to sidestep any ideology altogether and claims that it represents a non-ideological, anti-political alternative to the established parties. Its program is based on the claim that it fights the corrupt elite and pursues the interests of the people, promising to enhance living standards' (p. 162).

of small RWP parties in Greece. In 1989, the Republikaner, a German far-right party elected six MEPs and joined the NF and MSI. This success, even if it was short-lived, shattered the German political landscape, as it was the first time that an RWP party had gained more than 5 per cent of the vote in the aftermath of Nazi Germany. Furthermore, two parties that would become some of most successful RWP parties in Europe made their entrance to the EP in 1989: the Belgian Vlaams Blok (one seat) and the Italian Lega Lombarda, which would later become the Lega Nord, won two. For the next two elections in 1994 and 1999 the vote share of the RWP parties remained stable at around 5 per cent of all deputies. Although some far-right parties were shaking up their national political scene in the early 2000s (the French far-right wing candidate Jean Marie Le Pen qualified for the run-off of the presidential elections in 2002), but RWP parties made no major breakthrough in the EP until 2004.

The 2004 European elections constituted the first EP elections after the enlargement of the EU to include many of the former communist countries of Central and Eastern Europe. In these elections, RWP parties made substantive gains, more than tripling their vote share (from 27 seats in 1999 to 94 in 2004). These striking gains in the electoral performance of populist parties would not have been not possible without the strong performance of populist parties in Poland, the Czech Republic and Hungary. Parties like the Polish Law and Justice, the Hungarian Fidesz and Jobbik and the Czech Občanská demokratická strana (Civic Democratic Party, ODS) sent more than 40 per cent of the total number of RWP MEPs (45 of 94 in 2004 and 41 of 99 in 2009) to Brussels and Strasbourg. This success points to the fact that in (some) former communist satellite states (Hungary, Poland and Slovakia), RWP parties had become mainstream and majoritarian (Adam, 2017, p. 19). In 2014, populist far-right parties increased their seat share further, winning 157 seats, which is a growth of 481 per cent compared with the European elections prior to EU enlargement.

In contrast, the entrance of LWP parties into the EP was more modest. With Sweden and Finland joining the EU in the mid-1990s and organizing their first European elections in 1995 and 1996 respectively, LWP parties made their entry into the EP. The Swedish Vänsterpartiet (The Left) elected four MEPs and the Finnish Vasemmistoliitto (Left Alliance) elected two MEPs. In 1999 these leftist populist forces were followed by the Dutch Socialistische Partij (Socialist Party) and five years thereafter by the Portuguese Bloco de Esquerda (Left Bloc), the Irish Sinn Féin and the Cypriot Progressive Party of Working People (AKEL). However, the presence of the radical left remained marginal until the 2009 EP elections. Yet, in the aftermath of the 2007–2008 economic crisis, several LWP parties entered the EP. This was the case of the Czech Communist Party of Bohemia and Moravia (KSČM) (four seats), the Lithuanian Labour Party (one seat), the German Die Linke (eight seats) and the Greek Syriza (one seat). Five years later, in 2014, Die Linke (seven seats), Syriza (six seats) and the Spanish Podemos (five seats) became the three largest LWP parties in the EP. However, these grains were far less than the RWP parties were able to achieve during the same period. Even in the 2014 elections where the LWP parties registered their best electoral performance to date, LWP MEPs did not exceed 5 per cent of the total number of MEPs. In addition, among the 193 populist MEPs sitting in Brussels and Strasbourg in 2014, 80 per cent had an affiliation with a RWP party and only 19 per cent with a LWP one. Therefore, we can state with confidence that RWP parties have driven the populist wave over the past 40 years of EP elections.

II. The 2019 European Election Outcome: Winners and Losers

In the 2019 European elections, at least one MEP was elected from among 42 populist parties (28 RWP, 13 LWP, one centrist populist party) with an average vote share of 17.3 per cent for RWP parties and 10.6 per cent for LWP parties (see Figure 3). Overall, the number of populist parties that achieved more than 30 per cent of the vote share in their respective national contexts are RWP: the Hungarian Fidesz (52.1 per cent), the Polish Law and Order (PiS) (54.4 per cent), the Italian Northern League (LN) (34.3 per cent), the Bulgarian National Movement (VMRO/BMPO) (31.1 per cent) and the UK Brexit Party (30.7 per cent). Among the 26 parties that passed the bar of ten per cent, we have 20 RWP parties and five LWP parties. The two most successful LWP parties during these elections were the Cypriot AKEL (27.5 per cent) and the Greek Syriza (23.8 per cent). These were followed by the Irish Sinn Féin (11.7 per cent). the Portuguese Bloco de Esquerda (10.6) and the Spanish Podemos (10.1 per cent).

When it comes to the number of seats, the picture is somewhat different, considering that in the EP the total number of seats allocated to a country depends on that country's population size. In total 230 seats were won by populist parties in the 2019 European elections (198 by RWP parties, 31 by LWP parties and one by the only centrist populist party in our data, the Estonian Centre Party) (see Figure 4). The percentage of seats in the EP held by RWP parties increased from 20.9 per cent in 2014 to 26.4 per cent in 2019. Meanwhile seats held by LWP parties decreased from 4.7 per cent to 4.1 per cent. The average number of seats won is seven for RWP parties and 2.3 for LWP parties; a finding that again confirms that populism in the EP is more of a right-wing phenomenon than a far left-wing one. The Brexit Party was the party to elect the most MEPs (29), followed by the Italian LN (28), the Polish PiS (26), the French National Rally (20), the Italian M5S (14), the Hungarian Fidesz

Figure 3: Populist Parties' Vote Share in the 2019 European Elections. [Colour figure can be viewed at wileyonlinelibrary.com]

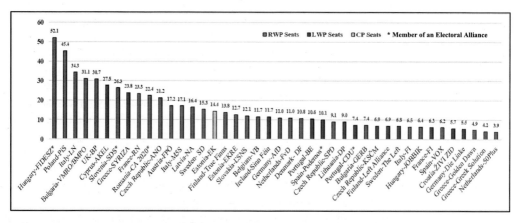

Sources: EP (2019), Norsk Senter for Forskningdata (2019).

(13) and the German Alternative for Germany (11). Figure 4 further shows that most of the populist parties elected have a parliamentary caucus of from one to ten MEPs. Parties in this category include the French La France Insoumise (six seats), the Czech Action of Dissatisfied Citizens (ANO) (six seats), and the Greek Syriza (six seats), among others. In addition, only one MEP was elected of 12 populist parties (the Dutch 50Plus and the Hungarian Jobbik).

Table 1 shows the change in shares of the vote and seats held by RWP parties between 2014 and 2019. The table indicates that three parties have driven the aggregate gains of RWP parties in 2019. The Italian Northern League (LN) vote share rose from to 6.15 per cent in 2014 to 34.3 per cent in 2019 (this triggered a 5.6-fold multiplication of its number of seats from five to 28 MEPs). In addition, the PiS vote share increased from 31.78 per cent to 45.38 per cent, allowing the party to gain 22 additional seats compared with 2014. We must add to these two parties the 'one-off Brexit Party with 30.74 per cent of the vote. The party won five extra seats compared to its UKIP predecessor five years previously (though UKIP took part in the 2019 European elections it did not win a seat). Among the RWP parties that entered the EP for the first time were the Bulgarian VMRO/BMPO (31.07 per cent; four MEPs), the Romanian Alliance 2020 (22.36 per cent; four seats), the Slovakian Kotlebists – People's Party Our Slovakia (L'SNS) (12.07 per cent; two seats) and the Italian Fratelli d'Italia (6.46 per cent; five seats).

However, not all RWP parties made gains in the 2019 European elections. This was particularly true of the Danish People's Party, one of the most well established and electorally strongest RWP parties in Western Europe. With diminished support, the

Figure 4: Populist Parties' Seat Share in the 2019 European Election. [Colour figure can be viewed at wileyonlinelibrary.com]

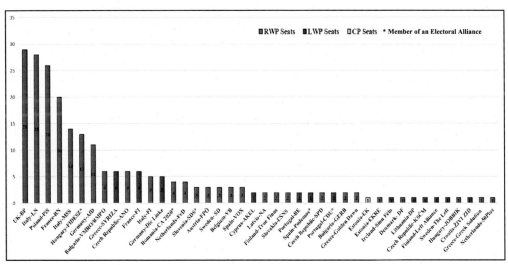

Sources: EP (2019), Norsk Senter for Forskningdata (2019).

Table 1: Vote and seat share of populist parties in 2014 and 2019

Country	Party	2019			2014			Variation	
		Vote share	Seats	Group	Vote share	Seats	Group	Vote Share	Seats
Austria	FPÖ	17.20	3	Identity and Democracy	19.72	4	NAM	−2.52	−1
Belgium	Vlaams Belang	11.68	3	Identity and Democracy	4.26	1	NAM	+7.43	+2
Bulgaria	VMRO/BMPO	31.07	6	EPP	10.66	2	ECR		+4
	GERB	7.36	2	ECR	30.40	6	EPP	−23.04	−4
Croatia	ŽIVI ZID	5.66	1	NAM	-	-		-	+1
	HSP-AS	-	-	-	41.40	1	ECR		−1
Cyprus	AKEL	27.49	2	GUE-NGL	26.98	2	GUE-NGL	+0.51	=
Czech Republic	SPD	9.14	2	Identity and Democracy	-	-			+2
	ANO	21.18	6	Renew Europe	16.13	4	ALDE	5.05	+2
	KSČM	6.94	1	GUE-NGL	10.98	3	GUE-NGL	−4.04	−2
	SVOBODNI	-	-		5.24	1	EFDC		−1
Denmark	People's Party	10.76	1	Identity and Democracy	26.60	4	ECR	−15.84	−3
Estonia	EKRE	12.70	1	Identity and Democracy	-	-			+1
	Centre Party	14.40	1	Renew Europe	22.4	1	ALDE	−8.00	=
Finland	True Finns	13.80	2	Identity and Democracy	12.90	2	ECR	+0.90	=
	Left Alliance	6.90	1	GUE-NGL	9.30	1	GUE-NGL	−2.4	=
France	National Rally, FN	23.31	20	Identity and Democracy	24.86	23	NAM	−1.55	−3
	FI	6.31	6	GUE-NGL	-	-			+6
Germany	AfD	11.00	11	Identity and Democracy	7.10	7	ECR	+3.9	+4
	Die Linke	5.50	5	GUE-NGL	7.40	7	GUE-NGL	−1.60	−2
	NPD	-	-		1.00	1	NAM		−1
Greece	Golden Dawn	4.88	2	NAM	9.39	3	NAM	−4.51	−1
	Greek Solution	4.18	1	ECR	-	-			+1
	SYRIZA	23.75	6	GUE-NGL	26.60	6	GUE-NGL	−2.85	=
	ANEL	-	-		3.46	1	ECR		−1
Hungary	FIDESZ	52.14	13	EPP	51.48	12	EPP		+1
	JOBBIK	6.44	1	NAM	14.67	3	NAM	−8.23	−2
Ireland	Sinn Féin	11.68	1	GUE-NGL	19.5	3	GUE-NGL	−7.82	−2
Italy	Lega Nord	34.33	28	Identity and Democracy	6.15	5	NAM	+28.18	+23
	M5S	17.07	14	NAM	21.15	17	EFDD	−4.08	−3

Table 1: (Continued)

Country	Party	2019 Vote share	2019 Seats	2019 Group	2014 Vote share	2014 Seats	2014 Group	Variation Vote Share	Variation Seats
	Fratelli d'Italia	6.46	5	ECR	-	-	-	-	+5
Latvia	National Alliance	16.40	2	ECR	14.25	1	ECR	+2.15	+1
Lithuania	Labour Party	8.99	1	Renew Europe	12.81	1	ALDE	-3.82	=
	Order and Justice	-	-	-	14.25	2	EFDD	-	-2
Netherlands	FvD	10.96	4	ECR	-	-	-	-	+4
	50Plus	3.91	1	EPP	-	-	-	-	+1
	PVV	-	-	-	13.32	4	NAM	-	-4
	SP	3.37	0	-	9.60	2	GUE-NGL	-	-2
Poland	PiS	45.38	26	ECR	31.78	4	ECR	+13.6	+22
	KNP	-	-	-	7.15	4	NAM	-	-4
Portugal	Bloco de Esquerda	10.56	2	GUE-NGL	4.93	1	GUE-NGL	5.63	+1
	CDU	7.41	2	GUE-NGL	13.71	3	GUE-NGL	-6.3	-1
Romania	Alliance 2020	22.36	4	Renew Europe	-	-	-	-	+4
Slovakia	LSNS	12.07	2	NAM	-	-	-	-	+2
	OL'ANO	-	-	-	7.46	1	ECR	-	-1
Slovenia	SDS	26.25	3	EPP	24.88	3	EPP	+1.37	=
Spain	Podemos	10.07	2	GUE-NGL	7.98	5	GUE-NGL	-	-3
	VOX	6.21	3	ECR	-	-	-	-	+3
Sweden	Sweden Democrats	15.34	3	ECR	9.67	2	EFDD	+5.67	+1
	Sweden; The Left	6.80	1	GUE-NGL	6.30	1	GUE-NGL	+0.5	=
UK	Brexit Party	30.74	29	NAM	-	-	-	-	+29
	UKIP	-	-	EFDD	26.77	24	EFDD	-	-24

Sources: European Parliament (2014a, 2019); Norsk Senter for Forskningdata (2019)

party's vote share shrank from 26.60 per cent to 10.76 per cent. It also lost three MEPs. Some other (smaller) RWP parties simply lost their representation in the EP (the Polish Congress of the New Right (KNP) (−4 seats), the Dutch Party for Freedom (PVV) (−4 seats), or the German NDP (−1)). In other countries, we found that one RWP won support to the detriment of another. One such example is Bulgaria. In this Eastern country the Citizens for European Development of Bulgaria (GERB) lost 23.04 percentage points in comparison to 2014 and was able to keep only two of the six seats it initially held. Yet this loss was more than compensated for by the new VMRO/BMPO coalition that won nearly one-third of the seats in Bulgaria. Something similar happened to UKIP, which lost all its seats to the Brexit Party (the Brexit party won six seats more in 2019 than UKIP did in 2014). A third group of RWP parties consolidated their position in this election with no or only a relatively slight change in their vote share. Among them, are the True Finns (13.80 per cent; two seats), the coalition of the Slovenian Democratic Party (SDS) (26.25 per cent; three seats) and the French National Rally (23.31 per cent; 20 seats).

When it comes to LWP parties, the performance of these parties was in slight decline in comparison to 2014 (see Table 1). Some of the successes within this party family were parties who either entered the EP as newcomers or were presenting their own autonomous list for the first time. Examples are the French La France Insoumise (6.31 per cent; six seats) and the Croatian Živi Zid (5.66 per cent; 1 seats). Probably the biggest election winner was the Portuguese Bloco de Esquerda, which doubled its vote and seat share from 4.93 per cent and one MEP in 2014 to 10.56 per cent and two MEPs in 2019. For a third group of LWP parties, the 2019 European election outcome was unfavourable. Examples are the Finnish Left Alliance (−2.4 percentage points; one seat), and the Greek Syriza (−2.85 percentage points; six seats).

III. Lessons to Draw from the 2019 EP Elections

Populist parties, in particular the populist right, fared very well in the 2019 EP elections. They continued their upward trajectory, gaining an additional 5 per cent of the vote and seats in 2019 compared with the 2014 elections. With 30 per cent of the seats, populist parties are a strong force in the current EP. This applies even more so because, the two centre coalitions, the European Peoples' Party and the Progressive Alliance of Socialists and Democrats lost their majority status for the first time in the history of the EP. Yet the 2019 elections were not the tsunami event expected to change the political landscape in Brussels and Strasbourg. Scattered across four party groups, RWP parties have remained a marginal force in the day-to-day business of the EP. The same applies to the radical populist left, which has stagnated at around 4 per cent of all MEPs in 2019.

Beyond this general observation, we can learn two lessons from these elections. First, populism in Europe remains predominantly a right-wing phenomenon. Despite the fact that since the 2009 European elections LWP parties have achieved important gains in same specific national contexts (Greece or Spain), the electoral successes of LWP parties has remained rather scattered so far. This implies that the electoral bases for LWP parties seem less consolidated, even in countries that have experienced a left-wing populist spring like Spain and Greece. Second, several RWP parties from Central and Eastern Europe, such as Fidesz and PiS have become normalized as political players in their national political system. The same does not fully apply to the traditional Western European RWP parties such as the French NF and the Italian LN, which still have a contested image. The 2019 European elections also show that these parties themselves are trying to maintain such a distinction through different European alliances. For example, RWP parties from former communist countries have mainly ran under the umbrella of the traditional right-wing European People's Party or the European Conservatives and Reformists Group. In contrast, Western European RWP parties are mainly aligned with the Identity and Democracy group or sit in the EP as non-attached members.

Quo vadis populism in Europe? Over the last 20 years populist parties, especially the right-wing variant, have gained unprecedented success, multiplying their vote share fivefold from 1999 to 2019. If this success continues they might be the strongest party family in 2024. Yet, in 2020, approximately a year after the 2019 European elections, the situation on the continent could not be more different from a year previously. Instead of the refugee crisis, Brexit, or climate change, the all-dominant topic is the coronavirus pandemic, which spread across the continent in the spring of 2020. As of 22 June 2020, it has led to more than 1.5 million infections and more than 150 thousand deaths on the continent (John Hopkins University Resource Center, 2020). The lockdown and the quarantine measures that most European countries imposed to contain the pandemic will most likely lead to the largest economic crisis in the 21st century. How will the EU, in combination with European nation-states, resolve this crisis? Will the EU manage to pass an emergency package that complements national efforts to contain it? Will the EU remain united in its response, or will the Covid-19 response weaken the EU? At the national level, will voters continue to endorse the crisis management of their national governments in most countries?

So far, RWP parties have been sidelined in the crisis response, and are rather have experienced a decline in citizens' support. While, it is still too early to say whether this trend will continue, it is at least possible that it will. Everything populism denounces, such as pragmatic leadership, science-based decision-making, international and European cooperation to find a vaccine and contain the crisis, are more important than ever to combat Covid-19. Populism embodies the antithesis of these attributes. It stands for dividing society in two blocks, one good and one bad, easy solutions for complex problems, and personalistic, non-science-based leadership. These characteristics are doomed to fail during a transboundary crisis such as Covid-19. A quick look across the ocean to the USA and Brazil illustrates these failures in effective crisis management. The Covid-19 response will be the dominant topic for months and years to come. If the centre-left and right coalition in the EU, as well as the mainstream national governments, succeed in manoeuvring successfully through the crisis, the growth curve of RWP parties may flatten and even reverse, in the same way as the Covid-19 curve had flattened by the end of June 2020 in most European countries. Yet we make this prediction with the caveat that the next EP elections are still 4 years down the road.

ANNEX 1: LIST OF POPULIST PARTIES IN THE EUROPEAN PARLIAMENT

First Entrance to the European parliament	English name	Domestic name	Acronym
AUSTRIA			
1996	Freedom Party of Austria	Freiheitliche Partei Österreichs	FPÖ
BELGIUM			
1994	National Front	Front national	FN
1989	Flemish Block/Interest	Vlaams Blok/Belang	VB
BULGARIA			
2014	Bulgarian National Movement	Българско национално движение	VMRO/BMPO
2009	Attack Party	Партия Атака	ATAKA
2007	Citizens for European Development of Bulgaria	Граждани за европейско развитие на България	GERB
CROATIA			
2019	Human Shield	Živi zid	ZZ
2013	Croatian Party of Rights Dr. Ante Starčević	Hrvatska Stranka Prava Dr. Ante Starčević	HSP-AS
CYPRUS			
2004	Progressive Party of Working People	Ανορθωτικό Κόμμα Εργαζόμενου Λαού	AKEL
CZECH REPUBLIC			
2019	Freedom and Direct Democracy	voboda a přímá demokracie	SPD
2014	Action of Dissatisfied Citizens	Akce nespokojených občanů	ANO
2014	Free Citizens' Party	Strana svobodných občanů	SVOBODNI
2009	Communist Party of Bohemia and Moravia	Komunistická strana Čech a Moravy	KSČM
2004	Civic Democratic Party	Občanská demokratická strana	ODS
2004	Independent Democrats	Nezávisli demokraté	NEZDEM
DENMARK			
1999	Danish People's Party	Dansk Folkeparti	DF
1979	Progress Party	Fremskridtspartiet	FrP
ESTONIA			
2019	Conservative People's Party of Estonia	Eesti Konservatiivne Rahvaerakond	EKRE
2004	Estonian Centre Party	Eesti Keskerakond	EK
FINLAND			

ANNEX 1: (Continued)

First Entrance to the European parliament	English name	Domestic name	Acronym
2009	True Finns	Perussuomalaiset	PS
1996	Left Alliance	Vasemmistoliitto	VAS
FRANCE			
1984	National Front/National Rally	Front national/Rassemblement national	RN-FN
2019	France Unbowed	La France insoumise	FI
GERMANY			
2014	Alternative for Germany	Alternative für Deutschland	AfD
2017	National Democratic Party of Germany	Nationaldemokratische Partei Deutschlands	NPD
2009	The Left	Die Linke	DL
1989	The Republicans	Die Republikaner	REP
GREECE			
2019	The Greek Solution	Ελληνική Λύση	EL
2014	Golden dawn	Χρυσή Αυγή	XA
2014	Independent Greeks	Ανεξάρτητοι Έλληνες	ANEL
2009	Coalition of the Radical left	Συνασπισμός Ριζοσπαστικής Αριστεράς	SYRIZA
2004	Popular Orthodox Rally	Λαϊκός Ορθόδοξος Συναγερμός	LAOS
1984	National Political Union	Εθνική Πολιτική Ένωσις	EPEN
1984	Political Spring	Πολιτική Ανοιξη	ANOIXI
HUNGARY			
2009	Movement for a Better Hungary	Jobbik Magyarországért Mozgalom	JOBBIK
2004	Alliance of Young Democrats	Fiatal Demokraták Szövetsége	FIDESZ
IRELAND			
2004	Sinn Féin	Sinn Féin	SF
ITALY			
2019	Brothers of Italy	Fratelli d'Italia	FDI
2014	Five Star Movement	Movimento Cinque Stelle	M5S
1989	Lega Lombarda/Northern League	Lega Nord	LN-LL
1994	National Alliance	Alleanza Nazionale	AN
1979	Italian Social Movement	Movimento Sociale Italiano	MSI
LATVIA			
2019	National Alliance	Nacionālā apvienība	NA

ANNEX 1: (Continued)

First Entrance to the European parliament	English name	Domestic name	Acronym
2004	For Fatherland and Freedom/LNNK	Tēvzemei un Brīvībai/LNNK	TB/LNNK
LITHUANIA			
2004	Liberal Democratic Party/Order and Justice	Liberalų Demokratų Partija/Tvarka ir teisingumas	TS-TT
2009	Labour Party	Darbo Partija	DP
LUXEMBOURG			
No party			
MALTA			
No party			
NETHERLANDS			
2019	50Plus	50Plus	50Plus
2019	Forum for Democratie	Forum voor Democratie	FvD
2009	Party for Freedom	Partij voor de Vrijheid	PVV
1999	Socialist Party	Socialistische Partij	PS
POLAND			
2014	Congress of the New Right	Kongres Nowej Prawicy	KNP
2004	Law and Justice	Prawo i Sprawiedliwość	PiS
2004	League of Polish Families	Liga Polskich Rodzin	LPR
2004	Self-Defence of the Republic of Poland	Samoobrona Rzeczpospolitej Polskiej	SRP
PORTUGAL			
2009	Unitary Democratic Coalition	Coligação Democrática Unitária	CDU (PCP–PEV)
2004	Left Bloc	Bloco de Esquerda	BE
ROMANIA			
2019	Save Romania Union	Uniunea Salvați România	USR
2009	Greater Romania Party	Partidul România Mare	PRM
SLOVAKIA			
2019	Kotlebists – People's Party Our Slovakia	Kotlebovci – Ľudová strana Naše Slovensko	ĽSNS
2014	Ordinary People	Obyčajní Ľudia a nezávislé osobnosti	OĽaNO
2009	Slovak National Party	Slovenská národná strana	SNS
SLOVENIA			
2004	Slovenian Democratic Party	Slovenska demokratska stranka	SDS
SPAIN			

ANNEX 1: (Continued)

First Entrance to the European parliament	English name	Domestic name	Acronym
2019	VOX	VOX	VOX
2014	We Can	Podemos	PODEMOS
1989	Group José María Ruiz Mateos	Agrupación de Electores José María Ruiz Mateos	Mateos
SWEDEN			
2014	Sweden Democrats	Sverigedemokraterna	SD
1995	The Left	Vänsterpartiet	V
UK			
2019	Brexit Party	Brexit Party	BP
1999	UK Independence Party	UK Independence Party	UKIP
2009	British National Party	British National Party	BNP

References

Adam, R. (2017) 'A Populist Momentum in the EU?' *Online Journal Modelling the New Europe*, Vol. 23, No. 1, pp. 19–30.

Boissieu, L. (2019) 'Europe Politique|europe-politique.eu'. Available online at: https://www.europe-politique.eu/

Bordignon, F. and Ceccarini, L. (2013) 'Five Stars and a Cricket. Beppe Grillo Shakes Italian Politics'. *South European Society and Politics*, Vol. 18, No. 4, pp. 427–49.

Bordignon, F. and Ceccarini, L. (2015) 'The Five-Star Movement: A Hybrid Actor in the Net of State Institutions'. *Journal of Modern Italian Studies*, Vol. 20, No. 4, pp. 454–73.

Boros, T., Bartha, D., Cuperus, R., Győri, G., Hegedus, D., Eszter, G.L. and Soos, P. (2016) *The State of Populism in Europe 2017: With Special Focus on the Populists in Austria, the Czech Republic, France, Germany and the Netherlands* (Budapest: Foundation for European Progressive Studies and Policy Solutions and Friedrich-Ebert-Stiftung).

Cyprus Ministry of the Interior (2014) 'European Elections 2014 Official Results'. Available online at: http://results.elections.moi.gov.cy/English/EUROPEAN_ELECTIONS_2014/Islandwide

Erlanger, S. (2019) '*European Elections Will Gauge the Power of Populism*'. The New York Times. Available online at: https://www.nytimes.com/2019/05/19/world/europe/european-parliament-elections-populists.html

European Parliament (EP) (2014a) '*European Elections 2014: List of Elected MEPs*'. DG Communication, Public Opinion Monitoring Unit. Available online at: http://www.europarl.europa.eu/pdf/elections_results/ElectedMEPs.pdf

European Parliamet (EP) (2019) 'European Elections Results'. Available online at: https://europarl.europa.eu/election-results-2019/en/national-results/cyprus/2004-2009/constitutive-session/

EP http://www.europarl.europa.eu/elections2014-results/en/country-results-at-2009.html

Havlík, V. and Voda, P. (2018) 'Cleavages, Protest or Voting for Hope? The Rise of Centrist Populist Parties in the Czech Republic'. *Swiss Political Science Review*, Vol. 24, No. 2, pp. 161–86.

Hooghe, M. and Oser, J. (2016) 'The Electoral Success of the Movimento 5 Stelle: An Example of a Left Populist Vote?' *Österreichische Zeitschrift für Politikwissenschaft*, Vol. 44, No. 4, pp. 25–36.

Jakobson, M. R., Balcere, I., Loone O., Nurk A., Saarts, T. and Zakeviciute R. (2012) *Populism in the Baltic States: A Research Report*. Tallinn University Institute of Political Science and Governance/Open Estonia Foundation. Available online at: https://oef.org.ee/fileadmin/media/valjaanded/uuringud/Populism_research_report.pdf

John Hopkins University (2020). Corona Resource Center. Accessed on June 28, 2020 from www.coronavirus.jhu.edu/map.htlm

Mudde, C. (2004) 'The Populist Zeitgeist'. *Government and Opposition*, Vol. 39, No. 4, pp. 541–63.

Norsk Senter for Forskningdata (2019) 'European Election Database'. Available online at: http://eed.nsd.uib.no/webview/

Pew Research Center (2014) 'Can the European Center Hold?' Available online at: https://www.google.com/search?sxsrf=ACYBGNRUfBs3YOmpIzm5ML_IxEeFXvr35w:1578762930384&q=Can+the+European+Center+hold,+Pew+2014&tbm=isch&source=univ&sa=X&ved=2ahUKEwiap5mdhvzmAhVKIqwKHU6yAe0QsAR6BAgJEAE&biw=1920&bih=920#imgrc=JNAjNOMyxtsjDM

RTE (2019) 'Elections Set to Quantify Rise of Populism in Europe'. Available online at: https://www.rte.ie/news/elections-2019/2019/0521/1050858-eurosceptic/

Segatti, P. and Capuzzi, F. (2016) 'Five Stars Movement, Syriza and Podemos: A Mediterranean Model?' In Martinelli, A. (ed.) *Populism on the Rise Democracies under Challenge?* (Novi Ligure: Edizioni Epoké), pp. 47–72.

Van Kessel, S. (2013) 'A Matter of Supply and Demand: The Electoral Performance of Populist Parties in Three European Countries'. *Government and Opposition*, Vol. 48, No. 2, pp. 177–99.

JCMS 2020 Volume 58. Annual Review pp. 43–56   DOI: 10.1111/jcms.13080

Green Versus Radical Right as the New Political Divide? The European Parliament Election 2019 in Germany

CARL C. BERNING[1] and CONRAD ZILLER[2]
[1]Johannes Gutenberg-University of Mainz, Mainz [2]University of Cologne, Cologne

Introduction

The European Parliament (EP) election 2019 in Germany was exceptional for several reasons. Most notably, Bündnis90/Die Grünen (the Green Party) nearly doubled its support compared with the EP election in 2014, while the CDU/CSU (Christian Union) and SPD (Social Democrats) had their worst results in the history of EP elections. Another characteristic that stood out in the 2019 EP election in general is the personalization of campaigns, including in TV debates with lead candidates (*Spitzenkandidaten*) for the European Commission presidency. Ironically, none of these candidates got the job. Following the large intake of refugees during the so-called refugee crisis and electoral successes of the radical right party AfD (Alternative for Germany) in several elections, AfD also received substantial electoral support in the 2019 election, with 11.0 per cent of the votes. However, while immigration had dominated public debate during the previous federal and in recent state elections in Germany, the EP election was a turning point in terms of the public and political salience of issues, with climate change and environmental protection taking the centre stage. In this article we examine the results of the EP election 2019 in Germany and emphasize the role of broader contextual developments. Empirical results from individual-level data in the European Election Study (EES) show that environmentalism represents one of the most relevant cleavages behind voting decisions in this election, which outpaced even the role of economic and immigration-related considerations.

Voting behaviour in EP elections is usually different from that of national elections. For the most part, EP elections have long been perceived as a residual political event, a second-order election (Reif *et al.*, 1997), and one that voters see as an opportunity to express their protests against and frustration with national politics, if they vote at all. While voting in the 2019 German EP election is in some respects not very different from a national one (such as the domination of domestic political cleavages and issues), it has been unique for the abovementioned reasons.

In this article, we aim to provide a deeper understanding of the driving factors of electoral behaviour in the 2019 EP election in Germany. To do so, we first provide an overview of the last 40 years of EP elections in Germany, together with a description of changes in turnout and results. Then we conceptualize the 2019 German EP election and its campaigns, and formulate our theoretical assumptions about political issues that mobilized the electorate. We test our assumptions with the German sample of the EES 2019 (Schmitt *et al.*, 2019). Using logistic regression analysis, we examine the determinants underlying voting decisions in the 2019 German EP election. Based on our results, we then compare the effects of the two most pronounced political issues, environmental protection and immigration, focusing on voting for Bündnis90/Die Grünen and the radical right AfD. In sum, our results show that environmental protection was the key and most relevant cleavage in the German 2019 EP election.

I. The EP Elections in Germany: from 1979 to the Present

In 1979 67.5 per cent of the German electorate turned out to vote in the first EP election (see Figure 1). However, over the years participation rates declined to an all-time low of 43.3 per cent in 2009. Yet after the 2009 EP election, it seemed that the tide has turned and in the most recent EP election in 2019 61.4 per cent of the electorate turned out to cast their ballot. That is the highest turnout since the reunification of Germany. We can link some of these trends to the rise of the populist radical right AfD in Germany but that is not the whole story. The increased turnout since the 2009 election is also a direct result of the personalization of campaigns. Since then, every major political group of the EP nominated a lead candidate (*Spitzenkandidat*) for the European Commission and there is empirical evidence that this has led to an increase in turnout (Schmitt *et al.*, 2015). However, the effects were moderate and large segments of the electorate were still not able to identify candidates correctly. In the 2014 elections, the visibility of the *Spitzenkandidaten* was rather low in Germany (Schulze, 2016). The 2019 campaigns tried to change that by promoting the visibility of the *Spitzenkandidaten* in multiple TV debates. Nonetheless, they were still not the focus of most campaigns.

In the 1980s and most of the 1990s the CDU/CSU and SPD dominated the EP elections. Together, they accumulated about 80 per cent of the votes. While together they still hold the majority of votes, their support has decreased steadily since the 2000s. Especially SPD suffered and substantially lost public support toward the end of Gerhard Schröder's

Figure 1: Turnout rate for the EP elections.

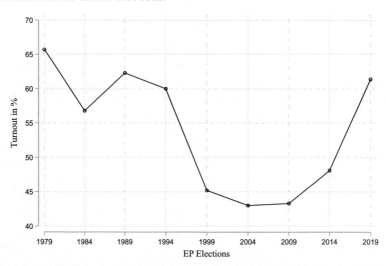

Source: Der Bundeswahlleiter, https://www.bundeswahlleiter.de/.

chancellorship in 2005. Even though Die Linke (the Left Party) and some smaller parties, such as Die Piraten (Pirate Party) or Freie Wähler (Free Voters) entered the political arena, the electoral support of these smaller parties stalled at around 10 per cent. Thus, the story of the last decades of the EP elections is one of the establishment of new (rather small) parties at the expense of Germany's traditional two big parties (instead of the rise of a third big one). Figure 2 displays the results of the EP elections since 1979 for the six largest parties (we present the results for all parties since 1979 in Appendix A).

Given the historical evolution of EP elections and the general trends described above, the results of the 2019 EP election in Germany were all the more exceptional. CDU/CSU received 28.9 per cent of the votes and Bündnis90/Die Grünen came in second with 20.5 per cent. SPD only got 15.8 per cent and the AfD received 11 per cent of the votes. Die Linke and FDP received around 5 per cent and none of the other parties collected more than 2.5 per cent of the votes, respectively. Evidently, the 2019 EP election in Germany changed the power relations in the party system and the underlying reasons for this call for further analysis.

II. Electoral Choice in the 2019 EP Election and the Case of Germany

In Germany, people perceived unemployment to be the most important problem over most of the previous two decades (Forschungsgruppe Wahlen, 2019). With a few exceptions, that was true until the so-called European refugee crisis took the spotlight in 2015. The rise of AfD in Germany catalysed the refugee and immigration issue into a political problem (Arzheimer, 2019; Arzheimer and Berning, 2019), which dominated the public and political agenda until the spring of 2019. The rallies and protests against climate change started in the fall of 2018, but received mass media and mainstream attention only

Figure 2: Results of the EP elections since 1979 for the six largest parties.

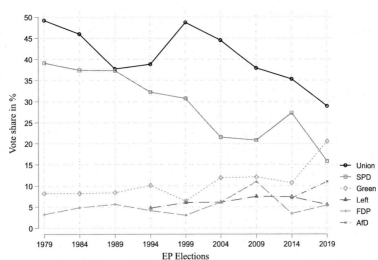

Source: Der Bundeswahlleiter, https://www.bundeswahlleiter.de/. [Colour figure can be viewed at wileyonlinelibrary.com]

in early 2019 (Haunss *et al.*, 2019). Specifically, the time before the EP elections was marked by protests by the 'Fridays for Future' movements and the first Global Climate Strike in March 2019.

In the German party system the few examples of successful single-issue parties are the Green party, promoting environmental protection, and AfD, opposing immigration. Following the theory of issue ownership, the closer the association of a party with an issue, the more competent this party perceived is to be by the electorate (Petrocik, 1996). While the immigration issue overshadowed the 2017 Federal election in Germany and paved the way for AfD to enter the German federal parliament as the third largest party, the climate change movement attracted most of the campaign attention right before the EP election in 2019. For the electorate of the populist radical right AfD, the immigration issue was nonetheless still very relevant to their voting decision (Arzheimer and Berning, 2019). At the same time, the populist radical right throughout Europe (including AfD) framed the EU mostly as a threat to national interests and identity (Lubbers and Coenders, 2017). More recently, these parties leveraged anti-elitism more generally in order to gain electoral support, especially from politically disenchanted voters (Berning and Ziller, 2017; Werts *et al.*, 2013; Ziller and Schübel, 2015).

The 2019 EP elections came at a bad time for the CDU/CSU and the SPD. A good year before these elections, both parties had negotiated the terms for a second-term grand coalition, after talks between the CDU/CSU, the FDP, and Bündnis90/Die Grünen failed. Both the CDU and SPD witnessed a steep decline in popularity and even party officials openly stated that another term would severely hurt them both.[1] This was not just because of their loss of popularity, but because voters generally respond to grand coalitions with an increase in votes for parties outside the governing alliance (Banaszak and Doerschler, 2012), and turn their back on junior coalition partners especially (Klüver and Spoon, 2020). Furthermore, the state elections in Bavaria and Hesse in October 2018 damaged the governing parties severely. In both elections, the CSU/CDU and SPD each lost more than ten percentage points of votes compared with the results of previous state elections. Therefore, Angela Merkel announced in 2018 that this would be her last term as a chancellor and that she would not seek re-election as the head of the CDU.[2] Crumbling national support for the CDU/CSU and SPD provided fertile ground for AfD and Bündnis90/Die Grünen to scoop up disappointed voters from the two main parties.

The spectrum of political issues has also become vastly more complex in recent years. It is no longer all economics, and has not been so for quite some time (Bornschier, 2010; Kriesi *et al.*, 2008). The issue (and the salience) of climate change in 2019 is one example of how another dimension of cleavage became the focus of political and public debates. Climate change was not the only issue that mobilized people, especially young citizens, to engage in mass protest in early 2019. The new Directive on Copyright in the Digital Single Market also mobilized segments of Germany's youth (Kuczerawy, 2019). Although these protests were much smaller than the anti-climate change movement and

---

[1]'Angela Merkel's Government Impasse: Grand Coalition Pros and Cons', retrieved from https://www.dw.com/en/angela-merkels-government-impasse-grand-coalition-pros-and-cons/a-41600717
[2]'Angela Merkel to Step Down as German Chancellor in 2021', retrieved from https://www.bbc.com/news/world-europe-46020745

were only temporary, they showed that the general public, again specifically the younger generation, also care about actual EU policies (see also Hobolt and de Vries, 2016).

All in all, public debates centred around climate change as well as migration. While economic issues took a back seat, they remained relevant particularly for the FDP and Die Linke. These parties continued to emphasize economic topics, because they struggled to find a clear and distinctive position on immigration or climate change (Akkerman, 2015; Steiner and Hillen, 2018). In the remainder of this article, we examine empirically the relative differences in the weight voters placed on several issues when opting for a political party in the 2019 EP election in Germany.

III. Determinants of Party Choice in the 2019 EP Elections in Germany

To analyse electoral behaviour in the 2019 EP election, we use the German sample of the EES 2019 (Schmitt *et al.*, 2019). The EES is a high-quality post-election survey of individual respondents, conducted subsequent to most EP elections in EU member states. In our analysis we use a sample of 816 respondents. The outcome variables under study are a set of binary variables of party vote, indicating whether respondents chose a respective party (variable takes on value 1), or not (variable takes on value 0). As main explanatory variables, we focus on three political issues: state regulation (in favour or against), liberal immigration policy (in favour or against), and support for environmental protection over economic growth (and vice versa).

While policy preferences have become more and more relevant, party identification is a stubbornly important factor for electoral behaviour (Johnston, 2006). Therefore, we include a binary measure of party identification as a covariate. Moreover, we also include a set of socio-demographic and structural control variables (gender, age, education, and region of residence). The operationalization of the variables included as well as descriptive statistics appear in Tables A2 and A3.

We base our empirical findings on a series of logistic regression models for each larger party and present them in Table 1.[3] Before we compare the relative impact of selected political issues across parties, we look at party choice and its determinants for each party individually. For CDU/CSU (Model 1), we find that the probability of voting for either the CDU or CSU increases with age (see also Goerres, 2008). The Christian Union managed, at least partly, to mobilize their core supporters, as party identification has a positive (yet only marginally significant) effect. Voting for the conservative CDU/CSU is further motivated by preferences for less state regulation and opposition to environmental protection. Similarly, SPD voters are older than other voters (Model 2). Apart from age, we only find a significant effect for party identification. Thus, the SDP were able to mobilize their core supporters as well.

Bündnis90/Die Grünen were the unofficial winners of the 2019 EP elections. They came second and practically doubled their support. Model 3 shows that Bündnis90/Die Grünen were especially popular among women and younger voters. Regarding political issues, the strong positive effect of environmental protection is hardly a surprise, as that has always been and remains their core issue. Our results also show a negative effect of

---

[3]All models are based on maximum likelihood estimation and we used robust standard errors. Furthermore, we use predictive margins to visualize our results.

Table 1: Logistic Regressions of Vote in the Last EP Elections

	Model 1: CDU/CSU		Model 2: SPD		Model 3: Bündnis90/Die Grünen		Model 4: Die Linke		Model 5: FDP		Model 6: AfD	
	Logit	S.E.	Logit	S.E.	Logit	S.E.	Logit	S.E.	Logit	S.E.	Logit	S.E.
Female	−.205	.185	−.065	.240	.347 +	.192	.298	.308	.255	.308	−.402 +	.235
Age	.022 ***	.006	.019 **	.007	−.011 *	.006	−.002	.010	.009	.010	.012 +	.007
Education												
Low	Ref.		Ref.		Ref.		Ref.		Ref.		Ref.	
Medium	−.299	.300	.332	.436	−.086	.301	.530	.581	.288	.600	.029	.279
High	−.257	.297	.369	.438	.299	.238	.486	.570	.471	.609	−.731 +	.404
East Germany	−.280	.235	−.140	.287	−.292	.238	−.250	.374	−.529	.464	.934 ***	.245
Party identification	.440 +	.235	.821 **	.312	.270	.217	.577	.399	−.245	.359	.436	.277
State regulation	−.070 +	.040	.053	.052	.050	.037	−.118 +	.063	−.271 ***	.052	.436 ***	.055
Immigration	.016	.027	−.030	.030	−.069 **	.028	−.036	.042	.019	.044	.090 *	.045
Environment	−.120 ***	.034	.048	.046	.288 ***	.043	−.010 +	.057	−.031	.051	−.262 ***	.048
Constant	−1.52 **	.503	−4.43 ***	.688	−3.21 ***	.510	−4.77 ***	.961	−2.34 **	.872	−1.59 **	.533
N	816		816		816		816		816		816	
R^2	0.0575		0.0399		0.1047		0.0367		0.0667		0.1190	
AIC	778.61		559.88		753.16		371.72		350.32		551.36	

Note: *** $=P<0.001$; ** $=P<0.01$; * $=P<0.05$; + $=P<0.100$. Unstandardized logits and robust standard errors are presented. Source: Own calculations

restrictive migration views on voting probability. In Model 4 we find that the probability of voting for Die Linke correlates with support for state regulation and the prioritization of environmental protection. The political issue of state regulation appeals to a leftist ideology and the effect of environmental protection probably comes from general opposition to the prioritizing of economic growth over anything else. In Model 5 we find that only opposition to state intervention in the economy influences the probability of voting for the FDP. During their campaign, the FDP struggled to find a clear position on environmental and migration issues. Lastly, Model 6 presents the results for support for AfD. Unlike left or liberal voters, the probability of voting for AfD correlates substantially with socio-demographic factors. This party mobilized mostly men, those who were older, and individuals with low education. Moreover, the probability of voting for the radical right is higher among East Germans, which has been highlighted in prior studies (Arzheimer, 2019). Finally, we find that support for AfD is motivated by support for restrictive immigration, but also, by opposition to the prioritization of environmental protection over economic growth.

In sum, our results are generally in line with the political agenda and thematic priority of these major parties. Most of the parties attract voters from a wide segment of the electorate, spanning traditional cleavages (such as religious denomination, urban–rural divides and occupation). Bündnis90/Die Grünen and AfD are the great exception: they attract support from very distinctive socio-demographic and ideological segments of the electorate.

In a next step, we compare the relevance of selected determinants across parties and thereby focus on the most exceptional parties in the 2019 EP election: Bündnis90/Die Grünen and the AfD. While immigration remains an important issue in 2019, protests against climate change pushed the environmental issue high on the political agenda. In the regression models presented above, we find that support for restrictive immigration and prioritizing environmental protection over growth matter for supporters of both Bündnis90/Die Grünen and AfD respectively. As discussed earlier, Bündnis90/Die Grünen can practically claim issue ownership over environmental protection and AfD can claim it over restricting immigration.

In Figure 3 we present the predictive margins of support for restrictive immigration policies on vote choice (that is, predicted probabilities with 95 per cent confidence intervals). The results show that the predicted voting probability at full opposition to restrictive immigration policy is three times higher for Bündnis90/Die Grünen than AfD. High levels of preferences for restrictive policies are related to a decreasing probability of voting for Bündnis90/Die Grünen, whereas the probability of voting for AfD increases.

We present the predictive margins of preferences prioritizing environmental protection on vote choice in Figure 4. The overall pattern highlights the importance of the environment for the 2019 elections. The predictive probability of voting for Bündnis90/Die Grünen at full prioritization of economic growth over environmental protection is nearly zero, while the probability of voting for AfD at this condition is around 37 per cent. With more favourable environmental protection preferences, the probability of voting increases for Bündnis90/Die Grünen and decreases for AfD. At full support for prioritizing environmental protection over economic growth, the probability of voting for Bündnis90/Die Grünen is about 36 per cent, while it is virtually zero for AfD. These results show that

Figure 3: Predictive margins of preferences for restrictive immigration policies on vote choice for Bündnis90/Die Grünen and AfD (CIs, confidence intervals).

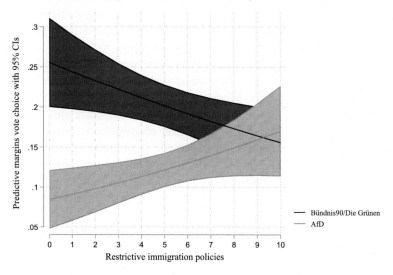

Source: Own Calculations.

Figure 4: Predictive margins of preferences prioritization of environmental protection on vote choice for Bündnis90/Die Grünen and AfD (CIs, confidence intervals).

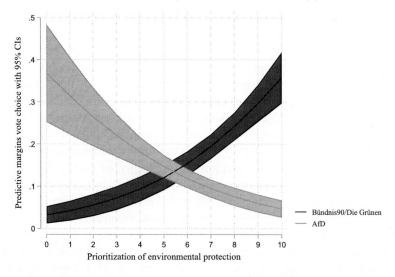

Source: Own Calculations.

the battleground of the 2019 EP election was fought on both the cleavage of immigration and that of environmental protection.

IV. Implications of the German 2019 EP Election

The 2019 EP elections in Germany broke many records. For one, the turnout rate was the highest since German reunification. Second, the two major parties, CDU/CSU and SPD, which dominated the political stage for most EP elections in terms of their combined vote share, received their worst results ever. Third, Bündnis90/Die Grünen more than doubled their support and came in third with an historic high.

In the run-up to the EP elections, the previously much-debated topic of immigration was largely replaced by a public debate about climate change. Large-scale protests and school strikes drew much of the political attention and created fertile ground for the emergence of Bündnis90/Die Grünen as a strong alternative party choice. Although the public salience of the immigration topic vanished to some extent, the radical right AfD still attracted a substantial share of votes, especially in East Germany. The economic issue as a determinant of party choice appeared to be relevant only for Die Linke and the FDP.

Using data from the German sample of the EES 2019 (Schmitt *et al.*, 2019), we examined determinants of voting behaviour in the EP elections. We find that party identification mattered only for the CDU/CSU and SPD, and that environmental protection and restrictive migration policies were the main driving factors for supporting the Bündnis90/Die Grünen and the AfD. Comparing their relevance across parties, we find that environmental protection was truly a defining issue in determining the outcome of the 2019 EP election in Germany.

In Germany, the recent years are testimony to the contemporary volatility of political behaviour. The time when the CDU/CSU and the SPD dominated Germany's political arena is over, not least because of a demographic change in Germany. The relevance of political issues (as well as individual politicians and political leaders) will become increasingly decisive for vote choices, while the impact of party identification and old cleavages has already started to diminish (Ferreira da Silva *et al.*, 2019). The extent to which the German 2019 EP election provided a new trajectory for the current and future political landscape in Germany remains an open question. Nonetheless, in the aftermath of the 2019 EP election, state elections in Brandenburg, Saxony and Thuringia (all in East Germany) resulted in losses for conservative and social democratic parties and gains for the AfD in particular and, to some extent, for Bündnis90/Die Grünen (in Brandenburg and Saxony). The enduring success of the Greens in public opinion polls has stimulated speculation of a potential coalition between the CDU/CSU and Bündnis90/Die Grünen, or even a Green chancellor in the next Federal election in September 2021. But that, of course, remains to be seen.

In terms of implications for the political landscape of the EU, the rise of AfD and the success of Bündnis90/Die Grünen also suggest there may be supranational changes in the balance of power. The next few years will be formative for the future and direction of the EU and the role of the EP. With continuing Brexit negotiations, the aim to make the EU carbon neutral by 2050, and several other EU projects, such as digitalization, a common foreign and security policy, as well as responses to the recent COVID-19 pandemic, the stakes could not be higher.

References

Akkerman, T. (2015) 'Immigration Policy and Electoral Competition in Western Europe: A Fine-grained Analysis of Party Positions over the Past Two Decades'. *Party Politics*, Vol. 21, No. 1, pp. 54–67.

Arzheimer, K. (2019) '"Don't Mention the War!" How Populist Right-Wing Radicalism Became (Almost) Normal in Germany'. *JCMS*, Vol. 57, No. S1, pp. 90–102.

Arzheimer, K. and Berning, C.C. (2019) 'How the Alternative for Germany (AfD) and Their Voters Veered to the Radical Right, 2013–2017'. *Electoral Studies*, Vol. 60, 102040.

Banaszak, L.A. and Doerschler, P. (2012) 'Coalition Type and Voter Support for Parties: Grand Coalitions in German Elections'. *Electoral Studies*, Vol. 31, No. 1, pp. 46–59.

Berning, C.C. and Ziller, C. (2017) 'Social Trust and Radical Right-wing Populist Party Preferences'. *Acta Politica*, Vol. 52, No. 2, pp. 198–217.

Bornschier, S. (2010) 'The New Cultural Divide and the Two-dimensional Political Space in Western Europe'. *West European Politics*, Vol. 33, No. 3, pp. 419–44.

Coffé, H. (2018) 'Gender and the Radical Right'. In Rydgren, J. (ed.) *The Oxford Handbook of the Radical Right* (Oxford: Oxford University Press), pp. 200–11.

Doyle, W.R. and Skinner, B.T. (2017) 'Does Postsecondary Education Result in Civic Benefits?' *Journal of Higher Education*, Vol. 88, No. 6, pp. 863–93.

Ferreira da Silva, F., Garzia, D. and De Angelis, A. (2019) 'From Party to Leader Mobilization? The Personalization of Voter Turnout'. *Party Politics*. https://doi.org/10.1177/1354068819855707

Forschungsgruppe Wahlen, M. (2019) *Politbarometer 1977–2017 (Partielle Kumulation)* (KölnZA2391 Datenfile Version 10.0.0: GESIS Datenarchiv) https://doi.org/10.4232/1.13243

Franklin, M., Lyons, P. and Marsh, M. (2004) 'Generational Basis of Turnout Decline in Established Democracies'. *Acta Politica*, Vol. 39, No. 2, pp. 115–51.

Giger, N. (2009) 'Towards a Modern Gender Gap in Europe?: A Comparative Analysis of Voting Behavior in 12 Countries'. *Social Science Journal*, Vol. 46, No. 3, pp. 474–92.

Goerres, A. (2008) 'The Grey Vote: Determinants of Older Voters' Party Choice in Britain and West Germany'. *Electoral Studies*, Vol. 27, No. 2, pp. 285–304.

Haunss, S., Rucht, D., Sommer, M. and Zajak, S. (2019) 'United Kingdom'. In Wahlström, M., *Kocyba, P., De Vydt, M. and de Moor, J. (eds) Protest for a Future: Composition, Mobilization and Motives of the Participants in Fridays for Future Climate Protests on 15 March, 2019 in 13 European Cities*. Pp. 32–41 Available at: http://eprints.keele.ac.uk/6571/7/20190709_Protest%20for%20a%20future_GCS%20Descriptive%20Report.pdf,.

Hobolt, S.B. and de Vries, C.E. (2016) 'Turning Against the Union? The Impact of the Crisis on the Eurosceptic Vote in the 2014 European Parliament Elections'. *Electoral Studies*, Vol. 44, pp. 504–14.

Hough, D. and Koß, M. (2009) 'A Regional(ist) Party in Denial? The German PDS and its Arrival in Unified Germany'. *Regional & Federal Studies*, Vol. 19, No. 4–5, pp. 579–93.

Johnston, R. (2006) 'Party Identification: Unmoved Mover or Sum of Preferences?' *Annual Review of Political Science*, Vol. 9, No. 1, pp. 329–51.

Klüver, H. and Spoon, J.-J. (2020) 'Helping or Hurting? How Governing as a Junior Coalition Partner Influences Electoral Outcomes'. *Journal of Politics*, https://doi.org/10.1086/708239.

Kriesi, H., Grande, E., Lachat, R., Dolezal, M., Bornschier, S. and Frey, T. (2008) *West European Politics in the Age of Globalization* (Cambridge: Cambridge University Press).

Kuczerawy, A. (2019) 'EU Proposal for a Directive on Copyright in the Digital Single Market: Compatibility of Article 13 with the EU Intermediary Liability Regime' In Petkova, B. and Ojanen, T. (eds) *Fundamental Rights Protection Online: The Future Regulation of Intermediaries* (forthcoming). Available at: «https://ssrn.com/abstract=3309099

Lubbers, M. and Coenders, M. (2017) 'Nationalistic Attitudes and Voting for the Radical Right in Europe'. *European Union Politics*, Vol. 18, No. 1, pp. 98–118.

Petrocik, J. (1996) 'Issue Ownership in Presidential Elections, with a 1980 Case Study'. *American Journal of Political Science*, Vol. 40, No. 3, pp. 825–50.

Reif, K., Schmitt, H., Norris, S. and P. (1997) 'Second-order Elections'. *European Journal of Political Research*, Vol. 31, pp. 109–24.

Schmitt, H., Hobolt, S. B., van der Brug, W. and Popa, S. A. (2019) 'European Parliament Election Study 2019, Voter Study'. Available at: http://europeanelectionstudies.net/european-election-studies/ees-2019-study/voter-study-2019

Schmitt, H., Hobolt, S. and Popa, S.A. (2015) 'Does Personalization Increase Turnout? *Spitzenkandidaten* in the 2014 European Parliament Elections'. *European Union Politics*, Vol. 16, No. 3, pp. 347–68.

Schulze, H. (2016) 'The *Spitzenkandidaten* in the European Parliament Election Campaign Coverage 2014 in Germany, France, and the United Kingdom'. *Politics and Governance*, Vol. 4, No. 1, pp. 23–36.

Steiner, N. D. and Hillen, S. (2018) 'How do Left-authoritarian Voters Decide? Issue Salience, Position Misperception and Left-Right Identification'. Paper presented at the ECPR General Conference, Hamburg, 22–25 August.

Werts, H., Scheepers, P. and Lubbers, M. (2013) 'Euro-scepticism and Radical Right-wing Voting in Europe, 2002–2008: Social Cleavages, Socio-political Attitudes and Contextual Characteristics Determining Voting for the Radical Right'. *European Union Politics*, Vol. 14, No. 2, pp. 183–205.

Ziller, C. and Schübel, T. (2015) '"The Pure People" versus "the Corrupt Elite"? Political Corruption, Political Trust and the Success of Radical Right Parties in Europe'. *Journal of Elections, Public Opinion and Parties*, Vol. 25, No. 3, pp. 368–86.

A: Appendix

Table A1: Results of the EP elections since 1979.

year	Turnout	CDU	CSU	B90/Die Grünen	SPD	AfD	Linke	FDP	Partei	FW	Tierschutz	OEDP	Familie	Völt	NPD	REP	Piraten
1979	65,7	39,1	10,1		40,8			6,0									
1984	56,8	37,5	8,5	8,2	37,4												
1989	62,3	29,5	8,2	8,4	37,3			5,6								7,1	
1994	60	32	6,8	10,1	32,2												
1999	45,2	39,3	9,4	6,4	30,7		5,8										
2004	43	36,5	8	11,9	21,5		6,1	6,1									
2009	43,3	30,7	7,2	12,1	20,8		7,5	11									
2014	48,1	30	5,3	10,7	27,3	7,1	7,4	3,4	0,6	1,5	1,2	0,6	0.7		1	1,9	1,4
2019	61,4	22,6	6,3	20,5	15,8	11	5,5	5,4	2,4	2,2	1,4	1	0.7	0,7			0,7

Source: Der Bundeswahlleiter, https://www.bundeswahlleiter.de/

Table A2: Operationalization of Variables

Type of variable	Label and reference to previous literature	Operationalization
Outcome variable	Christian Union	All outcome variables are based on respondents' vote choice in the last EP elections. Respondents were asked: 'Which party did you vote for in the European Parliament elections?' Binary measure for vote choice (CDU/CSU=1, all others=0)
	Social Democrats	Binary measure for vote choice (SPD=1, all others=0)
	Green Party	Binary measure for vote choice (Bündnis 90/Die Grünen=1, all others=0)
	Left Party	Binary measure for vote choice (Die Linke=1, all others=0)
	Liberal Party	Binary measure for vote choice (FDP=1, all others=0)
	Radical Right	Binary measure for vote choice (AfD or NPD=1, all others=0)
Explanatory variables	State regulation	Respondents were asked 'What do you think of state regulation and control of the economy' on a scale from 0 'You are fully in favour of state intervention in the economy' to 10 'You fully opposed of state intervention in the economy'; reversely recoded.
	Immigration	Respondents were asked indicate their views towards immigration on a scale from 0 'fully in favour of a restrictive policy on immigration' to 10 'fully opposed of a restrictive policy on immigration'
	Environment	Respondents' answers ranged from 0 'Environmental protection should take priority even at the cost of economic growth' up to 10 'Economic growth should take priority even at the cost of environmental protection'; reversely recoded.
	Party identification	Party identifiers are all respondents, who named any party, when asked 'Do you consider yourself to be close to any particular party?' with all others as a reference category.
Control variables	Gender (Coffé, 2018)	Binary measure for gender (female=1, male=0)
	Age (Giger, 2009)	Age in years.
	Education (Franklin et al., 2004; Doyle and Skinner, 2017)	Measured with three binary variables (low education, medium education, high education)
	East Germany (Hough and Koß, 2009; Arzheimer and Berning, 2019)	Binary measure for living area (East Germany=1, West Germany=0)

Table A3: Descriptive statistics

Variable	Mean	SD	Min.	Max.
Female	.48	.50	0	1
Age	49.64	16.57	18	83
Low education	.124	.33	0	1
Medium education	.433	.50	0	1
High education	.444	.50	0	1
East Germany	.22	41	0	1
Party identification	.72	.45	0	1
State regulation	4.60	2.43	0	10
Immigration	5.05	3.22	0	10
Environment	6.53	2.78	0	10

Note: Mean, arithmetic mean; SD, standard deviation; min, minimum value; max, maximum value.

JCMS 2020 Volume 58. Annual Review pp. 57–68   DOI: 10.1111/jcms.13081

Macron versus the RN? The Battle Lines of French Politics Following the 2019 European Elections

GABRIEL GOODLIFFE
Instituto Tecnológico Autónomo de México, Mexico City

Introduction

As elsewhere in other EU member states, the 2019 European Parliament (EP) elections in France broke new ground. Overshadowed by the prospect of a populist surge, the election campaign in the country introduced a real debate regarding the future character of European integration, ranging from a 'Europe of nations' projected by eurosceptic radical populists to a 'federal Europe' envisioned by europhile neofunctionalists. As a result, the elections yielded a fractured partisan landscape, distinguished by a clear dividing line between opposing eurosceptic populist and europhile federalist parties (see Table 1). In a repeat of the 2014 EP election result, the radical-right populist Rassemblement National (RN)[1] candidate list came first in front of the governing party joint list comprising La République en Marche (LREM) and the Mouvement Démocratique (MoDem). These were succeeded in third place by the list presented by Europe Écologie Les Verts (EELV), mirroring the breakthroughs registered by Green party lists elsewhere in Europe. Conversely, the former governing parties continued their electoral slide that has started during the 2017 presidential and legislative elections, with the lists presented by Les

Table 1: 2019 European Elections Results in Comparative Perspective (n, per cent)

	EP 2019% (seats)	Leg. 2017 (% 1st rd.)	Pres. 2017 (% 1st rd.)	EP 2014% (seats)
RN/FN	23.3 (23)	13.2	22.9	24.9 (24)
LREM/MoDem	22.4 (23)	28.2/4.12	23.1	9.9 (7)†
EELV	13.5 (13)	4.3	–	9 (6)
LR/UMP	8.5 (8)	15.8	17.8	20.8 (20)
LFI/FdG	6.3 (6)	11	20.8	6.3 (3)‡
PS	6.2 (6)	7.4	5.7	14 (13)
DLF	3.5 (−)	1.2	6.1	3.9 (−)
Génération.s	3.3 (−)	–	–	–
UDI	2.5 (−)	3	–	†
PCF	2.5 (−)	2.7	–	‡

† MoDem + UDI Source: Ministère de l'Intérieur ‡ includes PCF *Notes:* DLF, Debout la France; EELV, Europe Écologie Les Verts; EP, European Parliament; FdG, Front de Gauche; FN, Front National; Leg., Legislative; LFI, La France Insumise; LREM, La République en Marche; LR, Les Républicains; MoDem, Mouvement Démocratique; PCF, Communist Party; PS, Socialist Party; rd. round; RN, Rassemblement National; UDI, right Union des Démocrates Indépendants; UMP, Union pour un Mouvement Populaire.

[1]This was the new name given to the former Front National (FN) by its leader Marine Le Pen at the March 2018 party congress, as part of the effort to revamp the party's image following her heavy defeat to Emmanuel Macron in the second round of the 2017 presidential election and the FN's poor performance in the June 2017 legislative elections.

Républicains (LR) and the Socialist Party (PS) each failing to reach the 10 per cent bar. Last but not least, the list presented by La France Insoumise (LFI) experienced a substantial setback compared with the party's 2017 presidential and legislative election performances. The other party lists presented by the right-wing populist Debout la France (DLF), former Socialist presidential candidate Benoît Hamon's Génération.s, the centre-right Union des Démocrates Indépendants (UDI) and the Communist Party (PCF) failed to garner any seats in the new EP. As elsewhere in Europe, these results were given legitimacy by a surge in voter participation, which rose to 51.12 per cent, an increase of nearly 9 per cent compared with 2014 and 10.5 per cent compared with 2009.

This article interprets these results from the way that European and domestic influences respectively informed the campaigns mounted by the principal parties and their impact on voters' choices and then assesses the European and domestic significance of the election results as well as their political and policy implications. Building on the results of the 2017 presidential election, the article argues that the 2019 European election crystallized the integration-versus-demarcation cleavage reflecting pro versus anti-European sentiments externally and liberal versus illiberal attitudes domestically that has emerged as the new fulcrum of competition ordering French politics.

I. The Campaign

The 2019 EP elections were conducted against the backdrop of fraught European and domestic contexts. At the first level, the successive crises that had struck the EU over the previous decade, notably the European debt crisis of 2010–12 and its aftermath of austerity policies, the migrant crisis of 2015 and the Brexit referendum of 2016, informed the different parties' European election campaigns. In France, as elsewhere, the debate over how to reform the eurozone's governance and institutional architecture in the wake of the debt crisis has driven both its European and domestic economic policy debate (Matthijs and Blyth, 2015). Similarly, the EU was unable to arrive at a common European immigration policy in the wake of the 2015 migrant crisis and reform the Dublin Regulation. This placed an undue burden on southern EU members as well as countries like France, where migrants were most likely to move, making immigration a more contentious campaign issue than it would otherwise have been (Achilli, 2019). Last but not least, the uncertainty generated by Brexit also influenced the 2019 European election in France, as one of the member states that would be most negatively impacted by Britain's departure from the EU.[2] Politically, the complications surrounding Brexit poured cold water on the sovereignist proposals of France's most eurosceptic parties in view of the 2019 European elections (Damgé et al., 2019). Reflecting the growing popular unease over European integration in the wake of these crises, the autumn 2018 Eurobarometer poll directly preceding the European elections indicated that 70 per cent of the French (compared with 52 per cent of Europeans as a whole) felt that 'things were going in the wrong direction in their country' while 63 per cent of them (versus 51 per cent of Europeans) believed that 'things were going in the wrong direction in the EU' (European Commission, 2018, pp. 58–61). This finding was echoed by a CEVIPOF survey from January

---

[2]One study estimated that the French economy would lose from €6.3 billion to €25 billion, corresponding to 34,500 to 141,320 job losses, depending on the proposals regarding British sovereignty—a 'soft' or 'hard' Brexit—with respect to the EU that materialized (Vandenbussche, 2019, pp. 22–3).

2019 which found that only 28 per cent of respondents had confidence in the EU (CEVIPOF, 2019, p. 27).

This difficult European context inevitably affected the policy platforms advanced by the different party lists through the 2019 election campaign. This was particularly the case in attenuating the programmes advanced by the most eurosceptic and europhile formations. Accordingly, the proposals advanced by the joint LREM-MoDem list were less ambitious than the extensive federalizing reforms that had been proposed during the 2017 presidential campaign and its aftermath. Notably absent from its programme was Macron's entreaty to establish a joint eurozone budget presided over by an EU-level finance minister as a preliminary step to achieving a fiscal union (Kriesi, 2018, p. 10). The most concrete European goal advanced by the LREM-MoDem list was to create a fund of one trillion euros to invest in clean energy and transport technologies, followed by general demands to agree a common migration policy, establish an EU-level collective security council, and harmonize European social policy (Durand *et al.*, 2019).

Conversely, among the eurosceptic parties the RN jettisoned its call to leave the euro and stage a Frexit referendum that anchored its European proposals in 2017, while LFI shelved its 'Plan A versus Plan B' approach to either change Europe by renegotiating the European treaties or else unilaterally depart from the EU (Cautrès, 2017, p. 177; Perrineau, 2017, p. 256). Instead, the former called for transforming the EU 'from the inside' in order to replace it with an 'alliance of the European nation states' while the latter demanded that the Fiscal Compact be repealed and European Central Bank finance an ecologically and socially progressive reflationary programme. However, LFI quietly abandoned its previous call for France to leave the EU were these conditions not met (Damgé *et al.*, 2019; Graulle, 2019).

For their part, the other party lists presented broadly pro-Europe programmes of the (centre) right or left. Apart from the customary themes of immigration and the assertion of national sovereignty on the right, and reform of European economic governance and bolstering social programmes on the left, the environment and urgency of tackling climate change emerged, as elsewhere, as a central issue in the campaign (Durand *et al.*, 2019).

At another level, a tense socio-political climate constituted the domestic backdrop informing the 2019 European election campaign. The ambitious fiscal and structural reforms enacted by the Philippe government became the object of widespread social protest

Table 2: Vote Transfers by Party between the 2017 Presidential (1st round.) and 2019 European Elections as Percentage of 2017 vote

2019 EP party lists	LFI	PS	LREM	LR	DLF	FN
LFI	37	3	1	–	1	–
Génération.s	2	21	1	–	1	–
PS-PP	7	29	7	–	4	1
EELV	17	26	20	2	3	2
LREM-MoDem	5	8	60	27	4	1
LR	–	–	2	38	7	2
DLF	2	2	–	4	37	2
RN	7	5	3	15	26	85

Source: Ifop, (2018), p. 22.

in the guise of the Gilets Jaunes (yellow vests) uprising that began in November 2018 and reached a crescendo in January 2019 before lessening in intensity from February and March 2019.[3] Attaining at its peak mobilization levels not seen since May 1968, this protest movement, channelling the social and economic anxieties of the France *d'en bas*, dramatically polarized the political environment in the lead-up to the 2019 European elections (Perrineau, 2019, pp. 63–118). The 'great national debate' that was organized by the administration in the form of public meetings and online consultations in order to address laypeople's concerns in future policy deliberations as well as measures to lessen the fiscal burden on the working poor failed to assuage the *Gilets Jaunes* in the run-up to the elections (Perrineau, 2019, pp. 119–62).[4]

Seen from this perspective, although the European election was ostensibly about choosing between the programmes the party lists would pursue if elected to the EP, it was also a referendum on Macron's tenure in office since his election in 2017 (Foucault, 2019). At one level, it stood as an electoral test of his ambitious supply-side economic agenda, which favoured upwardly mobile, relatively well-off and educated urban constituencies who benefit from globalization at the expense of low-class, less educated peripheral groups who lose out from it (Perrineau, 2019, pp. 68–9). At a second level, the election cast judgement on Macron's governing style and persona, specifically the imperious – 'Jupiterian' – manner in which he has pursued his reforms, frequently relying on executive decrees in order to force them through in the face of widespread public and partisan opposition (Confavreux, 2018). Last but not least, contestation of the election around the figure of Macron was ensured by his hands-on management of the LREM-MoDem campaign. Presenting himself as the bulwark against the forces of euroscepticism on the European stage and those of populism domestically, Macron reduced the political debate underlying the election campaign to a binary choice between embracing or repudiating the EU on the one hand and of economic and cultural liberalism versus protectionism on the other (Salvi, 2019).

II. The Results

This programmatic polarization evident at both European and domestic levels was reflected in the 2019 European election results. In the first place, the latter confirmed the political cleavage that had asserted itself with the 2017 presidential and legislative elections which saw the collapse of the former governing parties – the PS and LR – and emergence of a new line of conflict between eurosceptic populism incarnated by the FN and Europhile liberalism enshrined by LREM (Kriesi, 2018, pp. 3–7). Testifying to the strength of this new cleavage, these two parties together accounted for 45.8 per cent of the vote in the 2019 European election (compared to 45.3 per cent in the first round of the 2017 presidential election). Conversely, LR and the PS together garnered only 14.7 per cent of the vote in 2019, a nearly 12 per cent drop compared to the 2017 presidential election. However, in contrast to the 2017 presidential election which saw the Socialist

---

[3]Foremost among these measures were the government's elimination of the wealth tax on financial assets, its reduction of housing subsidies for the poor, its augmentation of the carbon tax on gasoline, and far-reaching reform of the Labour Code.
[4]In addition to repealing the gas tax in December 2018, these measures included reducing taxes on low-wage earners by €5 billion, indexing pensions of €2000 or less a month to inflation, and ending the closure of rural schools and hospitals.

vote collapse compared to 2012 (6.4 per cent for Benoît Hamon versus 28.6 per cent for François Hollande) while the mainstream right held comparatively steady over the two elections (20 per cent for François Fillon versus 27.2 per cent for Nicolas Sarkozy), in 2019 the electoral collapse principally affected the latter, with the LR-led list winning only 8.5 per cent of the vote. The erstwhile governing parties thus took their place alongside more marginal political formations in a fragmented partisan landscape emerging alongside the new LREM-RN cleavage. This fragmentation was particularly pronounced on the left, in which five separate lists – EELV, LFI, PS-Place Publique, Générations.s, and PCF – garnered a total of 31.7 per cent of the vote.

These findings are confirmed if we compare the stability of the respective parties' electoral bases between the first round of the 2017 presidential election and the 2019 European election. Whereas the RN and LREM enjoyed the greatest degree of voter stability (i.e. the proportion of their voters from 2017 who voted for them again in 2019), LR, the PS, and LFI experienced the greatest voter defection (see Table 2).

DLF, Debout la France; EELV, Europe Écologie Les Verts; EP, European Parliament; FN, Front National; LFI, La France Insoumise; LREM, La République en Marche; LR, Les Républicains; MoDem, Mouvement Démocratique; PS, Socialist Party; PP, Place Publique; RN, Rassemblement National.

The Rassemblement National (RN)[5] list came first in front of the governing party joint list comprising La République en Marche (LREM) and the Mouvement Démocratique (MoDem). These were succeeded in third place by the list presented by Europe Écologie Les Verts (EELV), mirroring the breakthroughs registered by Green party lists elsewhere in Europe. Conversely, the former governing parties continued their electoral slide initiated during the 2017 presidential and legislative elections, with the lists presented by

Table 3: Sociology of the Vote for Seat-winning Parties in the 2019 European Election (%)

Social category	RN	LR-UDI	LREM-MoDem	EELV	PS-PP	LFI
SPC+	18	7	29	16	6	6
Shopkeepers/small business owners	30	8	26	9	3	5
Liberal professions/upper management	11	6	30	20	8	5
Intermediate professions	15	4	18	20	7	7
SPC-	38	4	13	10	4	9
Service employees	32	5	14	11	4	8
Industrial workers	47	2	11	7	4	11
No Bac or technical degree	31	9	23	5	5	5
Technical degree	40	8	14	8	7	8
Bac+2	19	7	25	13	6	7
More than Bac+2	11	9	31	18	8	5
Rural communes	30	8	19	12	6	7
Urban communes	23	8	23	12	7	6
Paris region	18	7	25	18	6	7

Source: Ifop, (2018), pp. 23–5.

[5]This was a new name given to the former Front National (FN) by its leader Marine Le Pen at the March 2018 party congress as part of the effort to revamp the party's image following her heavy defeat to Emmanuel Macron in the second round of the 2017 presidential election and the FN's poor performance in the June 2017 legislative elections.

Les Républicains (LR) and the Socialist Party (PS) each failing to reach the 10 per cent bar. Last but not least, the list presented by La France Insoumise (LFI)

Once again, the parties of the left, notably PS-PP as well as LFI, experienced the greatest level of voter defection between the two elections. In this sense, the 2019 European election confirmed the implosion of the French party system that was first observed in the 2017 presidential race. Specifically, a new principle of division emerged with the rivalry between LREM and the RN on the one hand and the fragmentation of support among the remaining parties on the other.

In turn, this simultaneously polarized and fractured landscape was sociologically and geographically refracted (see Table 3). First, diametrically contrary class, sectoral and geographical divisions distinguished the respective electorates of the two winning parties, the RN and LREM. Like Macron in 2017, the latter won a plurality of voters among the higher socio-professional categories (SPC+), the affluent and the better-educated while suffering its lowest score among the working classes (SPC-), the unemployed, the poor, and the least educated segments of the electorate.

Bac, Baccalauréat; EELV, Europe Écologie Les Verts; LFI, La France Insoumise; LREM, La République en Marche; LR, Les Républicains; MoDem, Mouvement Démocratique; PS, Socialist Party; PP, Place Publique; RN, Rassemblement National; SPC, socio-professional categories; UDI, Union des Démocrates Indépendants.

Conversely, in a mirror image of the LREM electorate, the RN performed best among working-class voters, the unemployed, the poor and the least educated while doing badly among the higher socio-professional categories, the affluent and best educated.

This polarization was replicated in the spatial and geographical distribution of the electorate. Whereas LREM dominated in urban centres, the RN attained its highest scores in rural communes as well as smaller provincial towns (31 per cent). Meanwhile, geographically, outside Île-de-France and a few isolated departments such as Haute-Savoie, Rhône and Pyrénées-Atlantiques, LREM's vote was highest in the western parts of the country while the RN's strongest areas were in the north and north-east as well as the Mediterranean basin. However, significantly, the latter also expanded its influence along parts of the Atlantic coast as well as within the *diagonale du vide* running from the Pyrenees to the Ardennes (Perrineau, 2019, p. 187). Commenting on the geographical correspondence between the *Gilets Jaunes* protests and the eurosceptic anti-Macron vote, the political geographer Christophe Guilluy observed that the 2019 European electoral map 'corresponds exactly to the dispersion of the working class on France's territory. Macron's electorate is besieged. They're living in these new medieval strongholds. And it's the periphery that is setting the agenda' (Nossiter, 2019).

Finally, reflecting the fractured partisan picture inherited from the 2017 presidential contest, the remainder of the electorate was sociologically and geographically dispersed among the former governing parties and secondary parties of the left. The first saw their catch-all electorates continue to dwindle under pressure from LREM and populist or formerly marginal alternatives. The PS's former pluralities among the intermediary professions (31 per cent of which had voted for Hollande in the first round in 2012), management executives (31 per cent), holders of advanced degrees (34 per cent), greater Paris (31 per cent) and rural commune (28 per cent) dwellers, and white-collar workers (28 per cent) respectively migrated to LREM or EELV in the case of the first four categories, or the RN with respect to the final two. Conversely, LR saw its erstwhile pluralities among the higher socio-professional categories (32 per cent of whom had voted for Sarkozy in 2012) migrate primarily to the RN in the case of shopkeepers and small business owners and to LREM in that of liberal professionals and upper management executives (Ifop, 2012, pp. 9–10; 2018, pp. 24, 26). Perpetuating a trend that first emerged in 2017, the remaining parties, namely EELV and LFI, continued to poach votes from the PS, the former particularly within the intermediary professions, holders of higher degree, and residents in greater Paris, and the latter among the lower socio-professional categories.[6]

In short, sociologically and geographically, the 2019 European election testified to a political contest between the partisan representatives of the France *d'en haut* versus the France *d'en bas*. As in 2017, this contest effectively exploded the cross-class coalitions that had underpinned the electorates of the former cartel parties, with the rump of the latter, particularly on the left, migrating to previously marginal or populist alternatives.

III. European Implications

As in the case of the 2019 European election campaign, the election's political effects can be parsed at the European and domestic levels. On the European dimension, at first blush the result appeared to be a good one for Macron and his party. The 23 seats won by the LREM list would give it the upper hand in the centrist Renew Europe (RE) party group, the new kingmaking faction within the EP now that the European People's Party and Social Democratic groups had lost their combined majority status (VoteWatch Europe, 2020). Yet, from the outset Macron found his position within RE and the broader EP under attack. The candidate he nominated to lead the RE group, LREM list head Nathalie Loiseau, was forced to renounce the position in favour of the Romanian Dacian Ciolos. She had alienated the other national delegations through her arrogant manner and bad-mouthing of key European players such as the European People's Party chief Manfred Weber and Angela Merkel (Ducourtieux and Stroobants, 2019). More crucially, Macron's dismissal of Weber to head the new European Commission under the established *Spitzenkandidaten* (lead candidate) system set the EP and a number of member states against him. His compromise choice of Ursula von der Leyen to head the Commission was approved with only a razor-thin majority of nine (out of a total of 751) votes in the EP. In an unprecedented swipe at his European prestige, Macron's preferred candidate to occupy the omnibus portfolio in charge of the internal market, industry, defence, space, digital affairs and culture in the Commission, his former Defence Minister Sylvie Goulard, was roundly rejected by the EP.[7]

In short, despite the strengthening of LREM's MEP delegation as a result of Brexit, the internal political dynamics at work within the EP in the wake of the 2019 EP elections did not bode well for Macron's capacity to achieve his federalizing goals regarding the eurozone budget and governance as well as fiscal harmonization internally, and his push

---

[6] EELV's success in winning the intermediary professions and coming second to LREM among voters in the liberal professions and upper management executives may have reflected the defection of former Socialist voters who had voted for Macron or LFI's Jean-Luc Mélenchon in 2017 but who, disappointed by the conservative economic policies espoused by the former and the increasingly autocratic and populist turn taken by the latter, instead opted for the Greens (Mestre, 2019).

[7] Highlighting the breadth of this rejection, 82 MEPs in the relevant committees voted against Goulard's appointment, versus only 29 in favour and one abstention (Malingre, 2019).

for a more independent and consolidated European defence and security identity externally (VoteWatch Europe, 2019). From this perspective, the EU Conference on the Future of Europe that was set up at Macron's initiative at the December 2019 European Summit in order to find 'new agreements on the future of European democracy' appears to have been an increasingly risky gambit that would not only further erode Macron's European standing but also compromise his re-election prospects at home (Malingre, 2020).

IV. Domestic Consequences

In turn, domestically, the 2019 European election confirmed a new populist 'ordinary citizens-versus-political establishment' cleavage at the heart of the French party system which first emerged in the 2017 presidential election. As we saw above, the crystallization of this cleavage was accompanied by the organizational and electoral implosion of erstwhile governing parties of the left and the right, and the correlative dispersion of the remaining political formations into a fractured counterpoise to this new political demarcation.[8] According to this new dispensation, the RN – following the collapse of LFI in this election – has established itself as the primary eurosceptic and populist opposition party in the country.[9] Meanwhile, Macron's LREM has packaged itself as the primary vehicle of pro-European economic and cultural liberalism. This suggests a fundamental reordering of the French party system according to an 'integration-versus-demarcation' cleavage turning around pro versus anti-European sentiment externally, and pro versus anti-immigrant attitudes and cultural liberalism versus illiberalism domestically (Hooghe and Marks, 2018; Hutter and Grande, 2014; Kriesi *et al.,* 2006). By the same token, the cycle between the 2017 presidential and 2019 European elections closed the traditional gap between first-order national and second-order supranational elections (Galpin and Trenz, 2019). For the first time in France, the results of a European election essentially replicated those of the preceding presidential contest.

Macron has been happy to take up the gauntlet thrown down by the RN as the principal party of opposition in France. He reckons that the fear and condemnation it continues to elicit will deliver majorities to his party down the road. However, this strategy is not without danger. Casting the RN as his principal opposition is likely to accelerate normalization of the party as voters become progressively inured to its nativist and eurosceptic claims (Dézé, 2015). In particular, Macron's plan to adopt a more repressive line on immigration to protect his flank against the RN's nativist critiques risks lending further credibility to the latter.[10]

More broadly, as attested to by the durability of the *Gilets Jaunes* movement, the liberalizing reforms pursued by Macron have proved quite unpopular, creating space for Le Pen's political resurrection following her defeat in 2017 and paving the way for the RN's

---

[8]Reflecting on this state of partisan dispersion at the level of political demand, Jerôme Fourquet has evoked the growing fragmentation of the French electorate into an 'archipelago' of distinct class, sectoral, religious, cultural, geographical and generational constituencies, evincing a diminishing core of common interests and values (Fourquet, 2019).

[9]This shift was confirmed in French public opinion. A June 2019 Ifop survey indicated that 51% of respondents believe the RN 'best represented the opposition to Macron' in the wake of the election, versus only 21% for LFI (Perrineau, 2019, p. 190).

[10]In a column for *Le Monde*, Françoise Fressoz observed that Macron was engaging a similar strategy of combining neoliberal economic reforms with a hard line on immigration that had been pursued by Nicolas Sarkozy during his *quinquennat* (Fressoz, 2019).

victory in the 2019 European elections.[11] This discontent has continued as the president moved to tackle the politically toxic themes of pension reform and climate-change mitigation during the second half of his *quinquennat* while his administration's controversial unemployment insurance reform came into effect in November 2019 (*L'Obs,* 2019; Pietralunga, 2019).

In particular, the public discontent provoked by Macron's pension reform proposal poses a serious threat to the government's political position and agenda. Triggering the longest strike action of the postwar era, which paralyzed the country for most of December 2019 and the first half of January 2020, in an ominous parallel to the *Gilets Jaunes* protests the movement spread from Paris to the provinces, sometimes descending into rioting and violence. Most worryingly for Macron, public opposition to the reform remains high despite the government's agreement to suspend its plan to increase the minimum retirement age from 62 to 64 years and granting exemptions from its universal pension scheme to workers in a growing number of sectors.[12] In this context, Macron's pension reform may prove, as in the case of the Juppé government in 1995, *la réforme de trop* (a reform too far), risking not just his administration's stability but also the viability of his reform agenda and prospective re-election.

Conclusion

In short, it remains to be seen whether Macron and LREM will go the same way as previous governments whose liberalizing economic and restrictive immigration formula failed and precipitated their downfall or whether, this time, this formula will yield the growth and legitimacy that may seal Macron's legacy as the historic reformer of contemporary France (Fourquet, 2019, pp. 362–68, 373–77; Kriesi, 2018, p. 11). The beginnings of an answer to this question were given in the municipal elections that were concluded in June 2020. Marked by a 'Green wave' that saw EELV candidates lead electoral alliances of the left to victory in a number of key cities, such as Lyons, Bordeaux, Strasbourg and Grenoble, or provide crucial support to other candidates of the left such as in Paris and Marseilles, the surge of the environmentalist vote – in many cases at the expense of LREM single-party or coalition lists – in the 2020 municipal elections both confirmed and built upon EELV's strong showing in the 2019 European elections.[13] Although it was marred by record low turnout (41.6 per cent), in this election the Greens emerged as the spearhead of a new post-materialist coalition of the left that will contest Macron's leadership of the forces of cultural and economic integration in France around a much less classically liberal, heterodox economic programme privileging environmental sustainability, social redistribution and the re-localization of production (Mestre, 2020). Given the RN's lacklustre performance as well as the former governing parties' inability to exceed

[11]This marks a remarkable comeback for Marine Le Pen, who was viewed as irreparably damaged by her calamitous performance in debate between the two rounds of voting in the 2017 presidential race (Laubacher, 2019).
[12]This sentiment was confirmed by an ELABE survey from 22 January, 2020 according to which 61% of respondents believed that Macron should take the strikers' demands into account and withdraw the reform (Lemarié and Faye, 2020).
[13]Underscoring LREM's relative lack of local political organization and ballast as well as its 3-year-long experience of national government, the president's party suffered a dark day at the polls, failing to win the mayoralty of any of the largest cities and instead seeing its candidates, either in single-party lists or 'anti-environmentalist' alliances fashioned with candidates of the right (LR), defeated by a resurgent Green-led coalition of the left. This setback will not only complicate Macron's task of governing the country over the remaining 2 years of his term, but also render his prospective re-election in 2022 much less straightforward than anticipated (Pietralunga and Lemarié, 2020).

expectations even though they are most durably locally implanted,[14] these elections have raised the prospect of a Green-inspired third force that complicates the cross-cutting integration-versus-demarcation dynamic that was set in motion with the 2017 presidential election and confirmed by the 2019 European election. As in the case of the latter, the 2020 municipal elections highlighted the questions of social equity, democratic account-ability and environmental sustainability as the key issues likely to inform future elections, starting with the 2022 presidential race.

Last but not least, this newly fluid electoral and political panorama is likely to be further complicated by the extraneous shock of the 2020 Covid-19 pandemic. By enhanc-ing the salience of new national vulnerabilities raised by globalization as well as by placing unprecedented focus on societal modes of production and consumption, the pandemic is likely to entrench further the integration-versus-demarcation divide that is fast emerging as the defining cleavage ordering democratic competition in France and Europe more generally.

References

Achilli, L. (2019) 'Why Are We Not Reforming the Dublin Regulation Yet?' *Euractiv*, 24 October. Available online at https://www.euractiv.com/section/justice-home-affairs/opinion/why-are-we-not-reforming-the-dublin-regulation-yet/. Last accessed 8 July 2020.

Belouezzane, S. (2020) 'Municipales 2020: les victoires en trompe-l'œil de la droite'. Le Monde, 29 June.

Cautrès, B. (2017) 'MéleLe vote disruptif'. In Perrineau, P. (ed.) *Les élections présidentielle et lég-islatives de 2017nchon: 'vainqueur caché de la présidentielle?* (Paris: Presses de Sciences Po), pp. 175–92.

Confavreux, J. (2018) 'Le macronisme au pouvoir: pouvoir fort ou pouvoir faible?' *Mediapart,* 15 April.Available online at https://www.mediapart.fr/journal/france/150418/le-macronisme-au-pouvoir-33-pouvoir-fort-ou-pouvoir-faible?onglet=full. Last accessed 8 July 2020.

CEVIPOF (2019) 'Baromètre de la confiance politique – vague 10'. January. Available online at https://www.sciencespo.fr/cevipof/sites/sciencespo.fr.cevipof/files/CEVIPOF_confiance_vague10-1.pdf

Damgé, M., Dagorn, G. and Cottin, D. (2019) 'Elections européennes: les eurosceptiques français en ordre dispersé'. Le Monde, 23 May.

Dézé, A. (2015) 'La 'Dédiabolisation': une nouvelle stratégie?' In Crepon, S. and Mayer, N. (eds) *Les faux-semblants du Front National: sociologie d'un parti politique* (Paris: Presses de Sci-ences Po), pp. 25–50.

[14]Despite winning the city of Perpignan, the first French city of over 100,000 inhabitants that the party has won since Tou-lon in 1995, the RN's performance in the 2020 municipal elections failed to substantially improve on its performance from 2014. The RN lost two towns, Mantes-la-Ville (Yvelines) and Le Luc (Var), as well as the 7th sector of Marseille that it had won in the previous municipal elections, but it also gained new municipalities, notably Bruay-la-Buissière (Pas-de-Calais), Moissac (Tarn-et-Garonne) and a collection of small towns in the Vaucluse (Johannès, 2020). For its part, despite winning just over 50% of French cities of 9,000 or more inhabitants, LR also experienced a mixed result, losing a number of its for-mer strongholds to the left or the far right (such as Marseilles and Perpignan) as well as proving unable to stop the Green-led left-wing surge through local alliances with LREM, such as in Lyons, Bordeaux and Strasbourg (Belouezzane, 2020). Fi-nally, by preserving its mayoralties in a number of key cities (such as Paris, Lille and Nantes) while gaining a number of new ones either on its own (Montpellier, Nancy and Saint-Denis) or in alliance with EELV (Marseilles and Lyons), the PS effectively arrested its electoral slide dating back to the 2017 national elections. However, momentum on the night un-questionably lay with the Greens who now find themselves in a position – unthinkable only 3 years ago – of supplanting the PS and LFI as the leading political force on the left (Zappi, 2020).

Ducourtieux, C. and Stroobants, J-P. (2019) 'Comment Nathalie Loiseau s'est sabordée à Bruxelles'. Le Monde, 13 June.

Durand, A.-A., Breteau, P., Sénécat, A., Dahyot, A., Talbot, R. and Cottin, D. (2019) 'Les décodeurs: elections européennes 2019: candidats, programmes, alliés ... explorez les 34 listes françaises'. *Le Monde,* 26 May.

European Commission (2018) 'Standard Eurobarometer 90 Autumn 2018'. 8 November. Available online at eb90_FiR_en. Last accessed 8 July 2020.

Foucault, M. (2019) 'Des enjeux européens, un débat d'idees français'. *Le Monde,* 21 May.

Fourquet, J. (2019) *L'archipel français. Naissance d'une nation multiple et divisée* (Paris: Seuil).

Fressoz, F. (2019) 'L'offensive menée par Macron sur l'immigration ressemble au tournant sécuritaire entamé par Sarkozy'. Le Monde, 24 September.

Galpin, C. and Trenz, H.-J. (2019) 'In the Shadow of Brexit: The 2019 European Parliamentary Elections as First-order Polity Elections?' *Political Quarterly*, Vol. 90, No. 4, pp. 664–71.

Graulle, P. (2019) 'La France insoumise et le "plan B": quatre années d'ambiguïté'. Media, 12 April. Available online at https://www.mediapart.fr/journal/france/120419/la-france-insoumise-et-le-plan-b-quatre-annees-d-ambiguite?onglet=full. Last accessed 8 July 2020.

Hooghe, L. and Marks, M. (2018) 'Cleavage Theory Meets Europe's Crises: Lipset, Rokkan, and the Transnational Cleavage'. *Journal of European Public Policy*, Vol. 25, No. 1, pp. 109–35.

Hutter, S. and Grande, E. (2014) 'Politicizing Europe in the National Electoral Arena: A Comparative Analysis of Five West European Countries, 1970–2010'. *JCMS*, Vol. 52, No. 5, pp. 1002–18.

Ifop (2018) 'Européennes 2019: profil des électeurs et clefs du scrutin'. 27 May. Available online at https://www.ifop.com/publication/europeennes-2019-profil-des-electeurs-et-clefs-du-scrutin/. Last accessed 8 July 2020.

Ifop (2012) 'Premier tour de l'élection présidentielle 2012: profil des électeurs et clés du scrutin'. 22 April. Available online at https://www.ifop.com/publication/sondage-jour-du-vote-22-avril-2012-premier-tour-de-lelection-presidentielle-2012-profil-des-electeurs-et-cles-du-scrutin/. Last accessed 8 July 2020.

Johannès, F. (2020) 'Municipales 2020: un scrutin au bilan mitigé pour le Rassemblement national'. *Le Monde*, 29 June.

Kriesi, H. (2018) 'The 2017 French and German Elections'. *JCMS*, Vol. 56, No. S1, pp. 1–12.

Kriesi, H., Grande, E., Lachat, E., Bornschier, S. and Frey, T. (2006) 'Globalization and the Transformation of the National Political Space: Six European Countries Compared'. *European Journal of Political Research*, Vol. 45, No. 6, pp. 921–56.

Laubacher, P. (2019) 'Le récit du retour de Marine Le Pen: 'Tout le monde me disait: Tu es dingue de faire cela!' L'Obs, 26 May.

Lemarié, A. and Faye, O. (2020) 'Réforme des retraites: pour l'exécutif, le bout du tunnel est encore loin'. *Le Monde*, 24 Jan.

L'Obs (2019) 'Macron exclut tout "changement de cap"'. 27 May.

Malingre, V. (2019) 'Commission européenne: l'échec de Sylvie Goulard, camouflet pour Emmanuel Macron'. *Le Monde,* 11 October.

Malingre, V. (2020) 'Les contours encore incertains d'une conférence sur l'avenir de l'Europe'. Le Monde, 22 January.

Matthijs, M. and Blyth, M. (2015) 'Introduction: The Future of the Euro and the Politics of Embedded Currency Areas'. In Matthijs, M. and Blyth, M. (eds) *The Future of the Euro* (New York: Oxford University Press), pp. 1–20.

Mestre, A. (2020) 'Municipales 2020: avec EELV, une vague verte historique déferle sur les grandes villes françaises'. *Le Monde*, 29 June.

Mestre, A. (2019) 'Elections européennes 2019: avec 13.4 % des voix et une 3e place, la surprise EELV'. *Le Monde,* 27 May.

Nossiter, A. (2019) 'European Vote Reveals an Ever More Divided France'. *New York Times*, 27 May.

Perrineau, P. (2019) *Le grand écart. Chronique d'une démocratie fragmentée* (Paris: Plon).

Perrineau, P. (2017) 'Marine Le Pen au premier tour: la puissance d'une dynamique, l'échec d'une ambition'. In Perrineau, P. (ed.) *Le vote disruptif. Les élections présidentielle et législatives de 2017* (Paris: Presses de Sciences Po), pp. 251–68.

Pietralunga, C. (2019) 'La rentrée tout-terrain d'Emmanuel Macron'. *Le Monde,* 27 August.

Pietralunga, C. and Lemarié, A. (2020) 'Municipales 2020: La République en marche encaisse une sévère déroute électorale'. *Le Monde*, 29 June.

Salvi, E. (2019) 'Le match installé par Macron a asséché la campagne des européennes'. Media, 22 May. Available online at https://www.mediapart.fr/journal/france/220519/le-match-installe-par-macron-asseche-la-campagne-des-europeennes?onglet=full. Last accessed 8 July 2020.

Vandenbussche, H. (2019) 'Sector-level Analysis of the Impact of Brexit on the EU-28'. Report to Flanders Department of Foreign Affairs, June. Available online at: https://www.flandersintheuk.be/en/sector-level-analysis-of-the-impact-of-brexit-on-the-eu-28-kuleuven. Last accessed: 8 July 2020.

VoteWatch Europe (2019) 'Von der Leyen Gets the Green Light, but the Biggest Challenges Are Yet to Come'. 27 November. Available online at https://www.votewatch.eu/blog/von-der-leyen-scrapes-through-but-the-biggest-challenges-are-yet-to-come/. Last accessed 8 July 2020.

VoteWatch Europe (2020) 'European Parliament: Current and Future Dynamics'. 21 January. Available online aty https://www.votewatch.eu/blog/european-parliament-current-and-future-dynamics/. Last accessed 8 July 2020l

Zappi, S. (2020) 'Les élections municipals 2020, un bon cru pour les socialistes, éclipsé par la percée écologiste'. *Le Monde*, 29 June.

JCMS 2020 Volume 58. Annual Review pp. 69–79   DOI: 10.1111/jcms.13079

Italy and the European Elections of 2019

ERIK JONES[1] and MATTHIAS MATTHIJS[2]
[1]Johns Hopkins University, Bologna [2]Johns Hopkins University, Washington, D.C.

Introduction

Traditionally, EU member state elections for the European Parliament (EP) get a bad rap. Average turnout tends to be 20 per cent lower than in national elections and the overall turnout for EP elections has fallen steadily over time, from 62 per cent in 1979 to around 43 per cent in 2014 (EP, 2019a). EP elections also tend to be dismissed as second-order contests by both the news media and national political parties. Rather than being dominated by EU-level issues, campaigns generally focus on national themes (van der Eijk and Franklin, 1996). Disgruntled voters frequently see EP elections as an occasion to cast a protest ballot against whichever party happens to be in power. The May 2019 EP elections, however, proved to be very different, and broke with the trend. Overall turnout across the Union went up from 43 per cent in 2014 to just over 50 per cent in 2019, and EU topics featured quite high on the agenda, especially in big member states like the UK and France.

Italy, by contrast, veered away from that broad EU tendency in 2019. Overall turnout in Italy continued its downward trend from 72 per cent (in 2004), to 66 per cent (in 2009), to 57 per cent (in 2014), to an all-time low of 54 per cent (EP, 2019a). In addition, EU issues were actually less prominent during the May 2019 elections for the EP than they were during the Italian national elections just a year earlier in March 2018. What the 2019 EP elections in Italy highlighted was the volatility of the Italian electorate as it showed dramatic shifts in voting patterns compared with 2014, with the right-wing Lega more than quintupling its vote share while the centre-left Partito Democratico (PD; Democratic Party) saw its vote share collapse from over 40 per cent to just below 23 per cent. As the causes of the electoral outcome have been analysed at length elsewhere, we focus on the effects of the Italian EP election results on three separate fronts. First of all, we argue that the result altered the perceptions of Italian political elites in a more eurosceptical direction. Second, we show how it changed the dynamics of EU institutions, especially when it came to the process of appointing a new Commission. And finally, we examine how it influenced behaviour on international financial markets, as increased electoral volatility and political risk led to jittery investment behaviour.

I. 2014 versus 2019: The Puzzling Tale of the Two Matteos

If you compare the Italian EP election results in 2014 and in 2019, the differences are sharp (see Table 1). The May 2014 elections were an overwhelming victory for centre-left Prime Minister Matteo Renzi and his PD, which managed to capture an unprecedented 41 per cent share of the vote. The closest challenger was

Table 1: EP Elections in Italy: 2014 versus 2019 Results

	2014 results (%)	2019 results (%)	Change (%)
Partito Democratico	40.8	22.7	−18.1
Forza Italia	16.8	8.8	−8.0
M5S	21.2	17.1	−4.1
Lega	6.2	34.3	+28.1
Fratelli d'Italia	3.7	6.4	+2.7
Other Parties	11.3	10.7	−0.6

Source: EP (2019).

founder-comedian Beppe Grillo's Movimento Cinque Stelle (M5S) or Five Star Movement, which garnered just 21 per cent – and that number was down from the more than 25 per cent that the M5S collected in the national elections of 2013. The centre-right party of Silvio Berlusconi, Forza Italia, won almost 17 per cent. The other political parties trailed much further behind. In 2014 the right-wing parties – Matteo Salvini's Lega (formerly Northern League) with 6 per cent and Giorgia Meloni's Fratelli d'Italia (Brothers of Italy) with just under 4 per cent of the vote were no more than an afterthought.

Fast forward to May 2019, and the picture looks radically different. Salvini's Lega came out on top in the EP elections with 34 per cent of the vote (double the 17 per cent share the party won during the March 2018 national elections). The PD, no longer led by Renzi, got 22 per cent, up from just under 19 per cent in the March 2018 national elections. The M5S got only 17 per cent, down from almost 33 per cent in the March 2018 contest. Berlusconi's Forza Italia party dropped below 9 per cent, and the Brothers of Italy rose above 6 per cent. If a week is a long time in politics, five years of Italian political development looked like an eternity.

The difference is particularly acute if you focus on the PD strongholds. For example, the PD or its centre-left predecessor parties have governed in the region of Emilia Romagna for almost 80 years. There the tradition of left-wing voting is so deeply embedded that it is almost taken for granted. Nevertheless, Lega was able to come out on top with just under 34 per cent of the vote, compared with just over 31 per cent for the PD. Moreover, this closeness was apparent only in the aggregate data. If you drill down to the provincial level, you find that the Lega dominated all the smaller provinces and the PD led by much smaller percentages in the larger ones – with Bologna being the only reason why the region-wide contest was not an even greater defeat for the centre left (see Figure 1). This pattern of strong Lega support in smaller communities and reduced dominance for the PD in larger communities is the same when you narrow down even further to voting patterns at the communal level.[1]

The key puzzle in these elections is to understand these contrasting outcomes and the changes of fortune that lay behind them (Chiaramonte et al., 2020). The answer cannot be found by merely pointing to whatever was happening in Europe. It is true that the EU's fumbling attempts to address the migration crisis played into the hands of Matteo Salvini and Lega. It is also true that perceptions of EU interference in banking resolution and

---

[1]It is worth noting that the PD overtook the Lega by a similar margin less than a year later in the January 2020 regional elections. The urban–rural division in terms of support remained the same, however.

Figure 1: Lega over Partito Democratico (PD) by Province in Emilia Romagna during 2019 EP Elections.

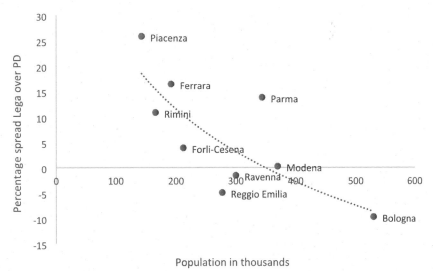

Source: Italian government (2019).

macroeconomic governance, especially fiscal affairs, generated frustration and even outrage among the Italian electorate. While scholars of Italian politics who try to understand the implosion of the PD in the March 2018 elections or the rise of M5S and Lega in that contest are quick to highlight these sources of tension (Caiani, 2019; Diamond and Guidi, 2019), it would be a mistake to assume that tensions in Europe are a powerful force for Italian political mobilization (Chiaramonte *et al.*, 2020; Valbruzzi, 2018; Vassallo and Shin, 2019). To begin with, many of the same frustrations existed in 2014 – particularly with reference to migration, but also in terms of macroeconomic governance (Lucarelli, 2015). After all, the May 2014 EP elections came right after what were possibly the most disastrous five years in European integration, with the economic damage done by the euro crisis still fresh on everyone's mind. This was particularly so in the Mediterranean countries of the eurozone's periphery, the so-called 'southern sinners' that had seen steep recessions and record high levels of unemployment (Matthijs, 2014, 2017; Matthijs and McNamara, 2015).

More important, perhaps, is that the pattern of mobilization in 2019 does not entirely fit the pattern of frustration. To paraphrase Maggini and Chiaramonte (2019), if the question is whether euroscepticism lay behind the victory of eurosceptical parties, then the answer is 'not exactly'. Europe was certainly talked about – even more so in the 2019 contest than in 2014 – and yet the tone of the conversation was measured (Cremonesi *et al.*, 2019) and the baseline attitudes of most Italians towards Europe were surprisingly positive despite their many frustrations (Fabbrini and Zgaga, 2019). As a result, the political debate during the campaign for the EP elections in 2019 was largely dominated by Italian domestic politics (Newell, 2019).

The best explanation for the change in the electoral outcomes among the two contests lies not in Italy's relationship with Europe or with the popular politicization of European integration, but with the underlying changes in the Italian political system and the subsequent weakening of Italy's traditional political parties (Ieraci, 2019; Pasquino, 2019; Pasquino and Valbruzzi, 2019a). This is hardly surprising to students of comparative European politics. What is true for Italy is true elsewhere in Europe. There is an international influence on Italian political developments but it is more transnational than European. It is continuous rather than being necessarily punctuated by European elections. And, in many ways, it is still very much an ongoing process (Silveri, 2019).

Where EP elections do have salience for the relationship between Italy and Europe is not so much in the voting patterns of the Italian electorate, but in three separate spheres. First of all, that relationship exists in the minds of Italian political elites. Second, it has a direct influence on the functioning of European political institutions. And finally, it manifests itself in the performance of Italian securities on international financial markets (Jones, 2017, 2018). These are three areas where the similarities between 2014 and 2019 are more important than the more obvious contrasts.

In the 2014 elections, for example, then Prime Minister Matteo Renzi came away with a renewed sense of self-confidence and a strong determination to assert a leadership role in the EU. He began to pursue Italian interests both directly in the European Council and through his promotion of his minister of foreign affairs, Federica Mogherini, to the EU's High Representative and Vice President of the European Commission. He also managed to create a renewed sense of optimism about Italy's economy and sovereign debt sustainability within the international financial community (Lucarelli, 2015; Jones, 2017).

If anything, the 2019 EP elections were even more important in shaping the perceptions of the Italian elite of Europe and European perceptions of Italy. In the run-up to the vote, then deputy Prime Minister Matteo Salvini used his winning status to try to forge a eurosceptical alliance around his idea of a 'Europe of Nations' (*Europa delle Nazioni*) that could muster a blocking minority in the EP. When the idea died on polling day because of the under-performance of the populist parties of other EU member states, Lega officials rehashed the old idea of a parallel Italian currency to exist alongside the euro. Financial markets quickly went into a tailspin, forcing Lega to back off. Then, Salvini was taken by surprise when his coalition partner, Luigi Di Maio from M5S, threw his support behind Ursula von der Leyen, the EU establishment choice for European Commission President. By the end of August of 2019, Matteo Salvini would meet the same fate as Matteo Renzi. When his efforts to topple the government were scuppered, he found himself out of power.

To borrow from Pasquino and Valbruzzi (2019b, p. 646), 'despite their alleged "second order" nature, the 2019 European elections have had first-order effects' in the case of Italy. Of course, the disturbing aspect of this parallel is that the honeymoon period for Renzi was short-lived and the 2014 EP elections ended badly. The consequences of the 2019 EP elections were just as nefarious with Salvini's meteoric rise and abrupt fall, and could prove to be even more dramatic down the line.

II. Italian Political Elites

The importance of the 2019 European elections in the Italian political context stems from the confluence of three factors. First, scepticism towards EU institutions, policies and rules was one of the only major points of congruence in policy terms between M5S and

Lega as governing parties. Neither party is close on the left–right dimension of the political spectrum or on the cleavage that contrasts "green, alternative, and libertarian" values with values that are more "traditional, authoritarian, and nationalist" (Valbruzzi, 2018, p. 471; Hooghe and Marks, 2018). The important bonds between the two parties lay in their joint appeal as anti-establishment parties and in the area of process rather than policy. They agreed on the need for substantial change, even if they disagreed on how that change should look (Marangoni and Verzichelli, 2019). As a result, it was difficult for either to distinguish themselves from the other on the EU dimension, even if it was clear to everyone that they were competitors in the 2019 EP elections.

Second, Lega and the M5S embody two very different forms of populism (Caiani, 2019). Lega is older and sits more easily on the nativist nationalist right side of the political spectrum. M5S has more left-leaning populist tendencies but draws broad support from across the left–right economic dimension (Diamanti and Lazar, 2018; Graziano, 2018). The ideological placement of Lega gave Matteo Salvini a distinct advantage over Luigi Di Maio. Salvini could meet other like-minded leaders, including Hungary's Viktor Orbán or France's Marine Le Pen, and he could even pretend to play a leading role in some kind of pan-European movement. Di Maio did not have any obvious European allies. He could meet the French *Gilets Jaunes* (yellow vest) protesters, but that hardly gave him the profile of a European leader and instead attracted the ire of French President Emmanuel Macron. As a result, Di Maio had to focus his campaign on domestic issues and therefore he started on the back foot.

Third, both Salvini and Di Maio were forced to make concessions to EU institutions as part of the wider procedures for European macroeconomic policy coordination. They may have started their governing coalition with bold plans to blow up the budget with a bang, but they ended fiscal negotiations with a whimper by compromising with Brussels (Fabbrini and Zgaga, 2019). This pattern could have been worse – and would have been worse if the French government were not also in violation of European norms for fiscal consolidation. The point is simply that their compromising position took some of the wind out of the sails of their eurosceptic arguments. During the electoral campaign in the spring of 2019, neither Salvini nor Di Maio could argue that they wanted to win support in order to change Europe, but they could not argue that they were prepared to destroy the EU or to take Italy out of the euro (at least not until after the vote). We will come back to this point when we discuss the knock-on effect of the 2019 Italian EP elections on European financial markets.

The above three factors explain why European issues were in the end somewhat absent from the Italian campaigns for the EP elections (Newell, 2019). The two governing parties could create more distance between themselves by focusing on domestic policy. Lega could play to its electoral base by touting Salvini's nativist connections in other parts of Europe, but only at the expense of alienating more centrist voters who did not really identify with right-wing politicians from France or Austria. M5S simply had no European counterpart. At the same time, the yellow–green Lega–M5S coalition government had learned the hard way that there was a real necessity for some reconciliation with Europe.

The European debate became relevant only once the May 2019 elections were over. As the scale of Salvini's victory became clear, it also became obvious that much of his support came from more right-wing elements that had previously voted for the M5S. This shift in support was less evident in the south than in the north. Yet it was sufficient to reveal the extent of the threat that Lega posed to M5S as well as the extent to which Salvini had succeeded in constructing Lega as a genuinely national political movement rather than a northern secessionist party (Pritoni and Vignati, 2018, 2019).

This success emboldened Salvini to stake out ever more extreme positions on Europe. At the same time, he tried to block much of the M5S's policy agenda within the government and started to push back more forcefully against European institutions. Here it is worth focusing on two illustrations: Salvini's threat to take Italy out of the euro and his refusal to name an Italian candidate for the European Commission.

The threat to take Italy out of the euro was a vestige of the original coalition agreement, which centred on the possible creation of zero coupon, small denomination government debt instruments (the so-called 'mini-BOTs') (Kaminska, 2019). Such a de facto parallel currency could be used to cover any arrears in government payments for goods and services, and could be accepted by the Italian Treasury as payment for tax obligations. These instruments were a threat to Italy's participation in the euro because, as European Central Bank President Mario Draghi skilfully explained in his press conference on 6 June, 2019, either the instruments were money, which would violate European law, or they were debt, which would violate European fiscal rules (Draghi, 2019).

The issue of the European Commission was even more quixotic. At the outset, Salvini focused on trying to block support within the European Commission for Ursula von der Leyen to be the new European Commission President. Then he shifted his focus to disrupting the formation of her new Commission team. This pattern went strongly against the message Salvini had promoted during the election about trying to change EU institutions from within. By winning the largest share of the vote in the European elections, Salvini also won the right to name someone close to Lega to represent Italy on the Commission. Initially it was rumoured that he wanted his close lieutenant, Giancarlo Giorgetti, to take up that position. However, Giorgetti did not want to leave either Lega or Italian politics. Rather than look for a replacement, Salvini simply let the position lie vacant (Reuters, 2019).

III. European Political Institutions

The M5S played an altogether different European game. Rather than trying to block the EP from supporting von der Leyen, M5S decided to vote in favour of her nomination. The M5S support turned out to be crucial, as von der Leyen won just 383 votes in the EP on July 16 – nine votes more than the 374 needed to secure a majority. Without the 14 M5S MEPs the European Council would have been forced to go back to the drawing board to nominate a new EC President. This surprise move by M5S drove a wedge between M5S and Lega in the Conte government (Pasquino and Valbruzzi, 2019a). Salvini would eventually use this 'betrayal' as part of his justification for bringing down the yellow–green coalition by the end of the summer of 2019. For the M5S, however, it created an opening with the new Commission. Moreover, as long as Lega failed to nominate a Commissioner, M5S support for von der Leyen offered at least the potential prospect that continuing budget negotiations within the framework of EU macroeconomic policy coordination would face looser constraints in the future.

This prospect bore fruit soon after Salvini decided to pull the plug from the first Conte government. The narrative here is tied to the European elections in so far as it rests on

Salvini's interpretation of the results and on subsequent polling. Lega had been ahead in the polls well into the EU contest (Cremonesi *et al.*, 2019). However, as any seasoned politician knows, being ahead in public opinion polling and winning elections are two different things. After the May 2019 EP elections, however, Salvini had greater confidence in his ability to translate polling into votes.

What he needed was sufficient cause to bring down the coalition government without provoking a backlash within the electorate. He also needed to ensure that the President of the Republic, Sergio Mattarella, could not appoint a prime minister who could cobble together an alternative majority in the two chambers of the Italian parliament. Salvini waited until the last days of the legislative calendar before parliament was to break up for the summer holidays. He then presented Giuseppe Conte with a fait accompli, telling him he had no choice but to resign as prime minister or face a vote of no confidence in parliament.

Salvini's actions were unprecedented. Historically, Italian politicians never go to the polls in the summer months, and holding elections in the autumn would come into conflict with the calendar for legislating the budget. Nevertheless, Salvini calculated that Conte would have no choice but to resign and Mattarella would have to admit to the need to dissolve parliament. He was wrong on both counts. Conte did not resign and Mattarella was able to encourage him to seek allies from other political parties. When the PD signalled its willingness to negotiate with M5S it took relatively little time for Conte to form a new government.

The reception of this new administration by other parts of Europe was immediately positive. It became even warmer when Conte announced that Italy would send former PD Prime Minister Paolo Gentiloni to the European Commission and it was further reinforced when the new Conte government elevated Roberto Gualtieri, former PD MEP and chair of the EP's economic and monetary affairs committee, to be the Italian Minister of Economics and Finance.

The M5S bet on supporting von der Leyen as European Commission President paid off handsomely – perhaps not as the party leadership expected at the time, but certainly in terms of greater flexibility from the European Commission and a more cooperative environment for pursuing its policy agenda. Meanwhile, Salvini found himself in opposition. This is what Pasquino and Valbruzzi (2019b) meant when they talked about the 'first-order effects' of the European elections.

IV. International Financial Markets

Those first-order effects were not limited to European political institutions. International financial market analysts monitored the European elections in Italy closely as well. They paid even closer attention to the aftermath. Financial market participants' reading of political events in Rome can be seen in the movement of relative sovereign bond yields as captured by the spread (or difference) between the rate of return on ten-year Italian government bonds and the rate of return on similar German government bonds (or *bunds*). These data are provided in Figure 2.

The magnitude of the spread is measured in terms of basis points, or one one-hundredth of a percentage point. What we observe is that the spread trends upward from about 250 basis points at the start of 2019, right after Italy reached agreement on

Figure 2: Yield Spreads between Italy and Germany on Ten-year Bonds. Source: *Il Sole 24 Ore* (2019). [Colour figure can be viewed at wileyonlinelibrary.com]

Source: Il Sole 24 Ore (2019)

its budget with the European Commission, to something closer to 267 basis points on 24 May, which is the last day the markets were open before Italy went to the polls for the EP elections. That increase may not sound dramatic, but it should be understood in light of the country's large stock of public debt (worth more than 130 per cent of gross domestic product at the time) and in comparison with other southern European countries. The equivalent figure for Spain, for example, was approximately half that amount.

The increase that takes place after the elections is due largely to speculation on the small-denomination debt instruments – the infamous mini-BOTs – and the risks they posed to Italy's participation in the euro area. Speculation calmed down as summer advanced, under the assumption that no Italian government would collapse during the holidays and no Italian president would dissolve parliament during the budgetary process in the autumn. The sharp spike in early August corresponds with Salvini's decision to bring down the government against precedent and conventional wisdom (Figure 2).

Once it became clear that Conte would not resign, however, and that the PD might join the M5S in forming a new government, the spread fell steadily and continuously. When the government was sworn in on September 5 the difference in relative borrowing costs was below 150 basis points (or 1.5 per cent). In practice, this means that the mere formation of the new Conte government quickly brought down Italy's borrowing costs, as old debt in October 2019 could be rolled over into new bonds at more than a full percentage point below the prevailing market rate just prior to the European elections in May 2019.

This reduction in borrowing costs was perhaps the most dramatic first-order effect of the European elections in Italy. It greatly expanded the ability of the second Conte government to meet its fiscal obligations within the European framework for macroeconomic policy coordination. Moreover, the less tension between the government and the European institutions, the readier investors were to buy or hold Italian government bonds. This meant that Italy's borrowing costs remained relatively stable and its fiscal position was relatively easier to manage. While the second Conte government did have some difficulties finalizing the 2020 budget toward the end of the calendar year, those fiscal challenges were considerably less than Conte would have faced if he had still been in charge of a yellow–green coalition.

V. How Long Can it Last?

Of course, the second Conte government faces what James Newell (2019, p. 110) calls 'the perennial question asked about Italian governments: For how long will it survive?' The 2019 European elections may have created the conditions for the movement from tension between Italy and Europe toward an easier, more collaborative relationship by creating the incentives for Salvini to bring down the yellow–green coalition, and for the PD to support a second Conte government. These first-order effects have been salutary from that standpoint and they are shown in more favourable financial market pricing of Italian government debt.

What the European elections have not resolved, however, are the long-term forces working to destabilize Italian politics by alternating the structure of societal cleavages and by weakening political parties. Those forces continue to operate whatever the current configuration of government, irrespective of the goodwill expressed by European officials and the relative indifference of market participants. As a result, it is not unreasonable to assume that Italy will continue to evolve in political terms throughout 2020 and beyond. It may even change enough for the next European elections to look completely different from those that have just passed, albeit for the same reason that the last elections looked so different from those that preceded them.

References

Caiani, M. (2019) 'The Populist Parties and Their Electoral Success: Different Causes behind Different Populisms? The Case of the Five-star Movement and the League'. *Contemporary Italian Politics*, Vol. 11, No. 3, pp. 236–50.

Chiaramonte, A., De Sio, L. and Emanuele, V. (2020) 'Successo di Salvini e Crollo del Movimento Cinque Stelle'. In Moschella, M. and Rhodes, M. (eds) *Politica in Italia 2019* (Bologna: Il Mulino).

Cremonesi, C., Seddone, A., Bobba, G. and Mancosu, M. (2019) 'The European Union in the Media Coverage of the 2019 European Election Campaign in Italy: Towards the Europeanization of the Italian Public Sphere'. *Journal of Modern Italian Studies*, Vol. 24, No. 5, pp. 668–90.

Diamanti, I. and Lazar, M. (2018) *Popolacrazia: La Metamorphosi Delle Nostre Democrazie* (Rome: Gius. Laterza & Figli).

Diamond, P. and Guidi, M. (2019) 'The PD and Social-democratic Parties in Europe'. *Contemporary Italian Politics*, Vol. 11, No. 3, pp. 251–62.

Draghi, M. (2019) 'Press Conference'. Frankfurt: European Central Bank, June 6.

European Parliament (EP) (2019) 2019 European election results: Results by national party (2019-2024) - Italy: official results. https://europarl.europa.eu/election-results-2019/en/national-results/italy/2019-2024/

European Parliament (EP) (2019) '2019 European Elections Results: Turnout by Year'. Available online at: https://europarl.europa.eu/election-results-2019/en/turnout/

Fabbrini, S. and Zgaga, T. (2019) 'Italy and the European Union: The Discontinuity of the Conte Government'. *Contemporary Italian Politics*, Vol. 11, No. 3, pp. 280–93.

Graziano, P. (2018) *Neopopulismi* (Bologna: Il Mulino).

Hooghe, L. and Marks, G. (2018) 'Cleavage Theory Meets Europe's Crises: Lipset, Rokkan, and the Transnational Cleavage'. *Journal of European Public Policy*, Vol. 25, No. 1, pp. 109–35.

Ieraci, G. (2019) 'Re-shaping the Political Space: Continuity and Alignment of Parties in the Italian Parliament'. *Contemporary Italian Politics*, Vol. 11, No. 2, pp. 158–76.

Il Sole 24 Ore (2019) https://www.ilsole24ore.com/

Italian Government (2019) Dipartimento per gli Affari Interni e Territoriali. https://elezionistorico.interno.gov.it/

Jones, E. (2017) 'Relations with Europe: Beyond the *Vincolo Esterno*'. In Chiaramonte, A. and Wilson, A. (eds) *Italian Politics: The Great Reform that Never Was* (New York: Berghahn Books), pp. 51–69.

Jones, E. (2018) 'Italy and the Completion of the Euro Area'. In Eriksson, J. (ed.) *The Future of the Economic and Monetary Union: Reform Perspectives in France, Germany, Italy and the Netherlands* (Stockholm: SIEPS), pp. 26–38.

Kaminska, I. (2019) 'Legality is Not the Problem with Parallel Currencies' *Financial Times*. August 6. Available online at: https://www.ft.com/content/e34402da-b799-11e9-8a88-aa6628ac896c

Lucarelli, S. (2015) 'Italy and the EU: From True Love to Disenchantment?' *JCMS*, Vol. 53, No. 1, pp. 40–60.

Maggini, N. and Chiaramonte, A. (2019) 'Europescepticism behind the Victory of Eurosceptic Parties in the 2018 Italian General Election? Not Exactly'. *JCMS*, Vol. 57, No. S1, pp. 77–89.

Marangoni, F. and Verzichelli, L. (2019) 'Goat-stag, Chimera or Chameleon? The Formation and First Semester of the Conte Government'. *Contemporary Italian Politics*, Vol. 11, No. 3, pp. 263–79.

Matthijs, M. (2014) 'Mediterranean Blues: The Crisis in Southern Europe'. *Journal of Democracy*, Vol. 25, No. 1, pp. 101–15.

Matthijs, M. (2017) 'Integration at What Price? The Erosion of National Democracy in the Euro Periphery'. *Government and Opposition*, Vol. 52, No. 2, pp. 266–94.

Matthijs, M. and McNamara, K. (2015) 'The Euro Crisis' Theory Effect: Northern Saints, Southern Sinners, and the Demise of the Eurobond'. *Journal of European Integration*, Vol. 37, No. 2, pp. 229–45.

Newell, J. (2019) 'Waiting for Something to Happen: Italian Politics in the Run-up to the European Elections'. *Contemporary Italian Politics*, Vol. 11, No. 2, pp. 109–11.

Pasquino, G. (2019) 'The State of the Italian Republic'. *Contemporary Italian Politics*, Vol. 11, No. 2, pp. 195–204.

Pasquino, G. and Valbruzzi, M. (2019a) 'The 2019 European Elections: A "Second-order" Vote with "First-order" Effects'. *Journal of Modern Italian Studies*, Vol. 24, No. 5, pp. 736–56.

Pasquino, G. and Valbruzzi, M. (2019b) 'Sovereignty in the Italian Polling Booths'. *Journal of Modern Italian Studies*, Vol. 24, No. 5, pp. 641–7.

Pritoni, A. and Vignati, R. (2018) 'Winners and Losers. Turnout, Results and the Flows of Vote'. *Journal of Modern Italian Studies*, Vol. 23, No. 4, pp. 381–99.

Pritoni, A. and Vignati, R. (2019) 'Turnout, Preferential Voting and Vote Flows in the EU Election'. *Journal of Modern Italian Studies*, Vol. 24, No. 5, pp. 691–715.

Reuters (2019) 'Italy's Salvini Says Giorgetti a Top Candidate for Economic EU Role'. World News. 15 July. Available online at: https://uk.reuters.com/article/uk-italy-salvini-eu-commission/italys-salvini-says-giorgetti-a-top-candidate-for-economic-eu-role-idUKKCN1UA1QU?feedType=RSS&feedName=worldNews

Silveri, U. (2019) 'The Italian Question: Systemic Crisis, Global Change and New Protagonists (1992–2018)'. *Journal of Modern Italian Studies*, Vol. 24, No. 3, pp. 393–401.

Valbruzzi, M. (2018) 'When Populists Meet Technocrats: The Italian Innovation in Government Formation'. *Journal of Modern Italian Studies*, Vol. 23, No. 4, pp. 460–80.

Van der Eijk, C. and Franklin, M. (eds) (1996) *Choosing Europe? The European Electorate and National Politics in the Face of Union* (Ann Arbor, MI: University of Michigan Press).

Vassallo, S. and Shin, M. (2019) 'The New Map of Political Consensus: What Is New in the Wave of Support for the Populists?' *Contemporary Italian Politics*, Vol. 11, No. 3, pp. 220–35.

JCMS 2020 Volume 58. Annual Review pp. 80–90   DOI: 10.1111/jcms.13078

Brexit and the 2019 EP Election in the UK

SOFIA VASILOPOULOU
University of York, York

Introduction

The 2019 EP election in the UK was called in the middle of an ongoing Brexit crisis and at a considerably short notice. Against all odds, Britons went to the polls to elect their country's Members of the European Parliament (MEPs) despite the fact that they had also voted by a majority to leave the European Union (EU) a few years earlier in the June 2016 EU referendum (Hobolt, 2016; Vasilopoulou, 2016). The UK parliament's rejection of the Brexit Withdrawal Bill essentially meant that the country would continue to be an EU member state and was, as such, legally obliged to hold the election. Against a background of intense political division on how to deliver Brexit, this unexpected vote became a proxy for a second referendum. In contrast to the 2017 general election which had strengthened the UK two-party system, in May 2019 voters rewarded small non-governing parties. On the one hand, two new parties, namely the Brexit Party and Change UK that campaigned on the single question of Brexit, ran for the first time in this electoral contest with the Brexit Party topping the polls. The Liberal Democrats whose campaign promised a second referendum came second, scoring their highest electoral result at any EP election. On the other hand, the mainstream Labour and Conservative parties recorded their lowest ever combined share of the vote since the first EP election in 1979. Support for the United Kingdom Independence Party (UKIP) also shrank and the party lost all its seats in the European Parliament (EP).

What set of events compelled the government to hold such an unexpected election? In what ways did Brexit feature in the political campaign? And how did the Brexit Party manage to achieve such an unprecedented electoral success? This contribution examines the debate in the run-up to the 2019 EP election arguing that – despite the fact that only two years earlier voters had opted for the two main parties that had pledged to honour the result of the EU Referendum – both the executive and the Parliament remained divided and unable to deliver on this promise. This led to Brexit becoming a key issue in both citizens' preferences and party campaigns. Voters rewarded smaller parties, sending a strong signal both against the government and the Labour Party. However, whereas the pro-EU vote was divided across many different political parties, the Leave vote was mostly united behind the Brexit Party, which had implications for parties' short- and medium-term strategies and British politics more broadly.

I. The Unexpected 2019 EP Election

The 2019 EP election was held across the UK on Thursday 23 May 2019 after the Conservative Prime Minister Theresa May's announcement only a few weeks earlier on 7 May. This election was held against a background of intense political divisions within the government and the Parliament. Following the British public's decision to leave the EU on 24 June 2016, the UK government invoked Article 50 of the Treaty of the EU on 29 March 2017, which legally commenced the withdrawal process with a maximum of a two-year negotiation period. Shortly after triggering Article 50, in April 2017, the Prime Minister had called for an early general election to take place in June 2017, in order to strengthen the government's hand in the UK–EU Brexit negotiations (Hobolt, 2018). Against most expectations, however, the snap election resulted in the Conservative Party losing seats and forming a minority government (Heath and Goodwin, 2017; Prosser, 2018). Despite the fact that the Conservative Party had a considerable lead in the polls a few months earlier, the 2017 general election instead weakened the Prime Minister's position both within her party and in parliament (Hobolt, 2018).

The following two years proved difficult for the government, which suffered from substantive internal division on the question of Brexit and its negotiation strategy. The leadership's position on Brexit lacked strong institutional underpinnings within the party (Lynch and Whitaker, 2018). Whereas some Remain MPs exerted pressure on the government to pursue a softer Brexit strategy, Leave MPs campaigned for a hard Brexit. Conservative Brexiteers were highly organized in parliament. They re-launched the European Research Group, for example, whose single focus was the country's withdrawal from the EU. Despite the fact that May's (2017) position included polices akin to a hard Brexit, namely leaving the single market, ending free movement and removing the UK from the jurisdiction of the European Court of Justice, her policy of maintaining frictionless trade with the EU in order to avoid a hard border with the Republic of Ireland became a contentious issue. As a result, May's withdrawal bill was perceived as a fudged compromise not satisfying either camp within the Conservative Party.

Being in a confidence and supply government arrangement with Northern Ireland's Democratic Unionist Party (DUP) complicated matters further. The deal between the two parties gave the DUP an unprecedented opportunity to exercise power in British politics. The 10 DUP MPs pushed for a Brexit deal that would not establish a UK border in the Irish sea. They consistently opposed the government's negotiation strategy, contributing to a period of instability. For the DUP, a different arrangement for Northern Ireland compared to the rest of the UK, for example by aligning to the EU single market rules in order to maintain an open border on the island, would create internal trade barriers within the UK, thus undermining the UK's constitutional integrity (Murphy and Evershed, 2019). This argumentation served to further justify Conservative MPs' opposition to the Prime Minister's deal and contributed significantly to the scale of Conservative backbench rebellion against the Withdrawal Bill (Sheldon, 2019).

Political division also characterized the British Parliament, which rejected the Prime Minister's Brexit Withdrawal Agreement on three occasions (15 January, 12 March and 29 March 2019) by 230, 149 and 58 votes respectively. A significant number of Conservative MPs voted against their own government (115, 75 and 34 respectively) defying party whips. In an already polarized political landscape, the government was unable to find cross-party support in order to pass the Withdrawal Bill, which was also rejected by the majority of Labour, Liberal Democrat, Scottish National Party, Green and Plaid Cymru MPs.

Theresa May had attempted to use the prospect of holding the EP election as leverage in order to convince MPs to vote for her Withdrawal Agreement and avoid the potentially embarrassing moment of holding the election. Lack of agreement in the Parliament, however, meant that the government had to request an extension of Article 50 and delay the country's withdrawal from the EU. As a result, and despite the government's previous statements to the opposite, the Prime Minister announced on 7 May that, by effectively remaining an EU member state, the UK was legally obliged to participate in the EP elections. This is because EU member states are bound by Treaty to give the right to vote to EU citizens. Refusing to organize the EP election in the UK would have likely resulted in the European Commission initiating infringement proceedings and the UK government having to face the European Court of Justice. Excluding the UK would have required EU Treaty reform, which was not a viable scenario given the time pressure.

Political divisions on the question of Brexit were also reflected in public opinion, which was split on a number of issues, including whether the UK should leave the customs union, whether it should prioritize access to the EU's single market over placing restrictions on the free movement of people, and the reciprocity of EU citizens' rights (Vasilopoulou and Talving, 2019). The public was also polarized on whether to hold an – otherwise unexpected – EP election (Table 1). Three camps remained relatively stable as developments in the British Parliament unfolded. Between 38 and 40 per cent of the population found the prospect of holding an election acceptable whereas 43–44 per cent described that possibility as unacceptable. Approximately a fifth of the electorate did not know. These responses provide an initial lens into public opinion, which was not only divided on the question of whether Brexit should happen or not, but also on whether the UK should hold the EP election.

II. A Brexit Campaign?

The political campaign was dominated by Brexit and ensuing domestic political divisions. Despite the fact that Brexit relates to the UK's relationship to the EU and as such has a European dimension, the focus of the debate was in essence national. For Brexiteers, the emphasis was primarily on how to deliver Brexit, with some asking for a 'clean break' from the EU and others cautiously supporting May's Withdrawal Bill. For those more

Table 1: How Acceptable or Unacceptable Would It Be for You if Britain Needs to Hold Elections for British MEPs to the European Parliament on 23rd May as a Consequence of Still Being an EU Member?

	15-Mar 19	*29-Mar-19*	*12-Apr-19*
	%	*%*	*%*
Acceptable	38	38	40
Unacceptable	43	43	44
Don't know	19	19	16

Source: Opinium data from the United Kingdom. https://whatukthinks.org/eu/questions/how-acceptable-or-unacceptable-would-it-be-for-you-if-britain-is-still-a-member-of-the-eu-on-the-23rd-may-so-will-need-to-hold-elections-for-british-meps-to-the-european-parliament/

favourable to the EU, for some the question was whether an alternative Brexit plan was a viable option whereas others campaigned explicitly for a second referendum. Pro-EU parties mentioned EU reform but overall the campaign hardly referred to European institutions. For example, issues related to the EP, such as the lead candidate (*Spitzenkandidaten*) process whereby the large EP party groups nominate their candidate for the European Commission Presidency, did not feature in the debate.

The primacy of domestic issues and Brexit in party campaigns was also a partial reflection of public opinion, which prioritized Brexit and values over candidates and policy. YouGov asked citizens two months prior to the election (14–15 March 2019) if Brexit were delayed and Britain had to elect MEPs, which factors would be the most important in deciding how to vote.[1] The issue of whether the party supported leaving or staying in the EU was the most popular answer (22 per cent) followed by whether the party represented the individual's broader values and principles (21 per cent). Reasons related to candidates and policy were instead of minor importance at seven and six percentage points respectively. Approximately a fifth of respondents did not know what would motivate them to vote in the 2019 EP election.

Given the Conservative Party's failure to deliver the UK's withdrawal from the EU within the two-year period designated in Article 50, it did not invest in a fully-fledged campaign ahead of the 2019 EP election. Party officials admitted that the party was likely to be punished in the polls and that voters would turn to Nigel Farage's new Brexit Party, which was launched in April 2019 by the former UKIP leader and MEP to 'ensure that the UK leaves the EU'. Some Conservative Party MPs admitted that they would not be campaigning while others said that they would not vote at all (*Financial Times*, 2019). Instead of a manifesto, the party issued a short leaflet which included a photograph of Theresa May and the slogan 'The only party which can get Brexit done is the Conservative Party'. The leaflet focused on how the EP election could be stopped and defended the Withdrawal Agreement as a deal that 'takes back control of our money, laws, and borders'. While calling for unity, the leaflet also pointed at those who had backed and those who had blocked the government's Brexit deal. It also warned that the new Brexit Party was standing for Nigel Farage's own personal gain and that voting for that party would not get the country closer to Brexit. The message was simple: if voters wanted Brexit, the Conservative Party was their best option.

The timing of the election also coincided with internal disagreements within the Labour Party, which was criticized as ambivalent in terms of its Brexit policy. During the 2017 general election campaign, Labour Party leader Jeremy Corbyn had promised to honour the 2016 Brexit referendum result and push for a 'Jobs First Brexit' (Hobolt, 2018). However, there was strong divergence between the leadership and the members' views on Brexit. In a survey of Labour Party members conducted in January 2019, 89 per cent of members thought that in hindsight it was wrong to leave the EU and 72 per cent wanted the party to fully support a new referendum on Brexit (Bale *et al.*, 2019). Dissatisfaction with Jeremy Corbyn's leadership, which included – beyond his Brexit policy – his handling of allegations of anti-Semitism within the party, led to the

[1] https://whatukthinks.org/eu/questions/if-brexit-were-delayed-and-britain-had-to-elect-meps-to-the-european-parliament-which-of-the-following-factors-if-any-will-be-most-important-in-deciding-how-you-vote-in-that-election/ Accessed on 28 March 2020.

resignation of seven Labour MPs in February 2019, including former leadership hopeful Chuka Umunna. Along with another four MPs, including the Conservative Anna Soubry who was very vocal in her criticism of the government, they registered as a party to run in the EP election under the name Change UK – The Independent Group.

The prospect of a new electoral contest added pressure on Labour leadership to put forward a clearer position on Brexit and to consider the prospect of supporting a second referendum. In its 2019 EP election manifesto, Labour opposed both the government's Withdrawal Agreement and the prospect of the UK exiting the EU with no deal. However, the party continued to resist the membership's wish for a pro-EU agenda. The leader's vision, as set out in the foreword, was to unite the country behind his alternative Brexit plan, which consisted of building a 'close and cooperative relationship' with the EU. This would include a new comprehensive customs union, close single market alignment, guaranteed rights and standards, and the protection of the Good Friday peace agreement in Northern Ireland. The manifesto promised a public vote on Brexit only in the absence of an 'agreement along the lines of our alternative plan, or a general election' (Labour Party, 2019). The manifesto also featured a section on what Labour Party MEPs have achieved in the EP on issues such as labour standards, climate and equality. A number of domestic issues were also included, for example ending austerity, tackling climate change, delivering protection at work and protecting citizens' rights, signalling that for Labour this election was not only about Brexit.

The Liberal democrats, the Scottish National Party, the Greens, Plaid Cymru and Change UK supported a referendum to stop Brexit and warned against the rise of nationalism, populism and anti-liberal forces. The question of Europe dominated their electoral campaigns, which criticized both the government's policy and Jeremy Corbyn's agenda of delivering Brexit. They all issued fully-fledged manifestos, which stressed their European values and the EU's achievements in promoting freedom, peace and stability. Their campaigns also emphasized the economic benefits of EU membership, including jobs, funding and trade, as well as questions of environmental protection and labour standards. They also mentioned what their candidates would do if elected and touched upon EU reform.

UKIP and the new Brexit Party, on the other hand, issued very short campaign documents. UKIP's two-page manifesto argued that 'Brexit is being betrayed' by the political class in Westminster. The party urged leaving the EU under the 'policy of unilateral and unconditional withdrawal' and offering the EU tariff-free trade under the rules of the World Trade Organization (WTO) (UKIP, 2019). The Brexit party issued a pledge card, urging voters to opt for them in order to 'change politics for good'. It claimed that the government's Brexit deal was 'Brexit in name only' and portrayed the adoption of WTO rules for trade as a great opportunity for the country. The Party's case for Brexit was justified both in terms of restoring trust in democracy through taking control of laws, borders and trade; and in economic terms, namely more investment in the country and reducing the cost of living.

III. A Proxy for a Second Referendum?

In contrast to the 2017 general election which strengthened the UK two-party system, in May 2019 voters rewarded small non-governing parties and punished larger mainstream

© 2020 The Authors. JCMS: Journal of Common Market Studies published by University Association for Contemporary European Studies and John Wiley & Sons Ltd

parties. This is consistent with both previous EP election results in the UK (Vasilopoulou, 2017) and the general trend of EP elections as 'second-order' electoral contests, namely platforms for protest against the government and large governing parties (Reif and Schmitt, 1980). Table 2 shows the vote and seat shares in 2019 and the change in vote share compared to the 2014 EP election. In an unprecedented success for a new party, the Brexit Party topped the polls with 30.8 per cent and 29 seats. The strongly pro-European Liberal Democrats came second with 19.8 per cent of the vote, its highest share at any EP election and a considerable improvement of 13.1 percentage points compared to 2014, which translated to 16 seats. Other parties with a clear pro-EU stance, including the Greens, the Scottish National Party and Plaid Cymru also increased their support. Change UK received 3.3 per cent of the vote, but did not secure any seats. On the other hand, the Labour and Conservative parties recorded their lowest ever combined share of the vote since the first EP election in 1979 (Cutts et al., 2019). Their support slipped by 11 and 14.4 percentage points respectively compared to the 2014 EP election. Labour came third with 13.7 per cent of the vote whereas the Conservative Party finished fifth with only 8.9 per cent, below the Greens.

The two major parties, however, were not the only electoral losers. UKIP only received 3.2 per cent of the vote, dropping by 23.6 percentage points compared to the 2014 EP election. This development was in line with a broader trend of electoral decline. UKIP support had already dropped from 12.6 per cent in the May 2015 general election to only 1.8 per cent of the vote in June 2017. For years, UKIP had campaigned for the UK's withdrawal from the EU. After the 2016 referendum, however, the party 'found itself lacking a clear purpose' (Prosser, 2018, p. 1228). Shortly after the referendum, Nigel Farage, its charismatic leader, resigned paving the way to a period of crisis. UKIP experienced internal division and held five leadership elections, as leaders struggled to unite the party. Progressively, UKIP shifted its focus towards immigration. It adopted a very strong anti-Islamic rhetoric and sought alliances with controversial figures, including ex-English Defence League leader, Tommy Robinson (see also Heath and Goodwin, 2017).

Turnout was 37 per cent, which represented a small increase compared to 2014 and was the second highest since the first EP election in 1979. Aggregate-level analysis has

Table 2: 2019 European Parliament Election Results in the UK

Party Name	Seats 2019	Votes 2019 (%)	Change in vote share since 2014
Brexit Party	29	30.8	+30.8
Liberal Democrats	16	19.8	+13.1
Labour	10	13.7	-11
Greens	7	11.8	+4.1
Conservative Party	4	8.9	−14.4
Scottish National Party	3	3.5	+1.1
Plaid Cymru	1	1	+0.3
Change UK	0	3.3	+3.3
UKIP	0	3.2	−23.6

Source: https://europarl.europa.eu/election-results-2019/en/national-results/united-kingdom/2019-2024/

shown that turnout was lower in places that had given strong support to leaving the EU in 2016 and that turnout increased in strong and moderate Remain areas (Cutts *et al.*, 2019). This suggests that those living in Remain areas might have mobilised in order to signal their disillusionment with Brexit. Still, most voters did not vote at all and turnout was much lower compared to the average across the EU (50.66 per cent) and the 2017 general election (68.8 per cent).

More broadly, it should be noted that the EP election results in the UK conformed with the wider European trend of fragmentation, declining support for the traditional left and right, and rising support for liberals and the greens. At the same time, they were indicative of voters' frustration with Brexit and the government's handling of it. Table 3 outlines the main reasons people gave for choosing the party they voted for. Approximately half of the respondents cast their vote on the basis of either the party's Brexit policy or in order to show their dissatisfaction with the government's negotiation position. This lends some support to the second-order elections model of voting behaviour whereby voters use elections to the EP in order to signal their discontent with domestic politics and government performance (Reif and Schmitt, 1980). Questions related to candidates and policies other than Brexit did not feature prominently in people's preferences. Interestingly, the Brexit party and Liberal Democrats achieved most of their support on the basis of voters' dissatisfaction with Brexit and the UK government's handling of it (at a total of 81 per cent and 68 per cent respectively). On the other hand, Labour and the Conservatives received most of their votes from people who always voted for them at 36 per cent and 34 per cent respectively. Competence was also a key reason for choosing the two large parties. Other prominent reasons for voting Labour included having the best policies on issues other than Brexit and for the Conservatives that they were the least bad option on offer.

This descriptive analysis of the most important reasons for citizens' vote choice indicates that Brexit and government performance were key predictors of the vote.

Table 3: Below are Some Reasons that People Have Given for Choosing the Party They Voted. Please Can You Rank Them in Order of How Important They Were in Your Decision

	Total	Brexit	LD	Lab	Green	Con	UKIP	ChUK
They had the best policy on Brexit	30	37	58	6	22	7	27	26
I wanted to show my dissatisfaction with the UK government's current negotiating position on Brexit	21	44	10	7	10	1	26	20
I always vote for that party	11	0	5	36	5	34	9	0
They seem the most competent of the parties on offer	8	2	8	12	11	16	8	10
I didn't like any of the parties, but I wanted to vote and this party was the least bad option	8	2	7	9	12	19	9	16
I wanted to show that I'm not happy with the party I usually vote for	7	8	7	2	12	2	8	18
They had the best policies on issues other than Brexit	6	1	2	13	20	6	6	3
They had the best leadership of the parties on offer	4	4	2	8	2	6	3	1
I voted for who I thought were the best candidates, regardless of their party	4	2	2	7	5	9	5	5

Note: First mentions in the ranking. Source: https://lordashcroftpolls.com/2019/05/my-euro-election-post-vote-poll-most-tory-switchers-say-they-will-stay-with-their-new-party/

Figure 1: Socio-demographic Model of the Brexit Party Vote.

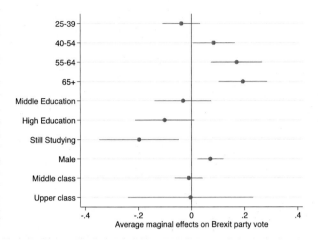

Source: European Election Study, Schmitt *et al.*, 2019.

We also know from aggregate-level analysis that the Brexit Party performed well in Leave areas and places with high levels of previous UKIP support, suggesting that it strongly benefited from pre-existing divides in British society (Cutts *et al.*, 2019: 505). To further understand the nature of these political divides and how they influenced the 2019 EP election result, we carried out individual-level analysis focusing on Brexit Party support and using data from the post-election survey of the European Election Study (EES) (Schmitt *et al.*, 2019) (for descriptive statistics and full results, see Supporting Information).[2]

We commenced by running a model that focuses on individuals' demographic characteristics. Research suggests that key socio-demographic changes, such as increases in life expectancy and the expansion of higher education, are contributing to the emergence of new cleavages in European democracies (Ford and Jennings, 2020). These divisions were also identified as key predictors of the Brexit referendum (Hobolt, 2016). If the divide is stable, it should also be present in the 2019 EP vote. Figure 1 shows the average marginal effects of age, education, gender and social class based on a logit model of Brexit Party vote with vote for all other parties as the reference category (Table A2, model 1). We observe that similarly to the referendum result, the effects of age and education are significant. Older citizens were more likely to opt for the Brexit Party. Specifically, compared to the reference category (18–24 years old), citizens over 65 years old were 19 percentage points more likely to vote for the Brexit Party. Individuals between 55 and 64 years old were similarly 17 percentage points more likely to choose the Brexit Party in the 2019

[2]This is a post-election study, conducted in all 28 EU member states after the elections to the EP were held between 23 and 26 May 2019. It asks a number of questions tapping into electoral behaviour. Party choices and general political attitudes, and covers respondents' background socio-demographic characteristics.

Figure 2: Attitudinal Model of the Brexit Party Vote.

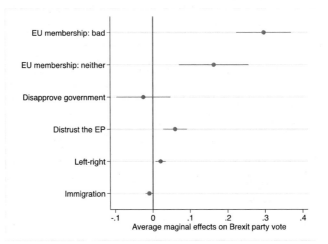

Source: European Election Study, Schmitt *et al.*, 2019.

EP election. Education was also a significant predictor with those still studying for a degree being 19 percentage points less likely to vote for the Brexit Party compared to those with low levels of education. This of course might also reflect the effect of age on vote choice. We also find that males were more likely to choose the Brexit Party, but that self-declared social class did not have an effect.

These findings indicate that the demographic divide was also present in the 2019 EP election. Hobolt et al. (2020) suggest that the Brexit referendum gave rise to affective polarization on the basis of individuals' views on Brexit. These Brexit identities cut across traditional party lines and can be as intense as partisanship. To what extent did these identities influence the vote in 2019 and how did they feature in people's minds in comparison to considerations traditionally associated with the second-order model of vote, such as the government's record? To test this, we proceeded to add a set of attitudinal variables to our vote choice model. Figure 2 presents the average marginal effects of people's views of the UK's membership of the EU[3] and their approval of the government's record to date while also controlling for trust in the EP, views on immigration and left–right self-placement (Table A2, model 2). The key observation here is the magnitude of the effect of individuals' opinions on their country's EU membership. Those who thought that the UK's membership of the EU is a bad thing were 30 percentage points more likely to opt for the Brexit Party compared to those that viewed EU membership positively. Interestingly, those who viewed membership as neither a good nor a bad thing were also more likely to choose the Brexit Party by 16 percentage points. Other attitudinal characteristics such as distrust in the EP, self-placement on the left–right dimension and immigration views were significant but did not carry as much weight in people's voting decision. Interestingly, the

---

[3] As a proxy for referendum vote, which is not included in the ESS, we are using the following question: Generally speaking, do you think that [country] membership of the European Union is...? (good thing; bad thing; neither).

extent to which citizens disapproved of the government's record did not seem to play a role in these preferences.

IV. Discussion

The 2019 EP election marked the 40th anniversary since the first election to the EP in 1979, and was conceivably the last EP election to be held in the UK. The results in the UK were striking. Smaller non-governing parties with unambiguous EU positions became unprecedented electoral winners. The newly-founded Brexit Party whose sole purpose was to ensure that the UK leaves the EU topped the polls. The Liberal Democrats campaigned on a second referendum ticket and finished second, scoring their highest ever result in an EP election. The two larger parties, on the other hand, which had promised to honour the referendum result but were fraught with internal division, were punished at the ballot box. They recorded their lowest ever combined share of the vote in an EP election.

To a large extent these results are in line with the broader European pattern where smaller parties won at the expense of the centre-left and the centre-right. Second-order elections, however, tend to be characterized by electoral volatility and as such one should be cautious about interpreting their results as an indication of electoral realignment and party system change. That said, voters' behaviour in EP elections have the potential to shape short and medium-term party strategies. Only one day after the vote on 24 May 2019 – and before the official results were declared – the Prime Minister announced her resignation. This paved the way for Boris Johnson being elected as the Conservative Party leader on 23 July 2019. Despite the fact that the Conservatives lost votes both to the Brexit Party and the Liberal Democrats (Cutts *et al.*, 2019), the new Conservative Party leader interpreted the 2019 election loss as a strong signal for adopting a hard line on Brexit. The pro-EU vote, however, was divided across a number of parties. This was perhaps an early warning that these parties had to pool their resources in order to create a unified front vis-à-vis the Brexit camp. Their inability to do so likely contributed to their weakening and the Conservatives' sweeping victory only a few months later in the December 2019 general election.

References

Bale, T., Webb, P. and Poletti, M. (2019) 'Love Corbyn. HATE Brexit'. Available at: https://esrcpartymembersproject.org/2019/01/02/love-corbyn-hate-brexit/#more-1588.

Cutts, D., Goodwin, M., Heath, O. and Milazzo, C. (2019) 'Resurgent Remain and a Rebooted Revolt on the Right: Exploring the 2019 European Parliament Elections in the United Kingdom'. *Political Quarterly*, Vol. 90, No. 3, pp. 496–514.

Financial Times (2019) 'Tories mount lacklustre campaign for European elections'. 8 May. Available at: https://www.ft.com/content/55da3c7e-719f-11e9-bf5c-6eeb837566c5.

Ford, R. and Jennings, W. (2020) 'The Changing Cleavage Politics of Western Europe'. *Annual Review of Political Science*, Vol. 23, No. 1, pp. 295–314. https://doi.org/10.1146/annurev-polisci-052217-104957

Heath, O. and Goodwin, M. (2017) 'The 2017 General Election, Brexit and the Return to Two-Party Politics: An Aggregate-Level Analysis of the Result'. *Political Quarterly*, Vol. 88, No. 3, pp. 345–58.

Hobolt, S.B. (2016) 'The Brexit Vote: A Divided Nation, a Divided Continent'. *Journal of European Public Policy*, Vol. 23, No. 9, pp. 1259–77.

Hobolt, S.B. (2018) 'Brexit and the 2017 UK General Election'. *JCMS: Journal of Common Market Studies*, Vol. 56, No. S1, pp. 39–50.

Hobolt, S.B., Leeper, T. and Tilley, J. (2020) 'Affective Polarization in the Wake of the Brexit Referendum'. *British Journal of Political Science*, 1–18. https://doi.org/10.1017/S0007123420000125

Labour Party (2019) 'Transforming Britain and Europe: for the many not the few'. Available at: https://labour.org.uk/wp-content/uploads/2019/05/Transforming-Britain-and-Europe-for-the-many-not-the-few.pdf

Lynch, P. and Whitaker, R. (2018) 'All Brexiteers Now? Brexit, the Conservatives and Party Change'. *British Politics*, Vol. 13, pp. 31–47.

May, T. (2017) *The Government's negotiating objectives for exiting the EU* (London, 17 January. Available at: www.gov.uk/government/speeches/the-governments-negotiating-objectivesfor-exiting-the-eu-pm-speech: Speech at Lancaster House).

Murphy, M.C. and Evershed, J. (2019) 'Between the Devil and the DUP: The Democratic Unionist Party and the Politics of Brexit'. *British Politics*, Vol. n/a, pp. 1–12. https://doi.org/10.1057/s41293-019-00126-3

Prosser, C. (2018) 'The Strange Death of Multi-party Britain: The UK General Election of 2017'. *West European Politics*, Vol. 41, No. 5, pp. 1226–36.

Reif, K. and Schmitt, H. (1980) 'Nine Second-Order National Elections: A Conceptual Framework for the Analysis of European Election Results'. *European Journal of Political Research*, Vol. 8, No. 1, pp. 3–44.

Schmitt, H., Hobolt, S.B., van der Brug, W. and Popa, S.A. (2019) *European Parliament Election Study 2019* (Voter Study).

Sheldon, J. (2019) 'Unionism and the Conservative Brexit Deal Rebellion'. Centre on Constitutional Change, Available at: https://www.centreonconstitutionalchange.ac.uk/opinions/unionism-and-conservative-brexit-deal-rebellion.

UKIP (2019) 'Vote UKIP: Vote to Make Brexit Happen'. Available at: https://www.ukip.org/pdf/EUManifesto2019-3.pdf

Vasilopoulou, S. (2016) 'UK Euroscepticism and the Brexit Referendum'. *Political Quarterly*, Vol. 87, No. 2, pp. 219–27.

Vasilopoulou, S. (2017) 'British Eurosceptic Voting: Anti-EU or Anti-government?' In Franklin, M. and Hassing, J. (eds) *The Eurosceptic 2014 European Parliament Elections: Second Order or Second Rate?* (London/Basingstoke: Basingstoke: Palgrave Macmillan), pp. 57–81.

Vasilopoulou, S. and Talving, L. (2019) 'British Public Opinion on Brexit: Controversies and Contradictions'. *European Political Science*, Vol. 18, No. 1, pp. 134–42.

Supporting Information

Additional supporting information may be found online in the Supporting Information section at the end of the article.

JCMS 2020 Volume 58. Annual Review pp. 91–104

DOI: 10.1111/jcms.13084

Media Personalization during European Elections: the 2019 Election Campaigns in Context[*]

KATJANA GATTERMANN
Amsterdam School of Communication Research, University of Amsterdam, Amsterdam

Introduction

The European Parliament (EP) placed great hopes in the *Spitzenkandidaten* (lead candidates) procedure, which was first employed in the 2014 European elections and entails that European party families nominate pan-European lead candidates for the president of the European Commission (EC). Following the nomination and subsequent election of former lead candidate Jean-Claude Juncker as Commission president in 2014, the EP evaluated the procedure as successful and argued, among other things, that the procedure 'fosters the political awareness of European citizens in the run-up to the European elections'.[1]

However, the election of Ursula von der Leyen as Commission president in 2019 led to the provisional abandonment of the procedure and casted doubt on the impact of the procedure on European Union (EU) politics in the long run. Although many of these concerns address inter-institutional relations (see Hobolt, 2014), low levels of recognising lead candidates (Gattermann and de Vreese, 2020; Hobolt, 2014) as well as their limited potential for mobilization (Schmitt *et al.,* 2015; Gattermann and Marquart, 2020) indicate that the *Spitzenkandidaten* have not yet fully resonated with European citizens. Why is this the case?

This contribution sheds light on this phenomenon by examining it through the lens of the personalization of politics at the EU level. Personalization implies that individual politicians come increasingly into focus at the expense of political parties and institutions (Rahat and Sheafer, 2007, p. 65). I argue that in order to understand the (limited) impact of European *Spitzenkandidaten* among European voters one needs to understand the personalization of EU politics in context. First, context is time dependent, which requires an assessment of the scope of personalization as a development over time. In other words, public attention paid to *Spitzenkandidaten* is likely to be contingent upon longitudinal changes in the personalization of EU politics more generally. In the absence of any such trend, it would hardly be surprising if the *Spitzenkandidaten* procedure failed to engage

[*]This study received funding from the Nederlandse Organisatie voor Wetenschappelijk Onderzoek (Veni grant, project no. 451–15-003). I would like to thank Paris Bethel, Catalina Gaete, Azade Kakavand and Manon Metz for excellent research assistance and acknowledge additional support from the European Research Council, grant no. 647316 (Principal investigator: Claes de Vreese). A previous version of this contribution was presented at the MAPLE Conference 'The Politicisation of Europe: A Citizens' Perspective' (Institute of Social Sciences, University of Lisbon, December 2017). I would like to thank all participants and particularly Marina Costa Lobo, Pedro Magalhães and Michael Lewis-Beck, together with Theofanis Exadaktylos of the JCMS Annual Review's editorial board, for their valuable comments.
[1]Decision on the revision of the Framework Agreement on relations between the EP and the EC, 7 February 2018 (2017/2233(ACI)).

voters. Second, context also varies at the domestic level, in terms of political cultures as well as media and electoral systems. Put differently, some domestic contexts are more prone to personalized politics than others (see Gattermann, 2018; Holtz-Bacha *et al.*, 2014; Kriesi, 2012; Šimunjak, 2017), which may explain potential cross-country variations in the attention paid to *Spitzenkandidaten*.

For these reasons, I analyse the personalization of EU politics in seven countries over the course of five European elections since 1999. I specifically examine the extent to which European broadsheets report on individual members of the European Parliament (MEPs) and *Spitzenkandidaten*. Media coverage is important for European voters to learn about candidates and issues at stake. If media do not report on candidates, and *Spitzenkandidaten* in particular, their impact on voter awareness and behaviour is likely to be limited. The findings indicate that EP election coverage generally does not become more personalized over time. This also holds for attention given to *Spitzenkandidaten* between 2014 and 2019, although they are often more visible than a typical MEP from the same party family. This leads me to conclude that the *Spitzenkandidaten* process is somewhat detached from mediated personalization developments at the national level. In the concluding section, I briefly discuss the implications of these findings.

I. European Elections in the Media

EP election campaigns have become more salient in European media outlets over recent years, although cross-country variation is still prevalent (Boomgaarden and de Vreese, 2016). Furthermore, scholars have observed that media coverage of EP elections has not become more European in nature, but continues to focus on domestic issues and political actors (Belluati, 2016; Boomgaarden and de Vreese, 2016; Schuck *et al.*, 2011). Yet political actors at both levels have often been studied as a collective, that is, no distinction has been made between politicians, parties and institutions, which impedes any examination of personalization trends.

We know relatively little about the media visibility of individual candidates during EP elections, with the exception of their activities on social media (Daniel and Obholzer, 2020; Koc-Michalska *et al.*, 2016). The *Spitzenkandidaten* have received slightly more scholarly attention (Belluati, 2016; Nulty *et al.*, 2016; Braun and Schwarzbözl, 2019; Schulze, 2016), and studies indicate that there is considerable variation in terms of media or campaign attention paid to *Spitzenkandidaten* among individual candidates, political parties and country contexts. However, it is difficult to assess whether these findings pertain to the very – pan-European – nature of the *Spitzenkandidaten* procedure and individual candidates put forward, or whether they actually align with personalization trends at the domestic level (or absence thereof). Put differently, existing research has rarely offered insights into media personalization trends with respect to EP elections.

II. Why Mediated Personalization of European Elections?

Proponents of the personalization of politics thesis have argued that mediated personalization is linked to three main factors (see also Gattermann, 2018; Gattermann and Marquart, 2020). First, scholars have observed a trend towards partisan dealignment as citizens have become more detached from political parties (Dalton and Wattenberg, 2000).

As a consequence, voting behaviour has become more volatile in recent decades, which impacts on party competition in the electoral arena and offers opportunities for personalized electoral behaviour (Garzia, 2014; Lobo and Curtice, 2015). Second, and most prominently, scholars have identified mediatization processes as being responsible for the changing relationship between media and politics (Mazzoleni and Schulz, 1999; Strömbäck, 2008). Journalists have become more independent over time and have gradually gained the upper hand in setting the campaign agenda, and political communication has been increasingly influenced by media logic as opposed to party or political logic, which entails a greater focus on individuals and personalities, among other things (see Mazzoleni, 1987; Strömbäck, 2008). Third, developments in political institutions, such as electoral system reforms, may trigger changes in the way the news media report on politics (Rahat and Sheafer, 2007).

Despite these developments, there does not appear to be any universal trend towards the increased personalization of media coverage because findings differ across countries (Langer, 2007; Šimunjak, 2017; Vliegenthart et al., 2011), also with respect to election campaign coverage (Holtz-Bacha et al., 2014; Kriesi, 2012; Rahat and Sheafer, 2007). Regarding the mediated personalization of EU politics, I could not confirm such a trend with respect to individual commissioners or the Commission president at the expense of the institution itself amid considerable variation across several EU member states (Gattermann, 2018). Although I have argued that a focus on individual politicians instead of institutions and political parties could potentially make EU politics less abstract and hence more tangible and accessible to its citizens (Gattermann, 2018, p. 347), the reverse appears to be the case with the EC. Commissioners are not directly elected by EU citizens and their party affiliation plays only a subordinate role to their work in the EC, which undermines the provision of additional heuristics that help the audience understand who they are. These circumstances, alongside the rising complexity of EU politics that entail an abundance of individual responsibilities, may explain why journalists opt to report on the institution at the expense of individual commissioners if their aim is to make EU politics accessible to their audiences. However, this may be different for the EP because '[i]ts members are directly elected and, hence, incentivized to gain media attention, and journalists have greater responsibilities to hold them accountable' (Gattermann, 2018, p. 362).

So, why would we expect mediated personalization of EP elections? As second-order national elections, EP elections are prone to low voter turnout and high voter volatility because parties and voters prioritize domestic issues (Reif and Schmitt, 1980). This may be a favourable condition for personalized voting behaviour, although a preliminary empirical assessment showed that it mainly occurs among sophisticated voters and that party preferences still play a more decisive role compared to candidate evaluations (Gattermann and de Vreese, 2017). Likewise, few voters actually recognize *Spitzenkandidaten* (Hobolt, 2014) and thus their impact on voter turnout and vote intention is somewhat limited (Schmitt et al., 2015; Gattermann and Marquart, 2020). This may also indicate that media coverage of EP election campaigns as main source of information for voters is not very personalized (see Belluati, 2016: Schulze, 2016).

Nonetheless, high volatility also provides incentives for personalized campaigning. Generally, EP election campaigns tend to be less professionalized compared with national ones (Tenscher and Mykkänen, 2014). However, over the course of eight EP elections, campaign posters of national political parties in the Netherlands and Italy have placed greater emphasis on individual candidates, suggesting that campaigning has become more professionalized in that respect (Gattermann and Vliegenthart, 2019). As professionalization and mediatization processes are interlinked (Strömbäck, 2008, p. 240) and notwithstanding the potentially limited scope of such developments, this may also indicate that mediated personalization of EP elections has taken place over time.

Lastly, the introduction of the *Spitzenkandidaten* procedure has clearly been a structural innovation in EP elections. As electoral reforms are considered to impact on mediated personalization (Rahat and Sheafer, 2007), they may also trigger more personalized media coverage of EP elections – not only with respect to *Spitzenkandidaten* themselves, but also regarding MEP candidates. However, such structural innovations have generally not led to more personalized broadsheet coverage of the EC, as new treaties have not had any impact on longitudinal changes (Gattermann, 2018). And while more contestation during EP election campaigns triggers more comprehensive media coverage (Schuck *et al.*, 2011), long-term trends of the politicization of EU integration (Hooghe and Marks, 2009; Hutter *et al.*, 2016) do not appear to play a crucial role for the mediated personalization of the EC (Gattermann, 2018).

Regardless of these considerations and given the mixed evidence from national politics, we are likely to find considerable variation across domestic contexts. While this may not necessarily hinder mediated personalization trends from emerging over time, as they could evolve at different levels of personalization, we should not ignore differences in media and electoral systems that potentially condition the scope of personalization trends (Holtz-Bacha *et al.*, 2014; Vliegenthart *et al.*, 2011). EP elections have been based on proportional representation since the coming into force of the uniform electoral procedures in 2002, but electoral institutions differ in terms of how much emphasis is put on individual candidates versus parties. For example, the Irish single transferable vote system allows voters to rank individual candidates across parties, whereas French voters choose between parties on the ballot. One assumption is that the more personalized the electoral system, the more personalized the campaigning of election contenders (Bowler and Farrell, 2011), which the media is likely to pick upon.

Likewise, traditional media systems differ in terms of levels of political parallelism, professionalization of journalists as well as commercialization and market competition, among other things (Hallin and Mancini, 2004). This has consequences for the degree to which media coverage is personalized. Studies, for example, find more pronounced personalization trends in the UK than in Germany (Holtz-Bacha *et al.*, 2014) and the Netherlands (Vliegenthart *et al.*, 2011), suggesting that the highly competitive British newspaper market plays a role in this. Differences in media systems are also reflected in the extent to which broadsheets personalize their news about the EC (Gattermann, 2018). Taken together, system-level differences at the domestic level may also explain why studies have found cross-country differences in the attention paid to *Spitzenkandidaten* (Belluati, 2016; Schulze, 2016), and it remains to be seen whether such patterns prevail with respect to the mediated personalization of EP elections over time.

III. Case Selection and Analysis

The study considers five EP elections (1999–2019) in seven countries, namely Ireland, the UK (England only), France, the Netherlands, Poland, Austria, and Italy. The countries are diverse in terms of the length of time they have been members of the EU; size and therewith number of elected MEPs; traditional media systems (Hallin and Mancini, 2004, 2012); and electoral systems, although proportional representation has been employed in all countries under study and at all points in time.

For the content analysis, one left-leaning broadsheet per country was chosen: *The Irish Times*, *The Guardian* (UK), the French *Le Monde*, the Dutch *De Volkskrant*, the Polish *Gazeta Wyborcza*, the Austrian *Der Standard* and the Italian *La Stampa* (note: *La Stampa* is considered rather centrist). As Poland joined the EU in 2004, only four elections are considered for *Gazeta Wyborcza*; the study period of the Austrian broadsheet comprises three elections since 2009 due to lack of data availability. I am aware that the newspaper selection does not include other media outlets with different political leanings or different types of media. However, newspapers are well suited for a study of personalization as a longitudinal process (Holtz-Bacha *et al.*, 2014; Langer, 2007; Vliegenthart *et al.*, 2011). Moreover, personalization trends are, for example, comparable between newspapers and television (Kriesi, 2012, p. 831).

For each election period, six weeks are considered, namely four weeks prior to the final election day and two weeks thereafter, which resulted in a total number of 21,423 articles collected (see Table A1).[2] The data collection and automated content analysis procedures are described in Gattermann (2018, p. 352) and the coressponding supplementary material. The data were retrieved from Nexis Uni by applying several keywords pertaining to EU institutions, MEPs in general and the elections themselves. These data were then analysed by searching the content for the names of all *elected* MEPs (and all *Spitzenkandidaten*) in each election, bar MEPs from Scotland, Northern Ireland, Wales, and French overseas territories (2004–14). Importantly, this means that we cannot generalize the findings at the individual level, because we do not take into account any news coverage of unsuccessful contenders. However, we are able to compare the results between periods before and after the elections (additional results are reported in the Appendix); the selection problem is no longer present after election day. A range of 291 to 313 elected MEPs is considered in each election across the respective countries (see Table A2). In 2014, there were six *Spitzenkandidaten*, while a total of 14 lead candidates contested the 2019 EP elections, because the Liberals presented a team of seven lead candidates. However, I consider only those nine *Spitzenkandidaten* from 2019 who took part in at least one of the pan-European televised debates (see Table A3).

To measure personalization trends, some studies have applied relative measures of individuals versus political parties (Kriesi, 2012; Vliegenthart *et al.*, 2011). With respect to EP elections, the party political reference points for MEP candidates and *Spitzenkandidaten* are more difficult to identify using uniform measures for several reasons: national parties could be referenced with respect to domestic politics instead of EU politics; many national parties have joined electoral lists under one umbrella organization (e.g., Olive Tree in Italy); *Spitzenkandidaten* compete for transnational party families and sometimes there is no successful national party affiliated to any of them (such as Liberals in Poland in recent elections). Moreover, there are some independent MEPs, especially in Ireland; in other countries, independents often join electoral coalitions.

---

[2]There may be articles missing from the Polish sample may after 2007 (Gattermann, 2018, p. 353). Over- time patterns have thus to be interpreted with caution.

Thus, to allow for comparability across countries and over time as well as between MEPs and *Spitzenkandidaten*, I analyse the absolute visibility of these politicians (for similar approaches see Langer, 2007; Šimunjak, 2017). Generally, all references to an MEP or *Spitzenkandidat's* last name were counted on the condition that each of them is mentioned at least once by their full name in an article. Variations and nicknames were included. References in the headlines count twice compared with references in the article text (see also Vliegenthart *et al.*, 2011, p. 99). The overall number of mentions were averaged per country and election across all respective MEPs and *Spitzenkandidaten* included in this study (or any subsets of MEPs; see below). After that, all scores were averaged per 100 articles in order to compare the results across elections and newspapers.

IV. Findings

Figure 1 shows the average number of references to MEPs (disregarding *Spitzenkandidaten*) in each newspaper and election. It distinguishes between pre and post-election periods. Generally, Irish MEPs are the most visible: a typical Irish MEP receives between 2.9 (2019, pre-election) and 8.5 mentions (2009, post-election) in the *Irish Times*. *Der Standard, La Stampa, De Volkskrant* and *Gazeta Wyborcza* follow, despite considerable variation over time. The average values for English and French MEPs in their respective newspapers are lowest of all. This may be an indicator of electoral system differences as these MEPs, as well as Polish MEPs, are elected via closed party lists, while

Figure 1: Average number of references to members of the European Parliament (MEPs), pre and post-elections.

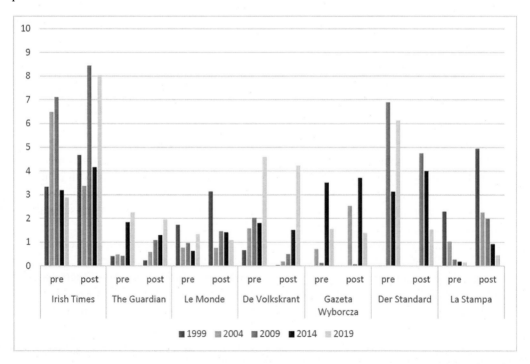

media system differences may not play a crucial role compared with the personalization of the EC (Gattermann, 2018).

However, we are mainly interested in variations over time to examine possible personalization trends. For most newspapers (*Irish Times*, *Le Monde*, *Gazeta Wyborcza* and *Der Standard)* there are no clear patterns. English MEPs receive continuously more attention in *The Guardian* over time (increasing from 0.2 to 2 references per MEP between 1999 and 2019 in the post-election period), as do Dutch MEPs in *De Volkskrant* (in the pre-election period values rise from 0.7 to 4.6 mentions). However, there is a reverse trend for *La Stampa*: over time, Italian MEPs receive less attention during pre and post-election periods (for the latter period, average mentions of MEPs drop from 4.9 in 1999 to 0.5 in 2019). In the Dutch case, the 2019 scores could be driven by the fact that two *Spitzenkandidaten* were Dutch, but mediated personalization had already taken place beforehand. Moreover, the depersonalization trend in *La Stampa* occurs despite the candidacy of Italian *Spitzenkandidat* Emma Bonino in 2019.

To examine whether these trends are driven by particular groups of MEPs, Figure 2 distinguishes between newly elected and returning MEPs. Newcomers could receive more attention than returning members. Alternatively, the latter have an incumbency bonus which may show up in newspaper coverage (Kriesi, 2012). Figure 2 shows that patterns are generally similar to the findings reported above. With few exceptions, returning MEPs often receive more attention on aggregate than newly elected MEPs in all newspapers bar the

Figure 2: Average number of references to new versus returning members of the European Parliament (MEPs)

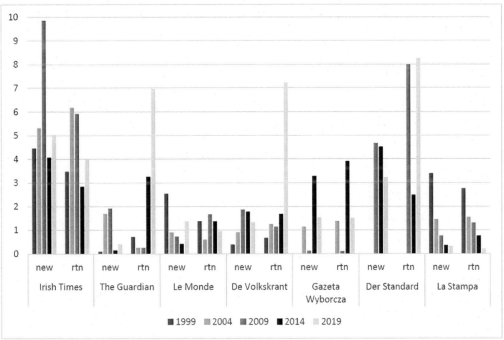

Note: Returning MEPs were in office at the end of the previous legislative term.

Irish Times. They also appear to be the main contributor to personalization trends in the British and Dutch newspapers, although newly elected MEPs sometimes receive more attention than returning MEPs in post-election periods (Figure A1).

As populist parties have gained more support in EP elections over time, Figure 3 distinguishes between MEPs from populist far-right domestic parties (based on the classification by Rooduijn *et al.,* 2019) and other MEPs. Personalization in *The Guardian* is more applicable for MEPs from the UK Independence Party and the Brexit Party compared with other English MEPs, while the previously reported (de-)personalization patterns are similar for Dutch and Italian MEPs from populist far-right and other parties, albeit at slightly different levels. On aggregate, the former group of MEPs often receives more attention than other MEPs, but this varies over time. Prominent individual MEPs, such as Nigel Farage, Marine Le Pen or Matteo Salvini, may be driving this pattern, which we cannot examine using the current study design. The patterns are similar if we only assess post-election periods (Figure A2), with the exception of *De Volkskrant* in 2019 and *Der Standard*.

Having received an overview of the rather limited personalization trends for MEPs in European newspapers, we now turn to the *Spitzenkandidaten*. Figure 4 shows the average number of *Spitzenkandidaten* references in 2014 and 2019, distinguishing between pre

Figure 3: Average number of references to populist far-right versus other members of the European Parliament (MEPs)

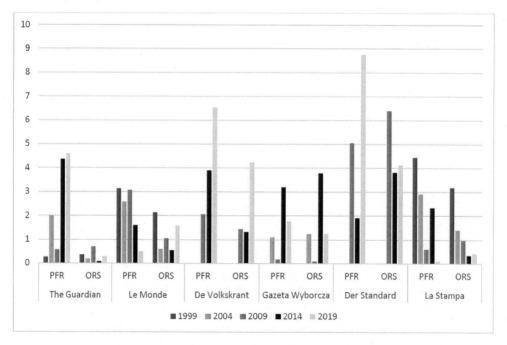

Note: PFR, populist far-right, ORS, other MEPs; there are no PFR parties in Ireland. PFRs considered: UK Independence Party/Brexit Party (England); National Front/National Rally (FR); Freedom Party, Forum for Democracy (NL); Freedom Party of Austria; Northern League, Brothers of Italy.

and post-election periods. Though similar to Figure 1, the scale is larger in Figure 4, meaning that on aggregate, *Spitzenkandidaten* receive more mentions in European newspapers than MEPs. The British, Dutch and Austrian newspapers pay most attention to them, followed by the French and Italian newspapers. Remarkably, with the exception of *De Volkskrant*, which probably reported on the two Dutch *Spitzenkandidaten*, the pan-European lead candidates received less attention in 2019 than before. Likewise, in many newspapers the attention paid to *Spitzenkandidaten* is higher after the elections than before, but this is not the case in *Gazeta Wyborcza* in both years, *The Guardian* and *Der Standard* in 2019 and *Le Monde* and *La Stampa* in 2014. In the latter case this may relate to the fact that a Frenchman, José Bové, stood for the European Greens and the Greek Alexis Tsipras headed an electoral list in Italy; none of them had been considered as Commission president after the elections.

The final analysis constitutes a comparison between references to MEPs of the European People's Party (EPP) and their *Spitzenkandidaten* as well as between MEPs and *Spitzenkandidaten* mentions among the Social Democrats (S&D group in the EP, Party of European Socialists (PES) for *Spitzenkandidaten*) in Figures 5 and 6, respectively.

Individual *Spitzenkandidaten* are often mentioned more frequently than a typical MEP from the same party family, which also holds for the post-election periods (Figures A3 and A4). The differences are most pronounced in the French, Dutch and Italian newspapers for both party families, as well as for the EPP in *Der Standard*. In the remaining newspapers, the differences are more marginal and reversed for the EPP in two instances: Manfred Weber received less attention in 2019 (6.3 mentions) than EPP MEPs in 2009 (seven mentions on average; but not post-election) in the *Irish Times*, and less attention compared to Polish MEPs in *Gazeta Wyborcza* in 2019 (0.9 versus 1.5 mentions). Nonetheless, there

Figure 4: Average number of references to *Spitzenkandidaten*, pre and post-elections

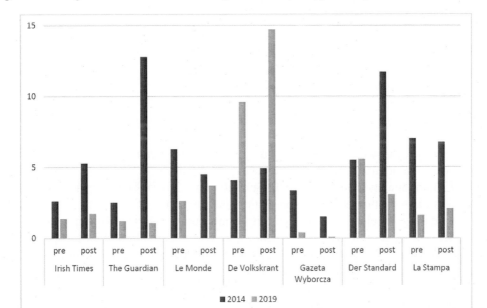

Figure 5: Average number of references to EPP members of the European Parliament (MEPs) and *Spitzenkandidaten* (SKs)

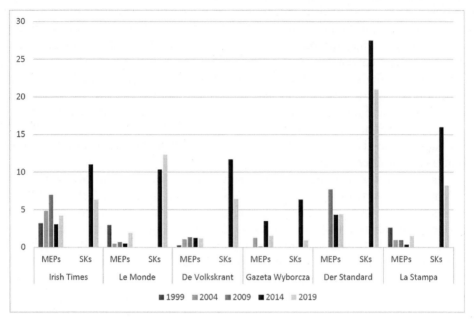

Note: The British Conservatives left the EPP in 2009 and are thus excluded.

does not seem to be a mediated personalization trend that relates references of *Spitzenkandidaten* to patterns of MEP visibility. Rather, *Spitzenkandidaten* appear to stand out from the respective national MEP delegation. Similar patterns are present only in *Gazeta Wyborcza*, which reports less often about both MEPs and *Spitzenkandidaten* between 2014 and 2019, while *Le Monde* reports more often about EPP MEPs and *Spitzenkandidaten* and *Der Standard* increased its coverage of social democratic MEPs and *Spitzenkandidaten* in 2019 compared with before; although these findings are not applicable if we consider only post-election periods.

Conclusion

The aim of the *Spitzenkandidaten* procedure was to raise voter awareness and participation. However, evidence suggests that their impact on electoral behaviour has been rather mixed (Gattermann and Marquart, 2020; Schmitt *et al.,* 2015). The purpose of this contribution was to study this phenomenon against the backdrop of mediated personalization processes during EP elections. As such, this contribution provides an important account of the media context in the 2019 EP elections, as voters learn about their prospective representatives through media coverage, which can ultimately inform their voting decisions. I argued that it is important to understand the *Spitzenkandidaten* procedure in the context of longitudinal developments and variations of personalized politics at the domestic level. Indeed, the findings show, first, that there are no universal personalization trends in the EP election coverage by European newspapers. Only *De Volkskrant* and *The Guardian* have

Figure 6: Average number of references to S&D/PES members of the European Parliament (MEPs) and *Spitzenkandidaten* (SKs)

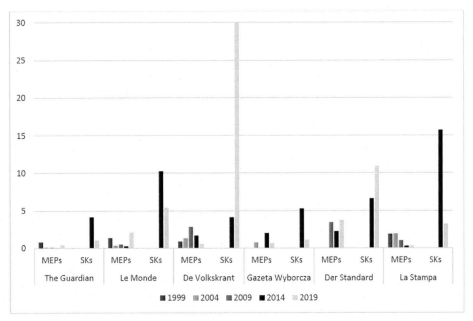

Note: Irish Labour MEPs have not been elected after 2009 and are thus excluded. The *Spitzenkandidat* value is 63.19 for *De Volkskrant* in 2019. Timmermans was excluded in the calculations of the Dutch S&D delegation.

paid increasingly more attention to elected MEPs over the course of five EP elections, while the reverse is the case for *La Stampa*. The patterns for the remaining newspapers are mixed. There is generally considerable variation across country, while returning MEPs and those representing populist far-right parties tend to receive slightly more attention than newly elected and other MEPs, respectively. However, these categories are not mutually exclusive, that is, patterns could be driven by returning MEPs *from* populist far-right parties. As the analysis excludes unsuccessful MEP candidates, additional research is needed to examine individual-level variation. Second, *Spitzenkandidaten* altogether received less attention in 2019 compared with previously, except in the Dutch press, which suggests that EP election coverage has also not become more personalized at the pan-European level. However, and third, *Spitzenkandidaten* of the EPP and PES often stand out compared with the newspaper attention that a typical MEP from the same party family receives. In other words, the *Spitzenkandidaten* are somewhat detached from mediated personalization processes during EP elections at the national level.

This has both positive and unfavourable implications. On the one hand, *Spitzenkandidaten* have received special attention, most notably when the procedure was first introduced, which is a positive precondition for European citizens to learn about them (see Gattermann and de Vreese, 2020). On the other hand, this particularity could also be a disadvantage because European voters, except perhaps Irish voters, are not necessarily used to personalized media reporting about EP election candidates. For example, as attention to individual candidates decreases in the Italian press, voters may have become less sensitized to the *Spitzenkandidaten* procedure. However, as mediated personalization in the Dutch press has already occurred prior to the *Spitzenkandidaten* procedure, voters here may have developed an apprehension for pan-European candidates, especially given that there were two Dutch *Spitzenkandidaten* in 2019.

If the procedure were to be revived, potentially enduring depersonalization trends would not enhance socialization with the procedure among European voters. One possible pre-emption would be to put forward candidates who already served in the EC. As the analysis showed, returning MEPs often tend to receive more media attention in European newspapers. Nominating *Spitzenkandidaten* with experience of serving in the EC would allow the media, and ultimately citizens, to hold them accountable for their past performance in future European elections, which would eventually mitigate the EU's accountability deficit (Hobolt and Tilley, 2014).

References

Belluati, M. (2016) 'Signs of Europeanization?: The 2014 EP Election in European Newspapers'. *Italian Political Science Review*, Vol. 46, No. 2, pp. 131–50.

Boomgaarden, H.G. and de Vreese, C.H. (2016) 'Do European Elections Create a European Public Sphere?' In van der Brug, W. and de Vreese, C.H. (eds) *(Un)intended consequences of European Elections* (Oxford: Oxford University Press), pp. 19–35.

Bowler, S. and Farrell, D. (2011) 'Electoral Institutions and Campaigning in Comparative Perspective: Electioneering in European Parliament Elections'. *European Journal of Political Research*, Vol. 50, No. 5, pp. 668–88.

Braun, D. and Schwarzbözl, T. (2019) 'Put in the Spotlight or Largely Ignored? Emphasis on the *Spitzenkandidaten* by Political Parties in Their Online Campaigns for European Elections'. *Journal of European Public Policy*, Vol. 26, No. 3, pp. 428–45.

Dalton, R.J. and Wattenberg, M.P. (2000) *Parties without Partisans: Political Change in Advanced Industrial Democracies* (Oxford: Oxford University Press).

Daniel, W.T. and Obholzer, L. (2020) 'Reaching out to the Voter? Campaigning on Twitter during the 2019 European Elections'. *Research & Politics*, Vol. 7, No. 2. https://doi.org/10.1177/2053168020917256

European Parliament (2018) Revision of the Framework Agreement on relations between the European Parliament and the European Commission, 7 February. Available at https://www.europarl.europa.eu/doceo/document/TA-8-2018-0030_EN.html Accessed 30 July 2020.

Garzia, D. (2014) *Personalization of Politics and Electoral Change* (Basingstoke: Palgrave).

Gattermann, K. (2018) 'Mediated Personalization of Executive European Union Politics: Examining Patterns in Broadsheet Coverage, 1992–2016'. *International Journal of Press/Politics*, Vol. 23, No. 3, pp. 345–66.

Gattermann, K. and de Vreese, C.H. (2017) 'The Role of Candidate Evaluations in the 2014 European Parliament Elections: Towards the Personalization of Voting Behaviour?' *European Union Politics*, Vol. 18, No. 3, pp. 447–68.

Gattermann, K. and de Vreese, C.H. (2020) 'Awareness of *Spitzenkandidaten* in the 2019 European Elections: The Effects of News Exposure in Domestic Campaign Contexts'. *Research & Politics*, Vol. 7, No. 2. doi: https://doi.org/10.1177/2053168020915332

Gattermann, K. and Marquart, F. (2020) 'Do *Spitzenkandidaten* Really Make a Difference? An Experiment on the Effectiveness of Personalized European Parliament Election Campaigns'. *European Union Politics*. https://doi.org/10.1177/1465116520938148

Gattermann, K. and Vliegenthart, R. (2019) 'The Writing is on the Wall: The Limited Professionalization of European Parliament Election Campaign Posters'. *Journal of European Integration*, Vol. 41, No. 6, pp. 763–82.

Hallin, D.C. and Mancini, P. (2004) *Comparing Media Systems. Three Models of Media and Politics* (New York: Cambridge University Press).

Hallin, D.C. and Mancini, P. (2012) *Comparing Media Systems beyond the Western World* (Cambridge: Cambridge University Press).

Hobolt, S.B. (2014) 'A Vote for the President? The Role of *Spitzenkandidaten* in the 2014 European Parliament elections'. *Journal of European Public Policy*, Vol. 21, No. 10, pp. 1528–40.

Hobolt, S.B. and Tilley, J. (2014) *Blaming Europe? Responsibility without Accountability in the European Union* (Oxford: Oxford University Press).

Holtz-Bacha, C., Langer, A.I. and Merkle, S. (2014) 'The Personalization of Politics in Comparative Perspective: Campaign Coverage in Germany and the United Kingdom'. *European Journal of Communication*, Vol. 29, No. 2, pp. 153–70.

Hooghe, L. and Marks, G. (2009) 'A Postfunctionalist Theory of European Integration: From Permissive Consensus to Constraining Dissensus'. *British Journal of Political Science*, Vol. 39, pp. 1–23.

Hutter, S., Grande, E. and Kriesi, H. (2016) *Politicising Europe. Integration and Mass Politics* (Cambridge: Cambridge University Press).

Koc-Michalska, K., Lilleker, D.G., Smith, A. and Weissmann, D. (2016) 'The Normalization of Online Campaigning in the Web.2.0 Era'. *European Journal of Communication*, Vol. 31, No. 3, pp. 331–50.

Kriesi, H. (2012) 'Personalisation of National Election Campaigns'. *Party Politics*, Vol. 18, No. 6, pp. 825–44.

Langer, A.I. (2007) 'A Historical Exploration of the Personalisation of Politics in the Print Media: The British Prime Ministers (1945–1999)'. *Parliamentary Affairs*, Vol. 60, No. 3, pp. 371–87.

Lobo, M.C. and Curtice, J. (2015) *Personality Politics? The Role of Leader Evaluations in Democratic Elections* (Oxford: Oxford University Press).

Mazzoleni, G. (1987) 'Media Logic and Party Logic in Campaign Coverage: The Italian General Election of 1983'. *European Journal of Communication*, Vol. 2, No. 1, pp. 81–103.

Mazzoleni, G. and Schulz, W. (1999) 'Mediatization of Politics: A Challenge for Democracy?' *Political Communication*, Vol. 16, No. 3, pp. 247–61.

Nulty, P., Theocharis, Y., Popa, S.A., Parnet, O. and Benoit, K. (2016) 'Social Media and Political Communication in the 2014 Elections to the European Parliament'. *Electoral Studies*, Vol. 44, pp. 429–44.

Rahat, G. and Sheafer, T. (2007) 'The Personalization(s) of Politics: Israel, 1949–2003'. *Political Communication*, Vol. 24, No. 1, pp. 65–80.

Reif, K. and Schmitt, H. (1980) 'Nine Second Order National Elections: A Conceptual Framework for the Analysis of European Election Results'. *European Journal of Political Research*, Vol. 8, No. 1, pp. 3–44.

Rooduijn, M., Van Kessel, S., Froio, C., Pirro, A., De Lange, S., Halikiopoulou, D., Lewis, P., Mudde, C. and Taggart, P. (2019) 'The PopuList: An Overview of Populist, Far Right, Far Left and Eurosceptic Parties in Europe'. Available online at: www.popu-list.org. Last accessed 24 July 2020.

Schmitt, H., Hobolt, S.B. and Popa, S.A. (2015) 'Does Personalization Increase Turnout? *Spitzenkandidaten* in the 2014 European Parliament Elections'. *European Union Politics*, Vol. 16, No. 3, pp. 347–68.

Schuck, A.R.T., Xezonakis, G., Elenbaas, M., Banducci, S.A. and De Vreese, C.H. (2011) 'Party Contestation and Europe on the News Agenda: The 2009 European Parliamentary Elections'. *Electoral Studies*, Vol. 30, No. 1, pp. 41–52.

Schulze, H. (2016) 'The *Spitzenkandidaten* in the European Parliament Election Campaign Coverage 2014 in Germany, France, and the United Kingdom'. *Politics and Governance*, Vol. 4, No. 1, pp. 23–36.

Šimunjak, M. (2017) '(De-)personalization of Mediated Political Communication: Comparative Analysis of Yugoslavia, Croatia and the United Kingdom from 1945 to 2015'. *European Journal of Communication*, Vol. 32, No. 5, pp. 473–89.

Strömbäck, J. (2008) 'Four Phases of Mediatization: An Analysis of the Mediatization of Politics'. *International Journal of Press/Politics*, Vol. 13, No. 3, pp. 228–46.

Tenscher, J. and Mykkänen, J. (2014) 'Two Levels of Campaigning: An Empirical Test of the Party-centred Theory of Professionalisation'. *Political Studies*, Vol. 62, No. S1, pp. 20–41.

Vliegenthart, R., Boomgaarden, H.G. and Boumans, J.W. (2011) 'Changes in Political News Coverage: Personalization, Conflict and Negativity in British and Dutch Newspapers'. In Brants, K. and Voltmer, K. (eds) *Political Communication in Postmodern Democracy* (Basingstoke: Palgrave Macmillan), pp. 92–110.

Supporting Information

Additional supporting information may be found online in the Supporting Information section at the end of the article.

Table A1: Data overview, number of articles collected.
Table A2: Number of elected MEPs who directly took up their seat, per election (considered in this study).
Table A3: Overview of *Spitzenkandidaten*.
Figure A1: Average number of references to new versus returning MEPs post-election
Figure A2: Average number of references to populist far-right versus other MEPs post-election.
Figure A3: Average number of references to EPP MEPs and *Spitzenkandidaten* post-election.
Figure A4: Average number of references to S&D/PES MEPs and *Spitzenkandidaten* post-election.

JCMS 2020 Volume 58. Annual Review . pp. 105–120   DOI: 10.1111/jcms.13104

Democratic Erosion? One Dominant Party and Ineffective Opposition

MAGDALENA SOLSKA
University of Fribourg, Fribourg

Introduction

2019 marked the 30th anniversary of the end of communism and the beginning of the post-communist system transformation towards democracy and a market economy for Poland and Hungary. Fifteen years after EU accession, heralded as the achievement of democratic consolidation in both countries, their democratic performance has been questioned. Regional experts have quizzed the depth and sustainability of democratic institutionalization (Krastev, 2016) and have expressed concerns over 'democratic backsliding' and 'illiberal tendencies' in the region (Greskovits, 2015). Both Poland and Hungary have been cited as examples of democratic decline in the recent years. Despite some ideological similarities between them, developments in Poland appear quite different from Hungary's more populist and one-sided turn.

Two approaches are used to explain different degrees of democratic decline: The structural approach, focusing on economic performance, political culture, historical legacies; and the agency-related approach, focused on actor-level dynamics, such as elite choices or their attitudinal shifts (Tomini and Wagemann, 2017, pp. 688–690). Using the agency approach, a successful transformation towards democracy requires political elites to be committed to democracy and ready to abide by the rules of the democratic political game even when it means losing power (Linz, 1997, pp. 408–409). For the same reason, democratic backsliding is more frequently associated with agency-related explanations (Waldner and Lust, 2018), in particular the ruling elite's behaviour when it is in the comfortable situation of having an absolute or constitutional majority in parliament. Structural factors, such as the state of democracy and the economy, can act as enabling conditions. Instead, agency-related elements account for the corresponding decline in democratic quality within the existing regime. Democratic backsliding implies that deliberate policies have been made that aim to strengthen the power of the ruling party, for instance, by placing its candidates in oversight institutions, such as constitutional courts, the (public) media and the civil service, one-sidedly changing the electoral law or regulations concerning civil society organizations. This practice is usually associated with populist, anti-establishment narratives that emphasize the previous elites' failures and corruption and the claim of the ruling party to be the true representatives of the will of the people (Bieber *et al.,* 2018).

Tomini and Wagemann (2017, p. 687) define democratic regression generally as a 'transition *within* democracy through a loss of democratic quality'. Waldner and Lust (2018 p. 95) point out that regression is an incremental process, which makes elections less competitive and gradually loosens the constraints of accountability. However, it is not clear when the process of backsliding ends and the democratic breakdown, that is, an outright system change towards authoritarianism, begins.

The authoritarian system is characterized by limited pluralism (Linz, 2000), that is, deliberate policies restraining political pluralism (such as political opposition and, political parties), societal pluralism (such as non-governmental organizations [NGOs] and the separation of economy from politics), and media pluralism (including freedom of expression and information, and diversity of media outlets). A systemic change towards authoritarianism would therefore entail explicit attempts by the ruling party to suppress parliamentary and extra-parliamentary opposition and deprive it of the possibility of controlling the ruling party and offering an alternative to it. While Tomini and Wagemann (2017) attempt to explain democratic regression or breakdown through a strong and disloyal opposition, this article examines how and to what extent *weak* opposition, defined as the lack of credible programme, feeble organization and lack of governmental (or coalition) capacity, observed in Hungary and Poland, contributes to the deterioration of democratic quality.

Drawing on comparative evidence from local elections in Hungary and parliamentary elections in Poland in 2019, where the opposition parties obtained their first, modest electoral gains, this article examines two hypotheses. First, if the weakness of the opposition in a country is self-inflicted, this contributes to a deterioration of its democratic quality. However, if the opposition is weakened and its functions are limited by deliberate policy changes introduced by the incumbents, a democratic breakdown is likely to happen. The focus is on parliamentary opposition in Poland and Hungary, illuminating the frequently overlooked dimension of the behaviour of opposition parties, as an indicator for a declining quality of democracy.

The first section reflects on the state of democracy in Poland and Hungary before the documented backsliding. The second section discusses the relevant policy changes conducted by respective ruling parties ('political engineering', to use Sartori's term). The third section addresses election results in 2019 in Hungary and Poland to review realignments and strategies of the respective opposition parties. This brings the discussion to other pertinent developments, such as the renewal of the Left in Poland, the split of the liberal-left forces in Hungary and conflict with the European Commission over the rule of law in both countries.

I. Post-communist Democracy in Poland and Hungary

Both countries are set up as parliamentary democracies, yet the Polish president is elected directly and has powers of veto, whereas the Hungarian president has symbolic representative functions. Parliamentarism in Hungary is accompanied by a need for supermajorities in a large range of policy areas (that is, approval by two-thirds of members of parliament). This arrangement should have strengthened the role of the opposition, but in the context of rising polarization, it has made the introduction of necessary reforms more difficult. One additional feature in Hungary and Poland has been their post-communist political culture, characterized by low levels of political engagement, low membership in parties and other political institutions, and low public trust in state institutions, parties and politicians (Gwiazda, 2015; Körösényi *et al.,* 2017).

The emergence of Viktor Orbán in Hungary was closely connected with his achievement in reshaping his own party and, consequently, the whole political landscape, by unifying all right-wing factions (Körösényi and Patkós, 2017; Mudde, 2016). As a strong, charismatic leader, Orbán has dominated the political right without challenge since 1998. Instead, in Poland since 2001 two political parties, the Civic Platform and Law and Justice (PiS), both stemming from the Solidarity movement, have gradually dominated the competition. The party system in Hungary was regarded as the most concentrated and consolidated in the region, whereas in Poland it was more loosely institutionalized (Enyedi and Casal Bértoa, 2018). Whereas any necessary reforms in Hungary were blocked by the requirement for a two-thirds majority, in Poland the profound reforms needed had been neglected by the previous Civic Platform and Polish People's Party government, due to its 'warm water in the tap' approach.[1]

In Hungary the 2006 political crisis[2] led to a dramatic loss of confidence in the liberal government, which was magnified by the 2008 financial crisis. Hungary was the first country to ask for help from the International Monetary Fund and to sign a bailout package. The austerity measures that followed fuelled public discontent and further undermined support for the government. The combination of these political and economic crises led to strong anti-elite sentiments. To illustrate, in a poll conducted after seven years in office of the socialist–liberal coalition (2009), three in four respondents (77 per cent) were dissatisfied with the way that democracy was working (Batory, 2016, pp. 291–292; Krekó and Mayer, 2015). 'In the eyes of many Hungarians, what unfolded in the twenty years since state socialism was liberal democracy – and it has failed' (Müller, 2011, p. 9). By contrast, Poland remained largely unaffected by the financial crisis in 2007–10 and experienced more than 3 per cent growth in GDP for several years. Nonetheless, an opinion poll in 2015 (Badora, 2015) showed that 31 per cent of Poles assessed their political system as 'bad and demanding fundamental changes' and 41 per cent said it was 'not good and require[d] many changes'. In sum, more than seven in ten respondents recognized the need for far-reaching reforms in the Polish political system. Thus, the reasons for the electoral victory of PiS were clear, but unavoidable 'pathologies of economic governance' (Karolewski and Benedikter, 2016a) in the post-communist period. Especially young people and senior citizens were in precarious positions (Matthes, 2016, p. 328), and over 2 million people had emigrated, seeing no career prospects in Poland. Perceptions of the ruling elite as corrupt, self-serving and detached were crucial in determining the 2015 electoral results in Poland.

The PiS and the Hungarian Civic Alliance (Fidesz) both rose to power aiming at profound reforms of their respective country's political system. For both parties, a new political social and economic order had to emerge from the grassroots, consistent with the nation's values and not to be imposed externally by appeal to supposedly universal principles and procedures. According to the PiS, for example, the procedures underlying the separation of powers in Poland between parliament, government and the judiciary were designed to serve the interests of the post-communist political and business elite, which, in turn, weakened the state (Kaczyński, 2011). This claimed inefficiency was hence not

---

[1]Bill and Stanley (2020, p. 4) describe this approach as technocratic managerialism.
[2]The crisis was due to the leaked speech of the re-elected socialist prime minister shortly after the 2006 elections, where he stated that his government lied to the people about the state of the economy.

just a structural problem that had been inherited from communism, but was also a result of the lack of political will to reform it (see Dąbrowska, 2019). The PiS government considered the problems to be so deep-rooted and serious (and completely misunderstood by the EU) that they required it to assume increased capacity to act, similar to a government of national unity (Benedikter and Karolewski, 2016, p. 3). Only an empowered government could break the vested interests and rectify the deficiencies of the current system. However, PiS did not forge an overarching alliance or attempt to reach consensus in public debate. In fact, the prime minister, Morawiecki, stated in an interview that it was impossible to break vested interests in a nice and subtle way.[3] Hence, from a PiS perspective, 'good change' justifies the use of unilateral measures and even the (temporary) deterioration of democratic quality.

Fidesz, in its turn, came to power with the promise to accomplish the 'insufficient transition' (Krekó and Mayer, 2015, p. 194). Fidesz equated the political right in Hungary with the defence of the nation-state and the left with liberalism and conspiring against the Hungarian nation. Orbán laid out his fundamental critique of liberalism in a speech in 2014: 'We had to state that a democracy does not necessarily have to be liberal. Just because a state is not liberal, it can still be a democracy. And in fact, we also had to and did state that societies that are built on the state organisation principle of liberal democracy will probably be incapable of maintaining their global competitiveness in the upcoming decades and will instead probably be scaled down unless they are capable of changing themselves significantly. [...] What this means is that we must break with liberal principles and methods of social organisation, and in general with the liberal understanding of society' (cited in Hegedüs, 2019, p. 11). With the achievement of a constitutional majority in parliament, the Fidesz-led government felt empowered to introduce deep-reaching policy changes.

II. Contested Policy Changes since 2010 in Hungary and 2015 in Poland

Despite some ideological affinities between PiS and Fidesz, there are crucial differences between the scope and quality of legislative changes in Poland and Hungary (Karolewski and Benedikter, 2016b). Together with the Christian Democratic party (KDNP), Fidesz held a majority of votes in parliament and could unilaterally introduce a new Constitution. According to many scholars and international organizations, the Fourth Amendment to the Fundamental Law of Hungary in 2013 undermines the independence of the judiciary, bringing universities under greater governmental control and classifying homelessness as a crime. PiS, on the other hand, achieved an absolute, but not constitutional majority in 2015, and thus it tended to bind and punctually breach the law to implement its political agenda. PiS contributed decisively to the weakening of constitutional tribunal through the appointment of additional, 'quasi-judges' (Bill and Stanley, 2020). Further, it initiated contested judiciary reforms while, among other things, lowering the retirement age for

---

[3]Polska Times (2017) 'Mateusz Morawiecki: Nie da się w białych rękawiczkach naruszyć zacementowanych interesów'. Available online at: https://plus.polskatimes.pl/mateusz-morawiecki-nie-da-sie-w-bialych-rekawiczkach-naruszyc-zacementowanych-interesow-wywiad/ar/11657068. Last accessed 28 July 2020.

judges,[4] amending the process of justices' selection,[5] and introducing a disciplinary chamber in the supreme court to make judges more accountable.

The Fidesz-led government changed Hungary's electoral law to benefit the largest party (Fidesz) and altered the boundaries of electoral districts.[6] The electoral system in Poland was reformed almost before every election over the years 1991–2005 (Benoit and Hayden, 2004) and is characterized by open lists and high proportionality (Casal Bértoa, 2017). While in both countries the public media remain clearly pro-government, in Poland, privately owned media, primarily funded by foreign companies, remain very critical, frequently acting as an opposition to government. Instead, in Hungary the government influences privately owned media using a new advertising tax (Karolewski and Benedikter, 2016b). A controversial law concerning the funding of NGOs from abroad was enacted in Hungary but not in Poland. In the run-up to electoral contests in 2019, the institutional policy changes in Hungary clearly benefited the ruling party Fidesz, especially when we consider that regulations on party funding remained lax,[7] allowing new 'business-firm parties' (Mazzoleni and Voerman, 2016) to emerge and therefore, contributing to the fragmentation of the opposition. In Poland the opposition parties still had 'their' media; the electoral law was not substantially changed and party funding regulations made all political parties dependent on the state.

In terms of their political methods or style of operation, both PiS and Fidesz are described as populist, illiberal, or even authoritarian. Their respective charismatic leaders dominate[8] the respective political party using radical language against corruption and the ineffectiveness of previous political elites and pointing to pathologies of the post-communist state. Furthermore, they employ exclusive and very rapid legislation processes, even on fundamental reforms. They also resort to frequent (verbal) animosity towards critical civil society organizations and political opponents, and express their constant and open criticism of liberal, 'cosmopolitan' and 'leftist' values as a threat to national tradition. Yet the political systems of Poland and Hungary differ from authoritarian regimes as elections are still free[9] and constitute the main source of the legitimization of the respective governments. The opposition can still fulfil its main function of presenting an alternative to the ruling party. In other words, political pluralism in both countries has not yet been constrained to the extent that the opposition

[4]Under pressure by the EU the government withdrew from that policy change.

[5]It was well known that there were issues with the judiciary and there was consensus on the necessity for judicial reforms.

[6]The Hungarian electoral reform increased not only the proportion of seats won in single member districts but also the threshold for electoral coalitions (to 10 per cent) and eliminated turn-out requirements and a two-round system (Várnagy and Ilonszki, 2018).

[7]All parties winning more than 1 per cent of votes in Hungary and 3 per cent in Poland have access to state funding. To register a political party needs 15 members in Hungary and 1,000 in Poland (Casal Bértoa and van Biezen, 2017, pp. 13–18).

[8]It is noteworthy that, whereas Prime Minister Orbán is the head of government in Hungary, the PiS leader Jarosław Kaczyński remains just a Sejm deputy and thus cannot be held responsible for government decisions. Hence, there are 'two poles of authority' in Poland (the PiS leader as the real decision-maker, and the prime minister who executes these decisions).

[9]Many authors argue that the elections in Hungary and in Poland are no longer fair, because of the biased public media (Krekó and Enyedi, 2018, p. 40, Markowski, 2020).

© 2020 University Association for Contemporary European Studies and John Wiley & Sons Ltd

parties cannot seriously challenge the incumbents, however their opportunity structure appears broader in Poland than in Hungary.[10]

III. The Opposition: Cooperation but Lack of Alternative Programme

There are high levels of political confrontation in both Poland and Hungary, in which the range of 'non-controversial issues', to use Fraenkel's (1991) phrase, has become very narrow. Features of 'populist polarization' (Enyedi, 2016) can be traced in both countries: hostile competition based on the use of disqualifying attacks on opponents, rejection of the constitutional status quo, quest to concentrate power, politicization of public administration, extra-parliamentary opposition and populist discourse and policies (see Casal Bértoa, 2017). This confrontation takes place between the government (including its parliamentary majority) and opposition parties.

By the 1990s the 'deliberate polarisation of the political scene' was a successful strategy employed by both governing and opposition parties in Poland (Wesołowski, 1997, p. 233). Today, the dominant line of conflict is drawn between the liberal and solidarity-driven forces in Poland and between the supporters of the liberal and illiberal state in Hungary. PiS and Fidesz, respectively, continually define the content of this main conflict and thus are able to stay in power (see Schattschneider, 1960). There is also a process of 'populism by contagion' (see Pappas, 2014), whereby the opponents resort to similar populist strategies, such as politics of outbidding, and become subordinate to the populist dichotomy underlying the main conflict.

European Parliament (EP) Elections (May 2019)

The EP elections in May 2019 resulted in decisive victories for the ruling parties in Poland and Hungary – PiS won 45.4 per cent and Fidesz 52.56 per cent of the votes, respectively. Both countries appeared to be split into two blocs between government and opposition supporters. Fidesz based its campaign on making numerous accusations that European Commission President Juncker was jointly responsible for mass immigration with George Soros (Róka, 2019). One of its main slogans was 'Don't let Soros have the last laugh'. Given that almost 80 per cent of the Hungarian media are under governmental control (Bertelsmann Stiftung's Transformation Index [BTI], 2020), this narrative made a huge impact on a vast majority of voters, especially those in the rural areas.

Although Fidesz again appeared as the most dominant political force in Hungary, the intra-opposition distribution of votes in Hungary changed. The left-liberal Democratic Coalition (DK) led by former Prime Minister Ferenc Gyurcsány became the strongest opposition party, capturing 16.05 per cent of the votes. A new liberal party, Momentum, emerged as the second strongest opposition party, garnering almost 10 per cent of votes. In turn, the Hungarian Socialist Party (MSZP) on the left and Jobbik on the far right fell behind and won 6.6 and 6.3 per cent of the votes, respectively (see Bíró-Nagy, 2020). The

[10]Additionally, many scholars stress the proliferation of obstacles faced by opposition parties and candidates in Hungary, pointing to the exclusion of paid political adverts from public television channels, the overlap between state and ruling party resources and the lack of distinction between government communication and governing parties' campaigns (Filippov, 2020; Kazai and Mécs, 2019).

Hungarian opposition appeared to be vaguely pro-European (but without a concrete programmatic profile) and, above all, fragmented.

Conversely, opposition parties in Poland – the centre-right Civic Platform, the agrarian Polish People's Party, the liberal Modern (Nowoczesna) and the successor to the communist party, the Democratic Left Alliance, attempted to cooperate by creating the 'European Coalition'. However, because of its eclectic ideological character, lack of credible policy alternative and lack of new, distinctive leadership, the European Coalition could not challenge the solid position of PiS, winning 38.5 per cent of the votes. The European Coalition tried to frame the campaign as a choice between 'joining European mainstream politics' or 'reducing and marginalising Poland's international position under PiS government' (Klimkiewicz and Szymański, 2019). The PiS vision of the EU is anti-federalist, stressing the sovereignty of member states. Nonetheless, it decisively reasserted its strong commitment to Poland's membership of the EU, refuting the opposition's claim that it wanted a 'Polexit'. Additionally, PiS ran the campaign on domestic issues (thus anticipating the upcoming parliamentary elections) and proposed new social policies known as Kaczyński's high five. They included the extension of the '500+' child subsidy programme, bonus payments for retirees and exemption from income tax for workers under 26 years of age (Prawo i Sprawiedliwość, 2019). As the party had mostly delivered on its previous electoral promises, its proposed programme appeared credible. Not even a nationwide teachers' strike and a controversial documentary targeting the Church, released a couple of weeks before the elections, could challenge the party's standing. The documentary triggered a debate about the institutional responsibility of the Polish Catholic Church in covering up child abuse crimes. Given the Church's proximity to the PiS, the party promptly introduced changes to the penal code aiming at increasing penalties and thus signalling its effectiveness (Klimkiewicz and Szymański, 2019).

Hungarian Municipal Elections (October 2019)

After Fidesz's decisive consecutive victories in three national elections, three local elections and two EP elections, opposition parties finally achieved their first electoral success in the municipal elections on 13 October 2019. The candidate of left-wing party Dialogue, Gergely Karácsony won the Budapest mayoralty,[11] whereas the united opposition parties won majorities in almost half the urban centres in Hungary.[12] What is more, this electoral success was achieved in the context of economic growth, rising wages and low unemployment, which usually favours the ruling party (Bíró-Nagy, 2020).

Electoral coordination and cooperation between an otherwise fragmented opposition was conducted consistently with little public bickering in the municipal elections. However, potential defections from the inter-opposition cooperation structures still constitute a major challenge. For instance, in the city of Győr, the local Jobbik party withdrew its

---

[11] Karácsony was described as follows: 'The opposition politician of the decade is undoubtedly Gergely Karácsony, a left-green leader, who in both thinking (technical coalition with Jobbik), determination (exit from the LMP and formation of Dialogue), tactics (cooperation with the MSZP) and in the introduction of innovative democratic procedures (pre-elections) has preceded his rivals'. Available online at: https://hungarianfreepress.com/2020/05/20/waiting-for-the-opposition/ . Last accessed 11 August 2020.

[12] In ten of 23 cities the mayor who won was supported by opposition political forces. The opposition also has 18 representatives in the metropolitan assembly, Fidesz–KDNP has 13 and there are two independent members (Kazai and Mécs, 2019).

support for the joint opposition candidate (Bíró-Nagy, 2020). Even so, all opposition parties are still weakly organized and lack a foothold in rural areas (BTI, 2020), which erodes their ability to challenge Fidesz incumbents in the longer term.

It is precisely these older, lower educated and rural voting groups on which Fidesz relies. The core supporters of the main opposition party, the DK, consist of elderly and left-leaning voters with strong anti-Fidesz sentiments. Momentum draws on young voters and intellectuals. It is trying to appeal to green voters (who were formerly attracted to the 'Politics Can be Different' party – [the LMP]) and moderate right-wing voters, as well as first-time voters (Bíró-Nagy, 2020). During its campaign the DK resorted to divisive rhetoric and 'tribalization', contributing thus to rising polarization. It built its base around the former prime minister Gyurcsány (who was seen as responsible for the economic and political crisis of 2006–10). Its supporters are loyal and it is now the most cohesive bloc of the opposition. The DK's goal has been to establish itself as the main opposition party (challenging the socialist MSZP) rather than winning elections. Unfortunately, this strategy has benefitted Fidesz the most. In contrast, Momentum avoids the duopoly and concentrates on issues such as corruption, transparency and appearing as a centrist anti-Fidesz force (Bíró-Nagy, 2020). Both the DK and Momentum are difficult to pin down ideologically. Momentum joined the centrist liberal Renew group, whereas the DK aligned itself with the Socialists and Democrats group in the EP. Interestingly, the DK voted against an EP resolution on the refugee crisis; a signal that the party tried to appeal to popular, anti-immigration sentiments in Hungarian public opinion.

Despite its low support in the municipal elections, MSZP has the biggest group of experienced staff in comparison with newer opposition parties. However, MSZP has suffered from leadership problems, changing six party presidents in ten years, and numerous scandals attached to prominent party figures have affect its public image. The other left-leaning party Dialogue for Hungary has so far collaborated with MSZP to reach the electoral threshold. It was Dialogue's candidate that won that mayoralty in Budapest and the party recorded some minor successes, including in the elite Castle district, one of Fidesz's bastions in Budapest (Bíró-Nagy, 2020).

Finally, the biggest defeat in the municipal elections belongs to Jobbik. Its 'mainstreaming strategy' (Bíró-Nagy and Boros, 2016; see also Böcskei and Molnar, 2019) that had started in 2013 was accompanied by the radicalization of Fidesz. As a result, Jobbik split and the new far-right formation 'Our Homeland' emerged. Anti-Semitic and anti-Roma messages have gradually disappeared from Jobbik's official statements (see Héjj, 2017) and its tone on EU integration has become softer. The party has not found yet a way to position itself strategically in the centre so it can meaningfully distinguish itself from other opposition parties. The success of Momentum in attracting young voters has become a challenge, alongside Jobbik's lasting problem of finding a leader that has comparable appeal to its former leader Gábor Vona (Metz and Oross, 2020). Due to minor infringements of party funding regulations (see Bos, 2018), Jobbik has been penalized by the Fidesz-controlled public authorities that oversee campaign funding. Also, Jobbik finds it even more difficult to access the media, as both Fidesz-controlled public and private media, and the remaining independent opposition media dismiss it due to its radical right legacy. However, the party is still the only opposition force with a sizeable rural base, which is why other opposition formations with less of a rural footprint cannot ignore it.

Several weeks after the municipal elections, the Fidesz–KDNP government tried to dampen down the electoral successes of the opposition forces, submitting a proposal on the use of local business tax revenues. This proposal would reduce control by the new Budapest Mayor Karácsony over the city's budget. The legislation – approved by National Assembly in December 2019 – forced local councils to direct business taxes to finance public transport before any other projects could be paid for (Bíró-Nagy, 2020). This move threatens spending in other areas, such as social services. Karácsony's electoral promises to turn Budapest into a green city and focus resources on improving health-care provision in the capital are thus endangered by this new legislation. However, the opposition-controlled Budapest City Council voted unanimously to back hosting the 2023 IAAF World Championships (which is particularly important for prime minister Orbán) if certain conditions were met, that is, it it received approximately €150 million from the central budget for health-care investments (Bíró-Nagy, 2020).

Nonetheless, the National Assembly passed an amendment to the Parliament's rules of procedure that may make it more difficult to the opposition parties to cooperate with each other (Filippov, 2020). Independent members of parliament can no longer join parliamentary groups. In fact, during the local election campaign many opposition politicians ran as independent candidates with informal party support. The new rules will not allow parliamentary groups to split either. If at the next elections parties decided to run on a joint list, they would be forced to stay in the same parliamentary group for the whole term.[13] At the same time, new finance regulations provide more funding to the opposition parties if they run separately (see Várnagy and Ilonszki, 2017).

Although all opposition parties are sensitive to socioeconomic issues, Fidesz still defines the terms of Hungarian political discourse and public debate and still determines the main battleground underlying inter-party competition. The policy changes made by the Fidesz government are clearly deteriorating democratic quality, hence, the self-acclaimed pro-democratic opposition should present a convincing vision of a democratic Hungary and promote necessary systemic reforms related to that vision. Yet many voters see the parliamentary opposition as part of the system of national cooperation (Batory, 2016), as some of its party members are still perceived to be corrupt and compromisers.[14] For instance, it was uncertain with whom several prominent MSZP members intended to cooperate.[15] For the opposition parties to be able realistically to challenge the ruling party in Hungary it requires moral soundness and taking an uncompromising stance against Fidesz. Moreover, it requires political unity, as conditioned by the Hungarian majoritarian electoral system. The unity, in turn, necessitates a nationwide organization of opposition parties, which is badly lacking today. It also requires opposition parties to present a convincing programme for future pro-democracy reforms.

---

[13]In general, electoral rules in parliamentary and local elections in Hungary prompt the coordination and cooperation of opposition forces. For instance, mayors are elected in a one-round, first-past-the-post procedure (see Kazai and Mécs, 2019).
[14]See https://hungarianfreepress.com/2020/05/20/waiting-for-the-opposition/. Last accessed 27 July 2020.
[15]The same applies to LMP, which was categorically against cooperation with left-wing opposition parties (see Kovarek and Littvay, 2019), and whose members apparently had some connections with the ruling party (see https://wyborcza.pl/7,75399,23488303,krajobraz-wegier-po-trzeciej-z-rzedu-wygranej-viktora-orbana.html) Last accessed 27 July 2020.

Polish Parliamentary Elections (October 2019)

In terms of cooperation, Poland appears to be quite similar to Hungary. Three opposition blocs could be identified in the run-up to the parliamentary elections: the Civic Coalition (KO), the 'Left' and the Polish Coalition.[16] These blocs were able to coordinate their political campaigns for the Senate (where first-past-the-post rules apply in single-member districts) and agreed not to run candidates against each other. The electoral campaign was characterized by little substantive debate on real policy alternatives, and more by the politics of outbidding. The main opposition bloc, the KO, notably came up with 'six-pack promises' to outbid the PiS's extensive social policies but without proposing any convincing alternative programme (Koalicja Obywatelska, 2019). It obtained 27.4 per cent of the vote. The Polish Coalition, in turn, received 8.55 per cent, which was perceived as an unexpected success, as its main party (the Polish People's Party) was inexorably losing its traditional rural followers, given the advancing modernization of Poland. After one term as an extra-parliamentary opposition, the 'Left' managed to return to parliament with 12.56 per cent, through a three-party coalition consisting of the old successors to communist party – the Democratic Left Alliance, the progressive left – Razem (Together) and the newly established (prior to the EP elections) – Wiosna (Spring). Another newcomer, Konfederacja, comprising several radical right parties and organizations, entered parliament in 2019 (6.8 per cent). It challenges PiS leadership on the right-wing of the party system. Konfederacja attracts the most radical voters from the broad conservative nationalist camp and criticizes PiS for being too soft in the sociocultural and nationalist domain and too leftist in its economic policies (Markowski, 2020, p. 1521).

The 2019 parliamentary elections were characterized by the highest electoral turnout of 62 per cent. Moreover, the share of wasted votes was the lowest ever in the history of elections in Poland, at below 1 per cent – down from almost 17 per cent four years earlier (Markowski, 2016, 2020). The idea of forming coalitions thus contributed to a fairer translation of votes into seats. With 43.66 per cent of the votes cast, PiS achieved its highest ever electoral result.[17] Nonetheless, although the party gained six points in electoral support from previous elections, it lost its majority in the Senate and achieved a narrow (but still absolute) majority in the Sejm. The emergence of a new radical-right party in parliament was also interpreted as a loss for PiS, because its long-term strategy was to absorb such tendencies, eliminate right-wing opponents and ensure it appealed to the broadest political spectrum (Bill and Stanley, 2020, p. 12). Opposition parties, together with some independents, now have a slim 51/49 majority in the Senate. The second chamber is less powerful than the Sejm, yet it can temporarily veto and de facto slowdown legislative processes, permitting to some extent a more effective debate.[18]

The electorate was polarized in terms of socio-demographic profiles, in particular those of the two main contenders – PiS and the KO – and largely resembles the Hungarian

---

[16]In fact, all the entities that entered parliament were de facto coalitions. However, they all registered as political parties to ensure they would meet the 5 per cent threshold. KO included the Civic Platform and Nowoczesna and several minor entities; the Polish Coalition included the Polish People's Party and Kukiz'15, and the 'Left' included Wiosna, Razem and the Democratic Left Alliance.

[17]This constitutes 26.6 per cent of all eligible voters and 235 of 460 parliamentary seats (see Markowski, 2020).

[18]The Senate has exercised its veto power only on 20 of all accepted bills from 1997 to 2015 and half of these were dismissed by the Sejm (Dudzińska and Betkiewicz, 2018).

political landscape. In the 2019 election 56 per cent of the oldest cohort voted for PiS, compared with 25 per cent for the KO. Furthermore, 64 per cent of individuals with primary education voted for PiS in 2019, and 12 per cent for the KO (Markowski, 2020, p. 1520). As a result, PiS currently represents almost two-thirds of the poorly educated and the elderly electorate, as well as those living in predominantly rural areas. The electorate of Konfederacja differs in two respects: it is disproportionately young (one in five of the 18–29 age cohort votes for them), and it is more than twice as popular with men than women.

Similar to Hungary, the cooperation of opposition parties resulted in their winning the Senate in Poland, but the liberal-centrist opposition has failed to develop a substantial and attractive programmatic alternative to the ruling party's social policies on the socioeconomic front. The opposition lacks a convincing leader to rally supporters. Civic Platform leader Grzegorz Schetyna lacked charisma and is Poland's least trusted politician. He was also the author of the hitherto ineffective strategy of 'total opposition', exerting pressure through street protests and international influence, especially through EU institutions.[19] The main political conflict has thus not been about redistribution policies, but about cultural issues, identities and emotions.

Both Fidesz and the PiS presented themselves as defenders of national identity, Christian values and culture and the traditional family. They argued these values stabilized social order, were in accordance with their country's tradition and history and promoted the common good (Bill and Stanley, 2020; Krekó and Enyedi, 2018). Both parties strongly opposed the EU's migrant relocation scheme, presenting Muslim migrants from the Middle East and North Africa as a threat to national security (Bill and Stanley, 2020; Bos and Pállinger, 2018). In addition, the vast majority of Poles and Hungarians opposed the EU's mandatory relocation scheme on the basis of cultural and security problems observed in many western European countries (Poushter, 2016). Both parties have also opposed what they call 'LGBT ideology', linking it to foreign ideas of western cultural liberalism or displaying it as the threat to the future of the nation and the institution of the family (Grzebalska and Pető, 2018). These issues touch upon basic moral and cultural values and thus polarize their respective societies. A defence of moral codes helps mobilize the core supporters of both parties in smaller towns and rural areas, where such traditional values are still cherished. And, while Poles appear to be increasingly tolerant of LGBT lifestyles, their acceptance declines decisively when it comes to issues of family life; for example, the role of parents in the primary sex education of children, same-sex marriage and adoption rights for same-sex couples (Bożewicz, 2019).

IV. Ongoing Disputes with the European Commission as a Common Theme

If the opposition does not act as a potential safeguard, should the EU play this role? Poland and Hungary have both engaged in an ongoing dispute with the European Commission over the rule of law and the absence of consensus on common values at the European level. In the past, this common ground was Christianity, to which both Poland and

---

[19]Representatives of opposition parties frequently voted against the Polish government, which was portrayed in the Polish public media as only pursuing their party's interest and not caring about the common good and Polish interests.

Hungary frequently refer. Recently, liberalism as a common reference has failed in both countries.

In 2016 the Commission initiated procedures against Poland under Article 7 of the treaties, related to its alleged systemic threat to democracy and the rule of law (Karolewski and Benedikter, 2016a). The Commission referred legislation on retirement provisions and the functioning of the ordinary courts to the European Court of Justice (ECJ), while Polish judges submitted a number of 'prejudicial questions' on these disputed reforms (see Bakke and Sitter, 2020). In 2019 the Commission filed another case to the ECJ against the new disciplinary chamber of the Polish supreme court, which, according to the Commission's argument, would fail to protect Polish judges from political control. The supreme court disciplinary chamber is made up of judges chosen by the national judicial council, in which some of its members are now selected by parliament (by a qualified three-fifths supermajority).[20] In fact, the ECJ issued negative opinions on the retirement question in November 2019, and some months later, it temporarily suspended the operation of the supreme court's new disciplinary chamber. Non-compliance with ECJ decision would trigger penalties and involve an open breach of EU rules. Concomitantly, the PiS defends the right of each country to reform its own judiciary system, and argues that the policy changes enacted are similar to mechanisms established in other western countries. Thus, according to the PiS, the Commission is not neutral but instead sides with the Polish opposition and the EU establishment. It dismisses an attempt by the Polish government to bring the judiciary closer to the public and make it more accountable.[21] The PiS argues that the rule of law is historically and socially embedded and cannot be evaluated according to an ideal, normative checklist developed elsewhere.

It was not until September 2018 that the EP voted to trigger Article 7 procedures against Hungary on the explicit risks that Fidesz was breaching EU values, primarily over media pluralism and the freedom of expression, as well as societal pluralism.[22] This action was taken with the consent of the European Peoples' Party group (EPP), to which Fidesz belongs. The Hungarian media portrayed the decision as revenge for Orbán's migration policy (Bíró-Nagy, 2020), while Fidesz criticized the EPP for abandoning the ideals of Christian Europe. The future EPP membership of Fidesz will be decided in 2020. In addition, both PiS and Fidesz faced difficulties in 2019 in securing the approval of their candidates to the EU Commission, showcasing their weak bargaining position and damaged image in Europe. Finally, both countries' governments attempted to hinder the Commission's intention to tie the disbursement of EU funds to 'rule of law compliance'. They sought to link these regulations to the transparent management of EU funds rather than systemic concerns which, as both governments argue, are difficult to assess objectively.

Overall, political developments in 2019, in terms of parliamentary elections in Poland, municipal elections in Hungary and the EP elections in both countries, have demonstrated there are persistent and largely self-inflicted weaknesses in their opposition parties. As Lust-Oskar (2005, pp. 34–35) argues, 'incumbents cannot dictate their opponents' actions, but they can influence them'. Especially in Hungary, new legislation introduced by Fidesz determines the rules of engagement that opposition parties need to follow in

---

[20]It must be noted that in most western European countries judges are chosen by parliament.
[21]Given that Polish judges tended to block any reform attempt by arguing that it would infringe on their 'judicial independence', many of them came to be seen as a juristocracy aligned with corporate interests.
[22]On why the EU reacted so late to Hungary's far-reaching policy changes, see Scheppele and Pech, 2018.

order to compete for power. The oppositions' electoral results in 2019 show that a strategy of coordination and of displacing the political conflict to EU institutions is not enough to win elections, especially in the context of economic growth and extensive social redistribution in both countries. The opposition parties still need to advance credible programmes of reform as well as develop their organizational structures. Their responsibility for previous the political mistakes must match their responsiveness towards voters' expectations.

References

Badora, B. (2015) 'Postulaty Dotyczące Zmian Systemowych w Polsce'. Centrum Badania Opinii Społecznej, July 2015, http://cbos.pl/SPISKOM.POL/2015/K_107_15.PDF Last accessed 22 June 2020.

Bakke, E. and Sitter, N. (2020) 'The EU's *Enfants Terribles*: Democratic Backsliding in Central Europe since 2010'. *Perspectives on Politics*. https://doi.org/10.1017/S1537592720001292

Batory, A. (2016) 'Populists in Government? Hungary's "System of national Cooperation"'. *Democratization*, Vol. 23, No. 2, pp. 283–303.

Benedikter, R. and Karolewski, I. P. (2016) 'Poland's Conservative Turn of 2015: Where Are Its Real Origins?' 4 May Policy paper, No 35. Centre international de formation européenne.

Benoit, K. and Hayden, J. (2004) 'Institutional Change and Persistence: The Evolution of Poland's Electoral System'. *Journal of Politics*, Vol. 66, No. 2, pp. 396–427.

Bertelsmann Stiftung's Transformation Index (BTI) (2020) 'Country Report. Hungary'. Available online at: https://www.bti-project.org/content/en/downloads/reports/country_report_2020_HUN.pdf Last accessed 28 July 2020.

Bieber, F., Solska, M. and Taleski, D. (eds) (2018) *Illiberal and Authoritarian Tendencies in Central, Southeastern and Eastern Europe* (Bern: Peter Lang).

Bill, S. and Stanley, B. (2020) 'Whose Poland Is It To Be? PiS and the Struggle between Monism and Pluralism'. *East European Politics*. https://doi.org/10.1080/21599165.2020.1787161

Bíró-Nagy, A. (ed.) (2020) *Hungarian Politics in 2019* (Budapest: Friedrich-Ebert-Stiftung and Policy Solutions).

Bíró-Nagy, A. and Boros, T. (2016) 'Jobbik Going Mainstream. Strategy Shift of the Far-right in Hungary'. In Jamin, J. (ed.) *L'extreme droite en Europe* (Bruylant: Brussels).

Böcskei, B. and Molnar, C. (2019) 'The Radical Right in Government? – Jobbik's Pledges in Hungary's Legislation (2010–2014)'. *East European Politics*, Vol. 35, No. 1. https://doi.org/10.1080/21599165.2019.1582414

Bos, E. (2018) 'Das System Orbán. Antipluralismus in Aktion'. *Osteuropa*, Vol. 68, No. 3–5, pp. 19–32.

Bos, E. and Pállinger, Z. T. (2018) 'Die Parlamentswahl in Ungarn 201'. *MIDEM-Bericht* 2 (Dresden).

Bożewicz, M. (2019) 'Komunikat z Badań nr 90/2019: Stosunek Polaków do związków homoseksualnych'. *Centrum Badania Opinii Społecznej*, July 2019. Available online at: https://www.cbos.pl/SPISKOM.POL/2019/K_090_19.PDF. Last accessed 28 July 2020.

Casal Bértoa, F. (2017) 'Polarizing Politics and the Future of Democracy: Georgia in Comparative Perspective'. Available online at: http://democracy-reporting.org/wp-content/uploads/2017/07/discussion_paper_polarising_politics_in_Georgia_en.pdf. Last accessed 22 July 2020.

Casal Bértoa, F. and van Biezen, I. (2017) 'Introduction. Party Regulation and Party Politics in Post-communist Europe'. In Casal Bértoa, F. and van Biezen, I. (eds) *The Regulation of Post-Communist Party Politics* (London: Routledge), pp. 1–30.

Dąbrowska, E. (2019) 'New Conservativism in Poland. The Discourse Coalition around Law and Justice'. In Bluhm, K. and Varga, M. (eds) *New Conservatives in Russia and in East Central Europe* (London: Routledge), pp. 92–112.

Dudzińska, A. and Betkiewicz, W. (2018) 'Poland: Opposition in the Making'. In de Giorgi, E. and Ilonszki, G. (eds) *Opposition Parties in European Democracies* (London: Routledge), pp. 171–90.

Enyedi, Z. (2016) 'Populist Polarization and Party System Institutionalization: The Role of Party Politics in De-democratization'. *Problems of Post-Communism*, Vol. 63, No. 4, pp. 210–20.

Enyedi, Z. and Casal Bértoa, F. (2018) 'Institutionalization and De-institutionalization in Post-communist Party Systems'. *East European Politics and Societies and Cultures*, Vol. 32, No. 3, pp. 422–50.

Filippov, G. (2020) 'Hungary. Executive Summary'. Nations in Transit. Available online at: https://freedomhouse.org/country/hungary/nations-transit/2020 Last accessed 28 July 2020.

Fraenkel, E. (1991) *Deutschland und die westlichen Demokratien* (Frankfurt am Main: Suhrkamp).

Greskovits, B. (2015) 'The Hollowing and Backsliding of Democracy in East Central Europe'. *Global Policy*, Vol. 6, No. S1, pp. 28–37.

Grzebalska, W. and Pető, A. (2018) 'The Gendered Modus Operandi of the Illiberal Transformation in Hungary and Poland'. *Women's Studies International Forum*, Vol. 68, pp. 164–72.

Gwiazda, A. (2015) *Democracy in Poland. Representation, Participation, Competition and Accountability since 1989* (London: Routledge).

Hegedüs, D. (2019) 'Rethinking the Incumbency Effect. Radicalization of Governing Populist Parties in East-Central-Europe. A Case Study of Hungary'. *European Politics and Society*, Vol. 20, No. 4, pp. 406–30.

Héjj, D. (2017) 'The Rebranding of Jobbik'. *New Eastern Europe*, No. 6, pp. 83–90.

Kaczyński, J. (2011) *Polska Naszych Marzeń* (Lublin: Akapit).

Karolewski, I.P. and Benedikter, R. (2016a) 'Poland's Conservative Turn and the Role of the European Union'. *European Political Science*, No. 16, pp. 515–34.

Karolewski, I.P. and Benedikter, G. (2016b) 'Poland Is Not Hungary. A Response to 'Poland's Constitutional Crisis'. *Foreign Affairs*. Available online at: https://www.foreignaffairs.com/articles/central-europe/2016-09-21/poland-not-hungary Last accessed 28 July 2020.

Kazai, V.Z. and Mécs, J. (2019) 'Local Elections in Hungary: the Results in Context'. VerfBlog. Available online at: https://verfassungsblog.de/local-elections-in-hungary-the-results-in-context/ Last accessed 28 July 2020.

Klimkiewicz, B. and Szymański, A. (2019) 'Poland: Mobilized, Divided and EU-positive'. In Bolin, N., Falasca, K., Grusell, M. and Nord, L. (eds) *Euroflections*. DEMICOM-report, No. 40, p. 39. Available online at https://www.miun.se/globalassets/ovrigt/euroflections/euroflections_v3.pdf Last accessed 11 August 2020.

Koalicja Obywatelska (2019) 'Twoja Polska: Program Koalicji Obywatelskiej'. Available online at: https://platforma.org/upload/document/86/attachments/121/KO%20Program.pdf Last accessed 28 July 2020.

Körösényi, A., Ondré, P., and Hajdú, A. (2017) 'A 'Meteoric' Career in Hungarian Politics'. In Bennister, M., Worthy, B. and Hart, P. (eds) *The Leadership Capital Index. A New Perspective on Political Leadership* (Oxford: Oxford University Press), pp. 82–100.

Körösényi, A. and Patkós, V. (2017) 'Liberal and Illiberal Populism. The Leadership of Berlusconi and Orban'. *Corvinus Journal of Sociology and Social Policy*, Vol. 8, pp. 315–37.

Kovarek, D. and Littvay, L. (2019) 'Where Did All the Environmentalism Go? 'Politics Can Be Different' (LMP) in the 2018 Hungarian Parliamentary Elections'. *Environmental Politics*, Vol. 28, No. 3, pp. 574–82.

Krastev, I. (2016) 'The Unravelling of the Post-1989 Order'. *Journal of Democracy*, Vol. 27, No. 4, pp. 88–98.

Krekó, E. and Enyedi, Z. (2018) 'Orbán's Laboratory of Illiberalism'. *Journal of Democracy*, Vol. 29, No. 3, pp. 39–50.

Krekó, P. and Mayer, G. (2015) 'Transforming Hungary – Together?' In Minkenberg, M. (ed.) *Transforming the Transformation? The East European Radical Right in the Political Process* (New York: Routledge).

Linz, J. (1997) 'Some Thoughts on the Victory and Future of Democracy'. In Hadenius, A. (ed.) *Democracy's Victory and Crisis* (Cambridge: Cambridge University Press), pp. 404–26.

Linz, J. (2000) *Totalitarian and Authoritarian Regimes* (Boulder, CO: Lynne Rienner).

Lust-Oskar, E. (2005) *Structuring Conflict in the Arab World. Incumbents, Opponents, and Institutions* (Cambridge: Cambridge University Press).

Markowski, R. (2016) 'The Polish Parliamentary Election of 2015: A Free and Fair Election that Results in Unfair Political Consequences'. *West European Politics*, Vol. 39, No. 6, pp. 1311–22.

Markowski, R. (2020) 'Plurality Support for Democratic Decay: The 2019 Polish Parliamentary Election'. *West European Politics*, Vol 43, No. 7, pp. 1513–25.

Matthes, C. (2016) 'Comparative Assessments of the State of Democracy in East-Central Europe and Its Anchoring in Society'. *Problems of Post-Communism*, Vol. 63, No. 5–6, pp. 323–34.

Mazzoleni, O. and Voerman, G. (2016) 'Memberless Parties: Beyond the Business-firm Party Model?' *Party Politics*, Vol. 23, No. 6, pp. 1–10.

Metz, R. and Oross (2020) 'Strong Personalities' Impact on Hungarian Party Politics: Viktor Orbán and Gábor Vona'. In Gherghina, S. (ed.) *Party Leaders in Eastern Europe: Personality, Behavior and Consequences* (Cham: Palgrave Macmillan), pp. 145–70.

Mudde, C. (2016) 'Viktor Orbán and the Difference between Radical Right Politics and Parties'. In Mudde, C. (ed.) *On Extremism and Democracy in Europe* (New York: Routledge), pp. 43–50.

Müller, J.-W. (2011) 'The Hungarian Tragedy'. *Dissent*, Vol. 58, No. 2, pp. 5–10.

Pappas, T.S. (2014) 'Populist Democracies: Post-authoritarian Greece and Post-communist Hungary'. *Government and Opposition*, Vol. 49, No. 1, pp. 1–23.

Poushter, J. (2016) 'European Opinions of the Refugee Crisis in Five Charts'. Pew Research Center, 16 September. Available online at: http://www.pewresearch.org/fact-tank/2016/09/16/european-opinions-of-the-refugee-crisis-in-5-charts/ Last accessed 19 July 2020.

Prawo i Sprawiedliwość (2019) 'Program Prawa i Sprawiedliwości: Polski Model Dobrobytu'. http://pis.org.pl/dokumenty Last accessed 28 July 2020.

Róka, J. (2019) 'European Parliamentary Elections of 2019 in Hungary'. In Bolin, N., Falasca, K., Grusell, M. and Nord, L. (eds) *Euroflections*. DEMICOM-report, No. 40, pp. 53. Available online at https://www.researchgate.net/publication/333967891_Euroflections_Leading_academics_on_the_European_elections_2019#pf35 Last accessed 11 August 2020.

Schattschneider, E.E. (1960) *The Semisovereign People: A Realist's View of Democracy in America* (New York: Holt, Rinehart and Winston).

Scheppele, K. L. and Pech, L. (2018) 'Why Poland and Not Hungary'. *VerfBlog*. Available online at: https://verfassungsblog.de/why-poland-and-not-hungary/ Last accessed 28 July 2020.

Tomini, L. and Wagemann, C. (2017) 'Varieties of Contemporary Democratic Breakdown and Regression: A Comparative Analysis'. *European Journal of Political Research*, Vol. 57, No. 3, pp. 687–716.

Várnagy, R. and Ilonszki, G. (2017) 'The Failure of Early Party Regulation and a New Beginning. The Hungarian Case'. In Casal Bértoa, F. and van Biezen, I. (eds) *The Regulation of Post-Communist Party Politics* (London: Routledge), pp. 106–23.

Várnagy, R. and Ilonszki, G. (2018) 'Hungary: The De(con)struction of Parliamentary Opposition'. In De Giorgi, E. and Ilonszki, G. (eds) *Opposition Parties in European Legislature. Conflict or Consensus?* (London: Routledge), pp. 151–70.

Waldner, D. and Lust, E. (2018) 'Unwelcome Change: Understanding, Evaluating, and Extending Theories of Democratic Backsliding'. *Annual Review of Political Science*, Vol. 21, pp. 93–113.

Wesołowski, W. (1997) 'Political Actors and Democracy: Poland 1990–1997'. *Polish Sociological Review*, Vol. 3, No. 119, pp. 227–48.

JCMS 2020 Volume 58. Annual Review. pp. 121–132

DOI: 10.1111/jcms.13102

Great Expectations, Structural Limitations: Ursula von der Leyen and the Commission's New Equality Agenda

GABRIELE ABELS[1] and JOYCE M. MUSHABEN[2]
[1]University of Tübingen [2]University of Missouri-St. Louis/Georgetown University, Washington, DC

Introduction

> Exactly 40 years ago, Simone Veil was elected as the first female President of the European Parliament ... I can say with great pride that **we finally have a female candidate for European Commission President.** I am that candidate thanks to all the men and women who have broken down barriers and defied convention. I am that candidate thanks to all the men and women who built a Europe of peace, a united Europe, a Europe of values. It is this belief in Europe that has guided me throughout my life and my career – as a mother, as a doctor and as a politician. It is the courage and daring of pioneers such as Simone Veil that are at the heart of my vision for Europe.

Ursula von der Leyen (2019a).

Ursula von der Leyen's election as the European Commission's first woman president in July 2019 confirms the fundamental transformation of the Union, as well as its politics and policies since the 1950s. Her first speech to the European Parliament invoked 'A Union that strives for more', promising to make gender equality a key component of her agenda (von der Leyen, 2019b). She generated great expectations by declaring that her Commission would consist of equal numbers of women and men, a plan immediately thwarted by two member states refusing to designate female nominees. Consisting of 12 women (44 per cent) and 15 men, the new Commission fall just short of parity, but her simultaneous appointment of the EU's first Commissioner for Equality, coupled with a new Gender Equality Strategy launched in March 2020 (marking International Women's Day and the 25th anniversary of the Beijing Action Platform), indicates that this Christian Democratic mother of seven is serious about advancing women's descriptive and substantive representation, by claiming a leadership position for herself, for the Commission and for the EU.

Limited to an analysis of her 'first 100 days', this study focuses on the new President's promises to 'complete, deepen and enlarge' the EU gender equality domain not only in

---

We pursue two arguments that, taken together, pose a 'glass half-full, glass half empty' conundrum. First, we contend that a leader's past performance is the best predictor we have when it comes to anticipating her future behaviour. Like her former boss, Chancellor Angela Merkel, von der Leyen entered German politics through the 'side door' in 1990 but quickly rose to national prominence. She is the only politician to have served in all four Merkel cabinets (2005–19), prior to her surprise nomination for Commission Presidency. Despite her refusal to label herself a feminist, von der Leyen generated a long list of gender policy achievements as Germany's Minister for Women and Family (2005–09), as Labour Minister (2009–13) and as its first female Defence Minister (2013–19), respectively. Her pro-active support for work–life balance policies, paternal leave, corporate board quotas and female mentoring in the *Bundeswehr* (armed forces) met with strong resistance within her own party, but these initiatives ultimately became the law of the land (Mushaben, 20122019b).

relation to substantive policies but also with regard to European institutions per se. We argue that von der Leyen has already recognized the gendered nature of leadership, linking it to more gender-inclusive policy ambitions and leadership requirements. Changes in policy performance can also affect wider perceptions of the EU's democratic legitimacy at a critical juncture. The new President will certainly face significant political-institutional obstacles. Member states inevitably place national interests above supranational politics in times of crisis, but crises also present great opportunities for exercising different kinds of leadership; Commission presidents can operate as 'policy entrepreneurs' by way of their agenda-setting power for the EU at large (Tömmel, 2013, 2019; Müller, 2017, 2020). What kind of difference could a female President make as a pro-active leader?

Von der Leyen's effectiveness at the national level provides grounds for feminist optimism, but her chances of turning her ambitious equality agenda into measurable policy outcomes are qualified by our second argument: structures matter when it comes to judging how leadership can be effectively exercised, but so do fundamental differences dividing decision makers at the national and EU levels. Each Commission sets its own goals and work-plan for advancing European integration, but von der Leyen will encounter significant challenges, owing to a fragmented European Parliament, a polarized Council, and new fault lines within the Commission itself.

These arguments fuel our efforts to incorporate a gendered leadership perspective as well. Having pursued national interests for 14 years, von der Leyen must undertake a supranational U-turn in order to champion European interests. This raises the question as to whether leadership skills accumulated at one level will automatically transfer to a multi-level governance framework. The ability to lead derives from a combination of *personal skills*, the *institutional context* and *policy-specific factors*; little EU scholarship has focused on leadership per se, much less on its gender dimensions. Prior to 2019, women accounted for 35 of 183 Commissioners, less than 20 per cent of the total across seven decades – hardly a women-friendly organization in relation to descriptive representation (Hartlapp *et al.,* forthcoming). Leading in transitional times is particularly demanding: 'great ambitions' not only raise great expectations but also greater national resistance to change. Concentrating on the transitional 100-day period, we raise the question: Would it be better for Ursula von der Leyen to aim very high, in hopes of achieving more, or should she avoid undermining her own credibility, and that of future women leaders, by overshooting the mark with promises she cannot keep?

We first consider gendered leadership, von der Leyen's successful transformation of the German gender regime, and potential disadvantages linked to her controversial nomination. Next we address the 'great expectations' she has raised, based on the bold promises of the 2020 Gender Equality Strategy, then zoom in on political-structural limitations inherent in multi-level governance. Finally, we address the imbalance between these great expectations and structural constraints, concluding with reflections on the proverbial 'glass half-full/half-empty' conundrum.

I. Leadership in EU Studies

Assessments of European governance from a leadership perspective are fairly new; even more rare are investigations of gendered leadership across all EU institutions, given women's lack of *critical mass* outside the European Parliament until 2019. Critical mass is linked to *positional* leadership, while the gendered way in which it is exercised centres on *behavioural* leadership (Müller and Tömmel, forthcoming), At issue is the link between descriptive and substantive representation: Will more women in power produce a reconfiguration of policies essential for gender equality? Establishing a correlation between the two is not a simple process in a multi-level system. In terms of symbolic representation, the first female President is certainly an important expression of the EU's ambition for stronger gender equality.

The EU involves a 'gender-specific environment moulded by "masculinist" norms and expectations' (Sykes, 2014, p. 691), forcing us to 'unpack' the role of gendered agency across all institutions, at all levels, to determine how it interacts with other gendered structures driving European integration processes. Contemporary European integration theories are often blind to the gendered nature of leadership (Abels and MacRae, forthcoming). There is a general consensus that '[C]risis leadership differs from leadership in routine times', because its 'stakes are much higher, the public is much more attentive, its mood more volatile, and institutional constraints on elite decision making are considerably looser' (Ansell *et al.*, 2014, p. 418 f.). The current, crisis-ridden EU offers a unique opportunity for analysing if, how and by whom leadership is exercised.

Existing scholarship stresses leadership crises, and/or the inability of the European states to 'lead'. The Commission President occupies a prominent place in such studies, due to the Commission's hybrid nature as a technocratic-administrative body and a political institution. Commission Presidents can exercise strategic leadership by transfer-ring 'political ambitions of a Pan-European scope into consensual agendas ... [that] can be effectively mediated through the intra- and inter-institutional arenas of decision-making at a European level ... and gain support among European public spheres' (Müller, 2017, p. 130). Three types of leadership – 'agenda-setting', 'mediative-institutional' and 'public' – guide our analysis, which we link to representation issues.

EU leadership is clearly multi-dimensional, multi-level and complex. Commission Presidents often act as policy entrepreneurs, linked to that body's agenda-setting power; they function as brokers in inter-institutional negotiations and as top managers within the Commission, given their power to reorganize an 'administration' consisting of 33,000+employees. Supranational agenda-setting is likely to be more successful when there is an effective outreach strategy, pushing the main agenda items at the beginning of a new term, when public attention is at its highest (Müller, 2017, p. 139). Juncker was the first to label his College a 'political Commission' (Kassim and Laffan, 2019); von der Leyen has proclaimed hers a 'geo-political Commission'. Her unique status as the first woman President, with high symbolic value, allows us to pose new questions, not all of which can be answered here. First, can a female-directed Commission provide strong leadership under crisis conditions (resurgent refugee waves, corona pandemic)? Second, what potential equality advances might we realistically expect from near-parity leadership in the Commission? Third, what particular legitimacy or credibility challenges will she face vis-à-vis the other institutions and the public?

The European Council's nomination of von der Leyen's in July 2019 contravened efforts to democratize the presidential selection by way of a *Spitzenkandidaten* (lead candidates) system. That mechanism's democratizing effect was viewed with scepticism when it was introduced in 2014 (Hobolt, 2014). While the conservative Manfred Weber

(EPP) proved unacceptable to France, the Visegrad countries rejected social-democrat Frans Timmermans (PES), who had initiated infringement proceedings against Poland for rule-of-law violations. Margrethe Vestager's party group (RENEW) had too few votes to cobble together a majority. The Parliament failed to rally behind any of the candidates. Christian Democrat von der Leyen did represent the EPP's winning plurality, as foreseen in Article 17 TFEU. Greens and social democrats refused to support her, requiring her to solicit votes from Europhobic MEPs as well as from right-wing rulers in the Council. She squeaked by with 383 of the 733 votes cast.

Progressives should have reviewed von der Leyen's policy-record regarding gender equality and social inclusion in Germany. Her promulgation of a national anti-discrimination law and monitoring agency in 2006, her 'radical' calls for family-work reconciliation policies, and a 40 per cent female quota on corporate boards subjected her to criticism of her content and style within her own male-dominated party. Her push for guaranteed child-care for infants and toddlers, paternal leave and internet regulations against child-pornography was closely aligned with EU mandates vetoed by chancellor Gerhard Schröder under an SPD–Green government (1998–2005).

Even as defence minister, von der Leyen established child-care portals, part-time/tele-work options and time-off 'savings accounts' for deployed parents. Basic training for all soldiers now includes modules on human rights, cross-cultural competence, diversity, equal treatment, sexual harassment, unconscious bias and other forms of discrimination. Mocked by military hardliners, she moreover upgraded family accommodations, introduced new uniforms for pregnant soldiers and ensured that family re-deployments would not occur in the middle of a school year, reforms that are quite popular among the troops (Bulmahn *et al.,* 2014; Kümmel, 2015; Richter, 2016; Wullers, 2016). These reforms underlie our argument that a leader's past performance is the best predictor available for anticipating her future behaviour. Von der Leyen's first speech as the presidential *candidate* emphasized the need for a 'Union of Equality', according gender equality a strategic, visible place on the supranational agenda and highlighting her ambition for more inclusive, gender equal leadership.

II. 'The Glass Half-Full': Mainstreaming the EU Gender Equality Agenda

The evolution of EU gender equality policies has been well documented, emphasizing three stages dating back to the 1957 adoption of Art. 119 EEC ('equal pay for equal work') (Abels and Mushaben, 2012; Jacquot, 2015; Ahrens, 2019). The Commission promoted multi-year Action Plans, Strategies and Road Maps, moving from equal treat-ment to positive action, to gender mainstreaming, codified in the 1996 Amsterdam Treaty, though the practice failed to live up to the theory.

Equality policies rarely enjoyed priority status among the Commissioners, despite lofty speeches and EU boasting about its status as 'one of the most gender-equal' institutions in the world (Fortin-Rittberger and Rittberger, 2014, p. 496). Engagement by previous presidents was modest at best, with the exception of Jacques Delors (1985–95). His pres-idency saw a flourishing of equality initiatives linked to the single market project, and the creation of the European Women's Lobby. According to MacRae (2012, p. 310), Romano Prodi at least understood 'the rhetoric of balanced participation', explicitly encouraging member states 'to put forward women's names for consideration to the College of

Commissioners'. José Manuel Barroso 'downsized' women's strength in the Commission (Hartlapp *et al.*, forthcoming), eliminating its High Group on Gender Equality. He orchestrated administrative reforms weakening existing gender equality institutions, shifting the equality portfolio from DG Employment to DG Justice (Hubert and Stratigaki, 2016, p. 28). European Parliament efforts to restructure competencies, institutionalize resources/expert networks and alter policy framing often met with Council resistance (Ahrens, 2019; Jacquot, 2020).

Pressured by the European Parliament, Jean-Claude Juncker tried, but failed to raise the number of female Commissioners, due to national governments' resistance (Dinan, 2015, p. 99). His gender-blind austerity policies undermined earlier initiatives (for example child-care provision) intended to level the playing field between women and men. Juncker floated ideas for a Road Map involving equal pay, public consultations and pay transparency in his Action Plan for 2017–19, but most were blocked by the Council. The work–life balance proposal (Directive (EU) 2019/1158) was his only real success, compared to his failure to recast the maternity leave directive. These developments at least 'tilled the policy field' (Hartlapp, 2017) for von der Leyen's plan for a Commission strategy on anti-discrimination. But Juncker's idea for the future of gender equality in the EU were, at best, very limited (Ahrens and van der Vleuten, 2019).

Encountering her first hurdle in attempting to secure parity representation in the College, the individual Cabinets, and across Commission services, the new President designated Helena Dalli the first Commissioner for Equality; her appointment offers another test-case for the argument that past performance is the best predictor of future leadership. Dalli displayed great tenacity as Minister for European Affairs and Equality and as Minister for Social Dialogue, Consumer Affairs and Civil Liberties in Malta. Her successful push for progressive LGBQTI legislation turned conservative, Catholic Malta into a 'gold standard' and 'beacon of hope' (Martin, 2017). Von der Leyen increased the number of Commission vice-presidents to eight, including three Executive Vice-Presidents charged with ensuring a holistic approach to policy formulation by linking dossiers. She placed long overdue reforms from Juncker's Action Plan on the priority list for her first 100 days, including pay transparency and the criminalization of domestic violence.

The fanfare marking the new Gender Equality Strategy (GES) 2020–25 (European Commission, 2020), launched to mark International Women's Day, came to a screeching halt with the onset of the corona-virus pandemic. All EU events involving 'external visitors' were cancelled in March. The urgent need for gender equality initiatives is documented in the 2019 Gender Equality Index (https://eige.europa.eu/gender-equality-index/2019), issued by the European Institute for Gender Equality (EIGE). It attests to the persistence of equality across all member states. Against the EU average (67.4 of 100 points), Sweden, scored 83.6, in contrast to Greece and Hungary, registering only 51 points at the time von der Leyen assumed office on 1 December 2019.

The GES recognizes the promotion of equality between women and men as 'a task for the Union, in all its activities'; it foresees the use of a dual approach, combining targeted measures with effective gender mainstreaming and the application of intersectionality as a cross-cutting principle. Gender equality experts display real excitement regarding its detailed contents (Iratxe *et al.*, 2020), which parallel many of the pledges outlined in von der Leyen's July speech. Combatting violence against women is paramount, because, as Dalli declared, '[n]obody can be free if they are under the threat of violence and impedes [sic] on their right to thrive in life'.[1] The GES commits the EU to 'doing all it can' to combat gender-based violence, sexual harassment, female genital mutilation, forced marriage, compulsory abortions or sterilizations. It promised to codify gender-violence as a 'Eurocrime' (to ensure prosecution) and calls for a Victims' Rights Strategy in 2020, to strengthen the Victims' Rights Directive. The GES aims to combat gender stereotypes, by bolstering women's participation in the arts, the media and the Artificial Intelligence domain. The Strategy specifies methods for closing persistent labour market gaps: measures include full implementation of the Work-Life-Balance Directive; using the Social Scoreboard and the European Semester to monitor adherence to the European Pillar of Social Rights (for example gendering structural reform programmes); mainstreaming gender in public administration, state budgeting and financial management; reforming taxation and social protection systems to end financial disincentives for second earners.

The GES further calls for gender-equal participation in start-up and entrepreneurial innovation initiatives, management of private equity and venture capital funds, and the Digital Education Action Plan (using the 'Women in Digital' scoreboard). Beyond demanding binding pay transparency measures, the Strategy mandates efforts to 'close the gender care gap', to free women for decision-making roles in business, industry and on corporate boards (40 per cent). The Commission moreover hopes to reach gender balance (50 per cent) at all levels of EU management by late 2024, by setting quantitative targets for female appointments and leadership development programs. Von der Leyen welcomes the very high bar established by the new GES; she has promised additional funding, as well as hard law, not merely soft law recommendations, in several fields, combined with strict monitoring. It would constitute a curious kind of 'reverse discrimination' for equality activists to expect the President to accomplish all of this on her own; given the principle of collegiality, she expects strong support from all Commissioners.

III. 'The Glass Half-Empty': Structural Limitations for an Ambitious President

Despite this ambitious agenda, von der Leyen and her Commissioners will encounter major structural constraints. The post-2019 landscape is imposing new limits on strong presidential leadership, owing to stronger polarization and fragmentation within and among the three bodies comprising the legislative triangle: the Commission, Council and European Parliament. Indeed, the growing use of 'trilogues' has weakened the Commission's ability to broker compromises, with detrimental effects for equality interventions (Mushaben, 2019a). In addition, developments linked to EU 'poly-crises' have enhanced the Council's prominence in EU governance and crisis-management. This has marginalized both the Commission (with few exceptions) and the Parliament in key areas, for example economic governance, in line with resurgent, intergovernmentalist conceptions of European integration. It will be more difficult for the new Commission to navigate the already complex inter-institutional dynamics and for the President to meliorate the inter-institutional tensions generated by the *Spitzenkandidaten* fiasco.

---

[1]https://ec.europa.eu/commission/presscorner/detail/en/SPEECH_20_413.

While von der Leyen aimed for gender parity, some national governments refused to nominate male and female candidates, forcing her to choose from an unbalanced list; several published their nominee names before consulting with her. Two female nominees were then rejected outright by the Parliament, following their hearings. Though she could not secure full parity, von der Leyen has appointed the largest number female Commissioners to date, reaching 44 per cent. Committed to 'leading by example', her Mission Letters urged her Commissioners to seek parity in their personal Cabinets, while appointing more women to top positions in the Directorates-General. The final list of Cabinet members falls far short of parity: While women occupy 53.4 per cent of the Cabinet positions they account for only 16 per cent of the cabinet heads but 63 per cent of deputy heads – characterized by some commentators as 'gender-washing' (Foote and Fortuna, 2019).

The Commission itself is more fragmented politically; its members now hail from five, instead of three political party groups, which will affect its decision-making dynamics. Party politics will presumably play a larger role. This is very likely in a self-declared 'political' (Juncker) or 'geo-political' (von der Leyen) Commission, though its President is always a political actor (Dinan, 2016). The President has the power to (re)organize this complex institution. Von der Leyen took immediately advantage of this prerogative by assigning key Commissioners to new positions as 'Executive Vice-presidents'. Several are likely to support her innovation agenda, including the new Equality Commissioner (Dalli), vice-president Timmermans (a self-declared feminist), three female Scandinavian Commissioners (Vestager, Johansson and Urpilainen), and second-term Commissioner Jourová, with whom Dalli jointly presented the GES.

Introducing an Equality Commissioner counts as another major innovation: Dalli is responsible for 'inclusion and equality' 'in all of its senses, irrespective of sex, racial or ethnic origin, religion or belief, disability, age or sexual orientation', required since the Amsterdam Treaty.[2] While responsible for relations with EIGE, Dalli lacks her own Directorate-General, however, and enjoys limited access to equality-relevant units of the DG Justice and Consumers and DG Employment, Social Affairs and Inclusion. Sharing could prove problematic, in view of likely conflicts with Commissioner Reynders over DG Justice and Schmit for DG EMPL; it also raises problems of accountability and the risk of hollowing out the agenda from within. Yet, Dalli chairs a new Taskforce on Equality, 'composed of experts from the Commission services' (European Commission, 2019, p. 8). This cross-cutting, gender mainstreaming approach has yet to prove its effectiveness (since previous attempts for mainstreaming at this level were less successful).

Insisting on 'collegial leadership', von der Leyen has further established 'clusters' of Commissioners jointly responsible for specific tasks. Dalli is member of two such clusters: 'Promoting our European way of life' and 'A new push for European democracy'.vFor a Commission President used to a degree of top-down control in German ministries (resort principle), holding disparate functional and partisan groups together and motivating them to rally around her agenda will pose a real challenge – especially

[2]https://ec.europa.eu/commission/commissioners/2019-2024/dalli_en.

with two strong executive vice-presidents, Timmermans and Vestager, who might position themselves to run for President again in 2024.

A Commission ally in the past, the European Parliament has also become more polarized since the 2019 election; it often requires a centre-left majority to pass equality legislation. Although the EP is poised to enter the 'gender-balanced zone' (40 per cent female), gains in descriptive representation are a mixed blessing.[3] Women's enhanced presence owes partly to a greater number of female MEPs allied with the new Eurosceptic, far-right Identity & Democracy (ID) group, now the fourth largest in the EP. Populist parties usually embrace traditional gender roles and anti-equality agendas. Eurosceptic groups like the ECR and ID have gained more seats. The EPP and S&D will need the support of other groups to muster a working majority and ensure party cohesion in an increasingly politicised policy field (Warasin et al., 2019). The centre-left, inter-group coalition capable of adopting equality policies in the past is no longer sufficiently strong (Kantola and Rolandsen-Agustín, 2016).

In addition, numerous MEPs still resent the European Council and certain national leaders for failing to abide by the *Spitzenkandidaten* model. Their actions precipitated von der Leyen's out-of-the-blue nomination, though she announced during her July 2019 speech that she would strengthen Parliament's role in initiating legislation and help to reform the lead-candidate selection model. Such expectations regarding institutional change also be hard to fill.

As to 'mediative-institutional leadership', von der Leyen will have to bridge gaps within the Council dating back, in part, to the big-bang CEE expansion of 2004/05. Eurosceptic and nationalistic leaders can now block Council actions; intensified conflicts stemming from the Euro and Schengen crises are now re-manifesting themselves by way of member state responses to the Corona pandemic. New mini-lateral groups are forming and flexing their muscles. The Council is not only polarized over austerity policies, migration/asylum, the EU budget and Corona issues but also over questions as to how much and what kind of integration to pursue per se, as witnessed during the nomination processes for top EU jobs or in the recent July 2020 European Council summit.

Finally, times of crisis also require exceptional displays of 'public leadership'. The Corona pandemic initially marginalized the Commission in relation to its co-ordinating role, given Council fights over the financing of assistance measures, while – as recent 2020 Special Eurobarometer data illustrate – the majority of Europeans are supportive of more EU competences and bigger budget to deal with crises such as the COVID-19 pandemic. So far, the Commission appears to be little more than a bystander, despite the pan-European nature of the threat, as governments attempt to seize the wheel in setting a common course. The long-term effects on European integration could prove dramatic.

Conclusion: Future Prospects for the von der Leyen Commission

What lessons can we derive at this early stage by adopting both a leadership and represen-tational perspective? As of this writing there is not sufficient evidence to judge whether von der Leyen's pro-active agenda-setting will result in successful policy change. The

---

[3] Initially, 40.6 per cent of MEPs were women, after UK withdrawal the number dropped slightly to 39.6 per cent.

ability of EU actors to generate concrete policy outputs depends on the institutional setting and contextual factors, which are shifting dramatically as a consequence of the corona pandemic. Leaders constitute a select group of actors; although mainstream studies neglect its impact, we believe that 'the little difference' can hold 'big consequences' (Schwarzer, 1975), but this says nothing about the direction or degree of change. There is empirical evidence inferring that descriptive and substantive representation are interlinked, albeit not in a straightforward manner. Significant changes require not only 'critical mass' but also 'critical acts' and 'critical actors'. Traditionally associated with certain types of masculinity, leadership is a gendered concept, even in the peculiar environment constituted by the EU.

Our assessment of von der Leyen's performance during the first 100 days comprises only a small slice of a larger study, examining the extent to which woman leaders might transfer lessons and approaches from one level to another. Despite her weak performance during the preliminary party-group hearings, von der Leyen demonstrated a capacity for rallying to the equality cause during her first speech to the European Parliament, which qualifies as a 'critical act'. Mindful of women's long march through the institutions in pursuit of equality, her opening tribute to Holocaust survivor Simone Veil revealed her grasp of the significance of symbolic and descriptive representation. 'Strategically setting Europe's agenda' constitutes a Commission President's 'primary political opportunity' to demonstrate leadership (Müller, 2017, p. 139), but keeping gender equality high on the integration agenda, to foster a 'Union of equality', will require even greater active leadership.

Regarding our own expectations, we welcome von der Leyen's assertive, ambitious start – for example, her effort to seek parity representation among the Commissioners and their Cabinets. We value her pledge to hold her Commissioners individually and collectively responsibility for securing equality and diversity in everything they undertake (as outlined in her Mission Letters), as well as her public embrace of the Gender Equality Strategy. Her use of the first 100 days to take visible steps towards legislative action on a long list of overdue gender reforms (equal pay, domestic violence) illustrates her recognition that leadership begins with agenda-setting, linking symbolic to descriptive and substantial representation.

But will she be able to deliver the goods? In fact, nobody is born a leader; leadership derives from learning-by-doing in different contexts. Von der Leyen is still learning how to 'become Madam President' and how to master the ambivalent expectations accompanying this role. Unforeseen in 2019, the Corona pandemic is concurrently challenging and accelerating the need for ambitious leadership. To the extent that 'past performance *is* the best predictor of future performance', von der Leyen's record to date evinces a long list of gender policy achievements, and the stamina to achieve them in the face of strong resistance, during her respective terms as a long-serving German minister. She also acquired substantial experience in dealing with the peculiarities of supranational policy-making in her various ministerial capacities. As Commission President she has made more equality promises than all of her predecessors combined, perhaps more than she will be able to keep over the next five years, but in the words of the great Canadian ice hockey player, Wayne Gretzky, 'you miss 100 percent of the shots you never take'.

Von der Leyen and her Commissioners must nonetheless anticipate major structural constraints at the EU level as she moves to fulfil those promises. Administrative reforms undertaken by her predecessors weakened the Commission's own institutional structure with respect to gender equality policy, which she aims to remedy with her own changes. Add to this greater partisan fragmentation within the College of Commissioners per see, along with possible tensions defining its relationship to the Council and the European Parliament, coupled with tense relations between the Parliament and the Council.

Von der Leyen's ability to engage in 'mediative-institutional leadership' also amounts to a key challenge. Party-political fragmentation is changing the political climate inside the European Parliament, afflicted by Europhobic parties; the Council is also facing internal divisions, owing to Eurosceptic heads of government and states. She must suddenly address a universal economic crisis already kicking in as a result of the corona-virus epidemic; this crisis is beyond her control, notwithstanding her professional training as a doctor. This could precipitate even bigger fault lines within the Council, exacerbating a break-down in historical consensus regarding European integration as a whole. Under these conditions, perhaps, she should not be making promises that will be very hard, if not impossible to keep. Would it be better for her to avoid the risk of undermining her own credibility, and that of future women leaders, by overshooting the mark?

Von der Leyen's (s)election as the first female Commission President provides us with an experimental setting for studying gendered leadership in the EU, along with the linkages among different dimensions of representation. At the symbolic level, the task of serving as the first woman will always pose new challenges in a still gendered environment, but von der Leyen appears willing to tackle this challenge as 'critical actor'. At the descriptive level, the fact that she heads the first ever Commission to boast of near-parity, coupled with her declared emphasis on gender equality and her first 'critical acts', at least opens the door to stronger substantial representation, as illustrated her outspoken support for the GES during the first 100 days. It is still too early to assess the linkage between a more 'feminized' Commission, the President's authority and leadership style, as well as the Commission's policy effectiveness. At least, we have realistic grounds to hope that this President will exercise strong leadership in striving for a more gender-equal Union.

References

Abels, G. and MacRae, H. (forthcoming) 'Searching for Agency: Gendering Leadership in European Integration Theory'. In Müller, H. and Tömmel, I. (eds) *Pathways to Power: Female Leadership and Women Empowerment in the European Union* (Oxford: Oxford University Press).

Abels, G. and Mushaben, J.M. (eds) (2012) *Gendering the European Union: New Approaches to Old Democratic Deficits* (Basingstoke: Palgrave Macmillan).

Ahrens, P. (2019) 'Birth, Life, and Death of Policy Instruments: 35 Years of EU Gender Equality Policy Programs'. *West European Politics*, Vol. 42, No. 1, pp. 45–66.

Ahrens, P. and van der Vleuten, A. (2019) 'Fish Fingers and Measles? Assessing Complex Gender Equality in the Scenarios for the Future of Europe'. *Journal of Common Market Studies*, Vol. 58, No. 2, pp. 292–308.

Ansell, C., Boin, A. and t'Hart, P. (2014) 'Political Leadership in Times of Crisis'. In Rhodes, R.A.
W. and t'Hart, P. (eds) *The Oxford Handbook of Political Leadership* (Oxford: Oxford University Press), pp. 418–33.

Bulmahn, T., Hennig, J., Hoefig, C. and Wanner, M. (2014) *Ergebnisse der repräsentiven Bundeswehrumfrage zur Vereinbarkeit von Dienst und Privat- bzw. Familienleben* (Potsdam: Zentrum für Militärgeschichte und Sozialwissenschaften der Bundeswehr: March).

Dinan, D. (2015) 'The Year of the Spitzenkandidaten'. *Journal of Common Market Studies*, Vol. 53, No. S1, pp. 93–107.

Dinan, D. (2016) 'A More Political Commission'. *Journal of Common Market Studies*, Vol. 54, No. S1, pp. 101–16.

European Commission (2019) 'European Commission 2019–2024: Allocation of portfolios and supporting services'. Available at «https://ec.europa.eu/commission/commissioners/sites/comm-cwt2019/files/team_attachments/allocation-portfolios-supporting-services_en_0.pdf» Accessed 28 March 2020.

European Commission (2020) 'A Union of Equality: Gender Equality Strategy 2020–2025'. COM (2020) 152 final, Brussels 5 March 2020.

Foote, N. and Fortuna, G. (2019) 'Gender-washing at the Commission?'. In *Euractiv* 6 December 2019. Available at «https://www.euractiv.com/section/future-eu/news/the-brief-gender-washing-at-the-commission/» Accessed 23 March 2020.

Fortin-Rittberger, J. and Rittberger, B. (2014) 'Do Electoral Rules Matter? Explaining National Differences in Women's Representation in the European Parliament'. *European Union Politics*, Vol. 15, No. 4, pp. 496–520.

Hartlapp, M. (2017) 'How Time Empowers Agency: Combining the EU Commission's Political Powers and its Administration's Advantage of Acting from a Long-Term Perspective'. *Journal of European Integration*, Vol. 39, No. 3, pp. 303–17.

Hartlapp, M., Müller, H. and Tömmel, I. (forthcoming) 'Gender Equality and the European Commission'. In Abels, G., Kriszan, A., MacRae, H. and van der Vleuten, A. (eds) *Routledge Handbook to Gender and EU Politics* (London: Routledge).

Hubert, A. and Stratigaki, M. (2016) 'Twenty Years of EU Gender Mainstreaming: Rebirth out of the Ashes?' *Femina Politica*, Vol. 25, No. 2, pp. 21–36.

Hobolt, S.B. (2014) 'A vote for the President? The Role of Spitzenkandidaten in the 2014 European Parliament Elections'. *Journal of European Public Policy*, Vol. 21, No. 10, pp. 1528–40.

Iratxe, G., Noichl, M., Stanishev, S. and Gurmai, Z. (2020) 'The EU Gender Equality Strategy is the Beginning of a New Chapter'. In *Euractiv*, 6 March 2020. Available at «https://www.euractiv.com/section/all/opinion/the-eu-gender-equality-strategy-is-the-beginning-of-a-new-chapter/» Accessed 31 March 2020.

Jacquot, S. (2015) *Transformations in EU Gender Equality: From Emergence to Dismantling* (Basingstoke: Palgrave Macmillan).

Jacquot, S. (2020) 'Small Decisions? The European Commission and the Transformation of the Role of Legal Expert Groups: The Case of Gender Equality and Non-Discrimination'. *Journal of Common Market Studies*, Vol. 58, No. 3, pp. 545–61.

Kantola, J. and Rolandsen-Agustín, L. (2016) 'Gendering Transnational Party Politics: The Case of European Union'. *Party Politics*, Vol. 22, No. 5, pp. 641–51.

Kassim, H. and Laffan, B. (2019) 'The Juncker Presidency: The "Political Commission" in Practice'. *Journal of Common Market Studies*, Vol. 57, No. S1, pp. 49–61.

Kümmel, G. (2015) 'The Bundeswehr and Female Soldiers: The Integration of Women into the Armed Forces'. *Connections – The Quarterly Journal*, Vol. XIV, No. 3, pp. 61–91.

MacRae, H. (2012) 'Double-Speak: The European Union and Gender Parity'. *West European Politics*, Vol. 35, No. 2, pp. 301–18.

Martin, I. (2017) 'Malta is the 'Gold Standard' of LGBT Reform, Says UN Equality Boss'. In *Times Malta,* 27 September 2017. Available at «https://timesofmalta.com/articles/view/malta-is-the-gold-standard-of-lgbt-reform-un-equality-boss.659017» Accessed 23 March 2020.

Mushaben, J.M. (2019a) 'Undermining Critical Mass: The Impact of Trilogues and Treaty Reforms on Gender-Sensitive Decision-Making in the European Parliament'. In Ahrens, P. and Rolandsen Agustín, L. (eds) *Gendering the European Parliament: Structures, Policies and Practices* (London: Rowman & Littlefield), pp. 69–84.

Mushaben, J. M. (2019b) '"Mutter der Kompanie": Ursula von der Leyen and the Marketing of the Bundeswehr as an Attractive Employer'. Paper presented at the European Conference of Politics & Gender, Amsterdam, 4–6 July.

Müller, H. (2017) 'Setting Europe's Agenda: The Commission Presidents and Political Leadership'. *Journal of European Integration*, Vol. 39, No. 2, pp. 129–42.

Müller, H. (2020) *Political Leadership and the European Commission Presidency* (Oxford: Oxford University Press).

Müller, H. and Tömmel, I. (forthcoming) 'Women and Leadership in the European Union: A Framework for Analysis'. In Müller, H. and Tömmel, I. (eds) *Pathways to Power: Female Leadership and Women Empowerment in the European Union* (Oxford: Oxford University Press).

Richter, G. (2016) *Wie attraktiv ist die Bundeswehr als Arbeitgeber? Ergebnisse der Personalbefragung 2016, Forschungsbericht No. 113* (Potsdam: Zentrum für Militärgeschichte und Sozialwissenschaften der Bundeswehr).

Schwarzer, A. (1975) *Der kleine Unterschied und seine großen Folgen. Frauen über sich, Beginn einer Befreiung* (Frankfurt/Main: Fischer Verlag).

Sykes, P.L. (2014) 'Does Gender Matter?' In Rhodes, R.A.W. and t'Hart, P. (eds) *The Oxford Handbook of Political Leadership* (Oxford: Oxford University Press), pp. 690–704.

Tömmel, I. (2013) 'The Presidents of the European Commission: Transactional or Transforming Leaders?' *Journal of Common Market Studies*, Vol. 51, No. 4, pp. 789–805.

Tömmel, I. (2019) 'Political Leadership in Times of Crisis: The Commission Presidency of Jean-Claude Juncker'. *West European Politics*, Vol. 43, No. 5, pp. 1141–62. https://doi.org/10.1080/01402382.2019.1646507

von der Leyen, U. (2019a) 'Opening Statement in the European Parliament Plenary Session'. As delivered. Strasbourg, 16/07/2019. Available at «https://ec.europa.eu/commission/presscorner/detail/en/speech_19_4230» Accessed 3 March 2020.

von der Leyen, U. (2019b) *A Union That Strives For More. My Agenda for Europe. Political Guidelines for the Next European Commission 2019–2024* (Brussels: European Commission).

Warasin, M., Kantola, J., Rolandsen Agustín, L. and Coughlan, C. (2019) 'Politicisation of Gender Equality in the European Parliament'. In Ahrens, P. and Rolandsen Agustín, L. (eds) *Gendering the European Parliament* (London: ECPR Press), pp. 141–58.

Wullers, D. (2016) 'Diversity Management: Wie die Bundeswehr bunter und fitter wird'. Bundesakademie für Sicherheitspolitik, No. 13.

JCMS 2020 Volume 58. Annual Review. pp. 133–146

DOI: 10.1111/jcms.13083

The EU's Socioeconomic Governance 10 Years after the Crisis: Muddling through and the Revolt against Austerity

AMANDINE CRESPY [iD]
CEVIPOL/Institut d'Etudes Européennes, Université libre de Bruxelles, Brussels

Introduction

Over ten years ago, at the end of 2009, Greece entered one of the most tumultuous periods in its contemporary history, and the entire Economic and Monetary Union (EMU) founded in 1992 threatened to collapse under the effects of the global financial crisis and the poor capacity of European governing elites to find rapid appropriate responses. After an initial Keynesian moment, 'austeritarianism' emerged from intergovernmental summits, with the Eurogroup, the informal gathering of the finance ministers of member states, with no legal existence in the EU's treaties, having the upper hand on decision-making. The strategy then embraced was one of internal devaluation in indebted countries, limited financial support by creditor members of the EMU conditional upon social retrenchment, and a collective commitment to stringent fiscal discipline. More than the financial crisis itself, it was the political response to it, guided by a questionable belief in expansionary fiscal consolidation (Blyth, 2013, pp. 212–16), which left EU countries struggling with a long recession. Ten years on, have Europeans recovered from the crisis? And where has the strategy of muddling through left the EU?

Before the outbreak of the coronavirus pandemic, decision-makers' discourse emphasized that the crisis was over. Not only had the EU's average growth rate stabilized at around 2 per cent, but the average unemployment rate in the EU had come down from 10.5 per cent in 2013 to 6.4 per cent in 2019. Yet the Euro crisis was never a pivotal moment bringing about a full recognition of the failure of financial capitalism and paradigmatic change. Instead, the meltdown of the banking system stumbling over excessive (private) debt eventually resulted in the remarkable resilience of neoliberalism (Crouch, 2011; Schmidt and Thatcher, 2013) which led to an acceleration of pre-existing trends, for instance, the 'infrastructural power' of financial markets over monetary policy (Braun, 2018) and the subordination of social policy to the economic imperatives of competitiveness and fiscal discipline (Crespy and Menz, 2015). In a world where politicians speak to the markets as much as they speak to the people (Schmidt, 2014), the prevailing discourse had been that 'there is no alternative' to prioritizing responsibility towards creditors over responsiveness to voters (Mair, 2013).

When the pandemic hit and confinement put economies to a halt in the spring of 2020, Europeans had been muddling through the recession for a decade. None of the structural issues affecting the socioeconomic governance of the EU had been adequately addressed. What is more, it is argued, the way the crisis was handled only exacerbated the loss of trust in political institutions and the revolt against governing elites. The first section of this article shows how the austeritarian response to the financial and debt crisis have left enduring marks on the EU as a union of peoples and states, despite a sensible inflection in policy-making away from austerity. The second section discusses the political deadlock that characterizes debates over EMU reforms, in particular, over needs for stabilization and democratization. The third section explains how the perceived lack of social justice in Europe feeds into social and political polarization, resulting in the strengthening of populist political forces.

I. The Enduring Legacy of Europe's Great Recession

The recession ensuing from the 2008 financial crisis unveiled the fragility of Europe's socio-economic foundations in two respects. On one hand, it accelerated the forms of social and territorial inequality resulting from the financialisation of the Europeans economies. On the other, it laid bare how the EU was struggling politically to depart from the structural ordo-liberal bias of its governance and proved little to manage socio-economic interdependencies in a timely and effective fashion.

A Divided Union of Peoples and States

A first way to look at the legacy of the crisis is to examine how it has affected levels of inequality in European societies. In this regard, rising levels of GDP per capita or declining levels of poverty hide a much more complex reality. Across Europe, the average share of national income captured by the top 10 per cent of earners has been on the rise since 1980, ranging from approximately 29 per cent in northern Europe to 32.5 per cent in western Europe in 2017 (Blanchet et al., 2019). However, it is possible to discern that the Euro crisis has aggravated the rise of inequality. First, the crisis put a halt to the fall in the poverty that Europe had experienced since 2000, stabilizing at around 21 per cent of people at risk of poverty (that is, with an income under 60 per cent of the median income nationally).[1] Behind the various fiscal and social systems to correct for inequality, some common trends can be identified. According to an Organization for Economic Cooperation and Development study, the improvement in average household disposable incomes in the recovery from the recession hides important disparities. In the vast majority of EU countries, the disposable income of the top 10 per cent of earners has grown much faster than that of the bottom 10 per cent (Organization for Economic Cooperation and Development, 2017). We also know that changes in disposable income depend on the structural evolution in labour markets. Flexibilization and the rise of precarious, part-time jobs have clearly affected income levels, with women being more affected than men; thus feeding into the gender pay gap. Meanwhile, rampant in-work poverty has become a reality across the board and has continued to rise from 8.9 per cent in 2012 to 9.6 per cent in 2018.[2]

Incomes are only part of the story, however. Looking at net wealth, including property, helps us to draw a more accurate picture. Strikingly, the decrease of median net wealth between 2010 and 2014 has been almost thrice less important for the top 10 per cent of earners (8.7 per cent) than for the bottom 10 per cent of earners across euro area countries (Sweeney and Wilson, 2018). Net wealth is also affected by the ability of welfare states to deliver services (such as childcare or health care) at affordable prices. Driven by the

---

[1]All figures are from Eurostat: www.ec.europa.eu/eurostat
[2]All figures are from Eurostat: www.ec.europa.eu/eurostat

objective of decreasing public expenditure, austerity packages systematically targeted public services in a way that has affected the welfare of those who cannot afford private services (Crespy, 2016, pp. 189–227).

The great recession has also exacerbated inequality between European societies. In some parts of Europe the absence of prospects has translated into a demographic haemorrhage, especially among qualified young people, to EU countries with more dynamic labour markets. Spain, Portugal, Latvia, Lithuania or Romania – to name a few – have been badly affected by the brain drain. At a macro level, the Euro crisis revealed that the socio-economic convergence the founders of the EMU had hoped for had not taken place. Structural disparities have proved enduring and there is a persisting gap in socioeconomic development between a core of rich northern and continental European countries and the southern and eastern peripheries (Makszin *et al.,* 2020). While GDP per capita remains higher in the south than in the east (about 45 per cent compared with approximately 30 per cent of that of the core), countries of the eastern periphery have remained on an ascending GDP trajectory throughout the recession. In contrast, southern Europe has experienced an important decline, which came to a halt only in 2016.

Politically, too, the Euro crisis has divided the continent, creating asymmetric power relations between creditors and debtors. The confrontations between Merkel's Germany and the Syriza government over bailouts and conditionality triggered unprecedented and shocking expressions of mutual hate, ranging from misplaced moral judgements to clichés and featuring images of Angela Merkel as a Nazi. Rather than recognizing the Euro area's systemic problems, the prevailing diagnosis of the crisis was essentially framed as a tale of 'Northern saints and Southern sinners' (Matthijs and MacNamara, 2015). Although the political climate seems to have eased over the past years, EU politics are shaped by a powerful 'Hanseatic league' of hawkish creditor states up to the present (Schild and Howarth, 2020). Clearly, a sense of mutual trust and recognition has been lost as a result of the financial crisis. Although the rate of unemployment has decreased on average since 2012, an entire generation of young people still experiences hardship, with youth unemployment ranging from 20 to 40 per cent in seven EU member states, including southern countries plus Croatia and France. Against this background, socioeconomic governance in the EU was one of mixed signals in terms of the social effects of the recession.

The Sluggish Shift of EU Governance Away from Austerity

Ten years after the Euro crisis broke out, it has been widely recognized that the EU's focus on adjustment by deflation and fiscal discipline has been to a large extent self-defeating. In 2013 the International Monetary Fund was first to criticize the EU's obsession with fiscal discipline. From 2014 onwards the Commission headed by Juncker initiated a shift away from austerity. When the new Commission president, Ursula von der Leyen, took over in November 2019, departing from muddling through and giving the EU a new political impetus appeared as the most pressing tasks.

From 2011 onwards, the European semester was set up as a broad governance framework encompassing the surveillance of budgets, with a legal hardening of the rules attached to the stability and growth pact, economic surveillance through the macro-economic imbalance procedure, and a soft coordination of social policies, that previously occurred through the social open method of coordination. After the initial phase that had clearly focused on austerity and fiscal consolidation under Barroso, the Juncker Commission partly acknowledged the need for a trade-off between fiscal consolidation and governments' capacity to enforce structural reforms that would generate growth in the medium term, and subsequently relaxed the former and stressed the latter. A number of initiatives have aimed to stimulate growth and tackle social issues. As Commissioner for Employment and Social Affairs under Barroso, Laszlo Andor was active in promoting a more social agenda by promoting, for example,the social investment package in 2013 and the youth guarantee in 2014. Relying partly on soft law and a mix of national and EU resources (from the European social fund), both instruments were meant to tackle the two main problems brought about by the crisis; namely skyrocketing youth unemployment and the debasing of public services. While these initiatives are to be welcome, they both exhibit the inadequate level of resources set aside to tackle the sheer size of the problems. The European-wide agenda for social investment, in particular, has been left to a large extent to the traditions, willingness and fiscal means of national governments.

At the same time, Juncker Commission operated a, important discursive turn towards investment. And the 'Juncker plan' (now rebranded InvestEU) was launched in 2015 as the Commission's flagship initiative to leverage private investment across Europe. Besides the plan's lack of capacity to boost growth on a large scale, an independent report from 2019 points to issues regarding the green earmarking of investments, the geographical coverage by the elected projects, and governance, transparency. It points, for instance, to the 'aggressive promotion and incentivization of PPPs for social and economic infrastructure financing (...), especially in sensitive public services sectors' (Network/Counterbalance, 2019). In 2018, public investment in the EMU's southern periphery had clearly not yet recovered, stagnating at its 2012 level after a dramatic decrease in 2009 (Seikel and Truger, 2019). The main initiative of the Juncker Commission has been the proclamation, in 2017, of the European pillar of social rights, a catalogue of 20 principles for ensuring decent life and work and to be enforced through a combination of soft law (recommendations) and hard law (new regulations). One of the main pieces of legislation so far has been the work–life balance directive in 2019. This relatively ambitious Commission proposal (creating a right to paternity leave or to carers' leave) has been largely watered down by the Council by leaving the practicalities (especially the levels of compensation offered) to member states. On the soft law front, the Commission is pushing for the creation of a child guarantee to tackle child poverty through a consultative process on the feasibility thereof conducted in 2019. Finally, when von der Leyen took office in November 2019 she committed the Commission to take action to ensure that a satisfactory proportion of European workers enjoy a fair minimum wage. As consultation of the social partners is still in process at the time of writing, it is not clear that the Commission will find sufficient political support (and a relevant legal basis) to adopt a binding instrument on this issue. Overall, the vast majority of social rights entailed in the pillar (notably related to work), are merely to be monitored through the European semester.

The European semester (also called new economic governance) serves to perform the multilateral monitoring of member states' fiscal, economic and social policy over a yearly cycle, steered by the Commission. This broad governance framework set up in 2011 encompasses stringent regulation of the stability and growth pact adopted in 2011–12 as well as the soft coordination of social policy (the 'Europe 2020' strategy) that formerly occurred via the open method of coordination. The literature dealing with the EU's new economic governance displays contrasting assessments of its nature and effects. Overall, a partial 'socialization' of the European semester has been detected (Zeitlin and Vanhercke, 2017). There has been a growing concern for social issues in the substantial messages sent by the Commission through its annual growth surveys and the country-specific recommendations. New instruments have been integrated to ensure the closer surveillance of social issues in the member states, as social and employment actors in the Council and Commission have fought back to extend their role in the process. Yet by adopting these strategies socially minded actors have had to moderate their ambitions (Copeland and Daly, 2018). Furthermore, a closer look at the substantial meaning and content of these recommendations in the realm of social policy provides two insights (Crespy and Vanheuverzwijn, 2017). First, the European semester has long remained focused on a typical neoliberal agenda centred on the liberalization of products and services markets, the deregulation of labour markets, and the reform of public administration. At the same time, structural reforms have from the outset encompassed calls for social investment as well as measures requiring retrenchment of social benefits. Thus, governments have found themselves facing contradictory injunctions to save (fiscal discipline) and to spend (social investment). A main policy outcome of the semester has been the implementation of labour market reforms which, overall, have 'operated mainly through the reduction of security for insiders, not by increasing job security for outsiders' (Arpe *et al.*, 2015, p. 50). From a critical perspective, thus, the fuzzy notion of structural reforms has allowed EU institutions to address these criticisms to some extent.

Against this background, the semester cycles of 2019 and 2020 clearly show a greater concern for fostering social investment and tackling exclusion and inequalities. As the consequences of the pandemic will exacerbate the need for effective social responses, political agreement over some fundamental underlying issues has so far proved elusive.

II. The Pending Agenda for A More Social and Democratic EMU

Shortly after Macron was elected as French president in 2017, he put forward an agenda for far-reaching reforms in the EU in a grand speech at Sorbonne University, calling for a 'sovereign, united and democratic Europe'. One of his proposals emphasized the need for new instruments to ensure stability and convergence in the Euro area, notably through a common budget based on new EU resources (among others). This was linked to a more integrated governance, featuring a common minister, greater control of the European parliament (EP), and social measures to fight against social dumping (a revision of regulations on the posting of workers and new rules guaranteeing minimum wages). Macron put these proposals at the centre of the Franco-German agenda, a discussion that rapidly got bogged down between reluctance and delays. It eventually became clear that the expected major overhaul of the EMU was not to take place, leaving the two main issues unsettled: stabilization and democratization.

Stabilization

Stabilization refers to the ability of the Euro area to cope with forthcoming external shocks such as financial crises or unexpected events (like a global pandemic) that may disturb European economies and trigger a new recession. Ten years on from the subprime crisis, is the eurozone fit to meet the next crisis? This debate took shape around essentially two policy ideas: the establishment of a European unemployment reinsurance fund and the creation of a eurozone budget.

The underlying idea of the first proposal was to compensate for the social costs of adjustment in the event of shocks in more vulnerable economies that are competing against more stable ones within a monetary union. Stabilization would therefore be facilitated by a form of automatic stabilizers such as a European unemployment benefits scheme. This idea has been long discussed, culminating in 2016, when high-ranking politicians and economists, including Marianne Thyssen, Pierre Moscovici, Pier Carlo Padoan, Sebastian Dullien and Paul De Grauwe, gathered together at the Centre for European Policy Studies to discuss alternative designs. The preferred option does not involve direct transfers from the EU to unemployed individuals. Rather, states would contribute to an insurance fund, which could be accessed by those countries most affected by external shocks and flow into national schemes (Andor, 2017). Even though the idea was mentioned in the 2018 Franco-German roadmap for the Euro area, it has not yet materialized as an EU policy.

These questions have generated fascinating academic debates about the normative underpinnings of EMU and the extent to which Europeans should be bound by financial and social solidarity. Drawing from Weber, Ferrera (2017) suggested, for instance, that the EU could be conceived as a neighbourhood community, underpinned not by mere altruism but by reciprocity *and* beneficence: a form of basic compassion taming economically motivated behaviour. Others have stressed that the EU should above all guarantee non-domination of some states over others and compensate for the unequal benefits stemming from integration due to the diversity of national social systems and their unequal capacity to adapt to economic and fiscal competition (Sangiovanni, 2013). On the political front, however, debates have revolved around the dichotomy between risk reduction and risk sharing. Here the concept of moral hazard has been key (Vandenbroucke *et al.,* 2016, pp. 9–11; Pierret, 2019), suggesting that sharing the financial burden of debt and recessions would act as a deterrent for less competitive member states to adopt sound policies for reducing debt and enforcing structural reforms. Thus, creditor countries put forward their concern that sharing risks through new financial instruments would de facto entail permanent financial transfers, hence advocating the reduction of risk through 'responsible' policies. In the same way that they had obliterated discussions around the creation of eurobonds in 2008–10, these underlying normative positions impeded decisions about a possible unemployment reinsurance fund or a eurozone budget.

After lengthy discussions and much resistance from a group of creditor states (especially the Netherlands, Finland, Ireland, Latvia and Lithuania), Macron's grand proposals for a eurozone budget resulted in 2018–19 in an agreement on a 'budgetary instrument for convergence and competitiveness' (BICC). The instrument, endowed with about 17 billion euro[3] from the EU budget, is to be distributed to member states on the basis of projects to 'finance packages of structural reforms and public investments' (Council of the EU, 2019). All commentators noted that the BICC fell far short of what could be regarded as a eurozone budget. Many economists have reckoned that the BICC was a first, albeit marginal step in the right direction, possibly 'leaving the door open for a

---

[3]The final amount dedicated to the BICC will be determined in the negotiations about the EU's multi-annual financial framework.

more meaningful instrument in the future' (Goncalves Raposo, 2019). But they have also stressed that the sheer size of the sum proposed (about 0.01 per cent of the eurozone's GDP) could under no circumstances perform a stabilization function. More strikingly, there is ambiguity as to the very objectives of the instrument for it to please both those who want to use it as a tool for boosting investment and convergence, and those who see it as a means to promote competitiveness through structural reforms. To conclude, rather than stabilization (let alone solidarity), it seems that the OHIO doctrine, according to which governments should put your 'Own House In Order' first, is still the game in town. It is now uncertain how the BICC will fare in the reconfiguration of EU resources aiming at fighting the consequences of the Covid-19 pandemic.

Democratization

The shake-up of the Euro area as a result for the financial and debt crisis triggered a debate about its incomplete, undemocratic governance. The key role of the European Council, and even more that of the Eurogroup, in particular, has raised questions as to the accountability of those deciding on issues that touch upon fiscal policy, the welfare state and budgets, all of which are the prerogatives of sovereign states and parliaments. In the 2015 'Five Presidents Report', key EU politicians advocated increasing EP control over the EMU. In academia, much more radical ideas were put forward. A group of French scholars (including Thomas Piketty) suggested the creation of a second assembly, made up of national MPs, which would decide on all the important socioeconomic matters in the Euro area, including the policy of the European Central Bank (Hennette et al., 2017). This institutional innovation, despite its cost, was, in their view, essential for reconnecting EMU governance to domestic political arenas and provide the necessary democratic legitimacy. Comparing the Bank of England, the US Federal Reserve Bank and the ECB, other scholars have shed light on the negative impact of central banking on inequalities, notably due to their embeddedness with financial markets. For this reason, they question the dogma of central bank independence.

In the political arena, Macron's proposals were were not as radical and, although they included the idea of increased control by the EP, greater emphasis was put on creating a post for a common finance minister, an idea echoing the long-standing French plea for a 'gouvernement économique' in the EU. However, strengthening the executive without matching it with parliamentary control would have been very questionable from a democratic point of view. In any event, discussions on eurozone reforms never seriously addressed democratization concerns. Instead, attention focused on improving the functioning of the European semester. When the Juncker Commission undertook a 'revamp of the European Semester' in October 2015, it called for enhancing the ownership of the EU's socioeconomic governance, meaning that the semester would be better endorsed and implemented if social partners and national parliaments, in particular, were better aware of the semester and able to feed into its objectives. Despite these good intentions, the semester has remained, to a large extent, a bureaucratic exercise serving to consolidate a European administrative space (through intense dialogue between the Commission and national administrations) but with little salience in national political arenas (Vanheuverzwijn and Crespy, 2018; Papadopoulos and Piattoni, 2019). Hence, overall the EMU remains distanced from the democratic credentials one would wish for in a policy area that shapes economic life, from banking activities to labour markets and welfare states.

III. 'The People' against Technocratic Governance

In the aftermath of the financial and debt crisis, the EU's political strategy of muddling through has been accompanied by the aggravation of long term social transformations. These have powerfully reshaped national party landscapes and boosted contestation against the kind of modernization project embodied by the EU.

From Social Polarization to Popular Revolts

One of the first effects of the great recession was to accentuate contemporary sociological cleavages on social mobilization on EU-related matters. Contemporary European societies find themselves divided around a new social line which opposes, roughly speaking, the winners and the losers of globalization and Europeanization (Kriesi *et al.,* 2008). While it is linked to contemporary forms of economic and social transformation, this new cleavage partly overlaps with older ones. The winners are typically urban professionals with a strong educational background and post-materialist values, while the losers tend to live in rural or deindustrialized areas and be more prone than winners to see immigrants and social diversity as a cultural and economic threat.

Against this background of structural transformations, the 2008 financial crisis and its aftermath have triggered a new cycle of protest and anti-austerity social movements (Della Porta, 2015). While activists of the Global Justice Movement, which had its heyday in the 2000s, belonged mainly to the educated middle class, anti-austerity protesters have more diverse profiles, including precarious or poor workers, unemployed people, people from rural areas, or students. While all criticize the effects of inegalitarian capitalism and the failure of representative democracy to serve the masses, they have also sometimes articulated contradicting demands. This has made it difficult for political actors wishing to capitalize on popular revolt to articulate coherent policy programmes or ideologies that could be backed by a majority.

The Yellow Vests (*gilets jaunes*) movement, which almost paralysed France from autumn 2018 and until the end of spring 2019, illustrates this cleavage best. Starting with a protest against new taxes on fuel, the movement's grievances rapidly enlarged to include a broad 'reformulation of the social question' around the issue of tax justice (Piketty, 2018; Spire, 2019) primarily by the citizens of the lower middle class, directing the revolt around precarity of work combined with unbearable fiscal burdens. The anger expressed by the movement focused mostly on Macron, who was accused of being the 'president of the rich' after decreasing taxes on the wealthiest citizens and on revenue from the capital. At the same time, the movement was criticized by many opinion leaders and by part of the public opinion for its excessive brutality and acts of vandalism, the incoherence of its demands, and its xenophobic and anti-Semitic flavour, as it was progressively infiltrated and captured by far-right forces.

While some parallels were made between the *gilets jaunes* and the *sans-culottes* of the French revolution, lessons can be drawn in terms of the two main challenges facing citizens and decision-makers alike. First, the mobilization of the *gilets jaunes* was successful in externalizing a pervasive and deep anger among the population. However, the diversity of backgrounds, views and demands impeded the emergence of spokespeople to represent the movement as a whole, to articulate coherent demands and to talk to decision-makers. The movement failed to unify its diverse consituent factions and faced much internal criticism. Ingrid Levasseur, a young nurse who had become a figurehead of the movement, failed to launch representatives for the European election and left the political scene in March 2019. Eventually, the division of the movement's representatives into three different lists (all receiving below 1 per cent of the vote) reflected the movement's inability to generate effective action in the political arena. Without the Yellow Vests' claims being adequately considered by established political actors, the motives of their revolt remained fundamentally unaddressed. The second lesson relates to the nature of these claims for social mobilization, considering that the movement was triggered by the rise of the tax on fuel. The 'social question' nowadays can only be conceived in terms of its articulation with the ecological transition and fiscal reforms. In this new context, fiscal policy has become the main instrument to ensure that the burden of the ecological adjustment will not only be borne only by the weaker members of society, leaving interests of powerful economic actors unaffected.

Inclusionary Populism Giving Way to Exclusionary Populism?

In 2000, prominent political scientists questioned how, notwithstanding dynamic eurosceptic parties, EU integration could profoundly alter the historically entrenched political cleavages in Europe, especially the left–right cleavage (Mair, 2000; Harmsen, 2005). The decade inaugurated by the financial crisis, however, has catalysed the transformations at stake, leading to the unimaginable remodelling of party systems in many EU member states. First, the EU has come to embody the values of cosmopolitan upper-middle class and elites, grounded on economic and political liberalism, while less affluent citizens have increasingly rejected it as a remote, faceless and undemocratic technocracy ruling from Brussels to serve the interests of the large corporations that lobby it. This change in political systems took various forms across different countries, shaped by historical legacies and institutional constraints and led by diverse emerging political actors. However, the most common development across countries was the new populist cleavage that has cut across the old left–right patterns, upsetting government and opposition dynamics and leading to political fragmentation and government crises in many countries.

From the outset of the recession, southern Europe has been a special place for observing the populist wave. The electoral rise of Syriza in Greece, Podemos in Spain and the Movimento Cinque Stelle (M5S) in Italy followed the social effects of the recession and austerity, as can be measured, for instance, by the decline of the social justice index in these countries (Kotroyannos et al., 2018, p.6). Despite national and cultural differences, all three parties exhibited similarities in their discourse, with their harsh critique of domestic and European political establishments, and the broad opposition between an indefinite mass of 'the people' against the elites. They can be defined as 'inclusionary' populist parties, stressing the need to enhance popular democratic participation and to give disadvantaged groups a voice; in contrary to 'exclusionary' populism focusing on anti-immigration and nationalism, and distributional and cultural exclusion by those entitled to be part of 'the people' (Mudde and Kaltwasser, 2013; Font et al., 2019).

Following recent electoral developments, we are arguably witnessing the end of an anti-austerity protest cycle which gave rise to inclusionary populism in southern Europe. Its strongest example, Syriza, which had governed Greece since 2015, handed power back to Greece's traditional right-wing New Democracy after losing the last Greek general election in July 2019. For some voters, Tsipras was seen to have betrayed socialist ideals whereas, for others, he was a victim of the ineluctable EU political diktat; and evidence that there is indeed no alternative to the neoliberal centrist mainstream in the current EU politico-economic order. In Italy M5S topped the polls with 32.7 per cent of the votes in the 2018 election and formed a coalition with the far-right Lega Nord. The unprecedented coalition of two populist parties called for an end to austerity and clashed loudly with the Commission over Italy's budget, forecasted to have a deficit over the 3 per cent threshold of the stability and growth pact. Nonetheless, due to many disagreements over a range of policies, the coalition was short-lived. Lega leader Salvini decided to withdraw his support strategically, hoping to rise to power. Yet MS5 then sided with the centre-left Partito Democratico to form a new coalition instead of calling an election. Meanwhile, the EP elections in May 2019 showed that the respective levels of support for the Lega and the M5S had reversed, with the latter halving its vote share to 17 per cent, while the former doubled it to 34 per cent. In Spain, Podemos (now under the coalition Unitas Podemos) experienced a stark decline from 21.15 per cent in 2016 to 12.9 per cent of the votes in November 2019. After repeated failed negotiations, Podemos eventually propped up a government coalition under Pedro Sanchez's Social Party. Meanwhile, the most notable result of this election was the rise of far-right Vox, which doubled its number of seats from 24 to 52 – compared with the earlier election in April 2019.

On the flipside, looking at the rise of exclusionary populism in the aftermath of the crisis, it is worth highlighting the resurrection of the long moribund far-right in Germany. The trajectory of Alternative für Deutschland (AfD) is interesting because it shows how initial contestation of the EMU can end up against EU socioeconomic governance can end up catalysing exclusionary populism. Founded as a single-issue party by a small group of anti-Euro academics, AfD changed leadership rapidly and transformed itsef into a classic anti-immigration party (Schmitt-Beck, 2017). This strategy was very successful, as we can see fromt AfD's electoral success, which within 4 years from its foundation became the third largest party in the 2017 general election (12.64 per cent of the votes). In the regional elections of 2019 it came second in the parliaments of Thuringia, Brandenburg and Saxony (with 23.4, 23.5 and 27.5 per cent of the votes, respectively). The rise of AfD has undeniably destabilized German politics by profoundly altering the available combinations for government coalitions, as the recent controversial political alliance between the Christian Democratic Union and AfD in Thuringia has shown. The German postwar political model and the normative grounds on which it was built have ended, which, in the medium run, could have implications beyond Germany.

To conclude, exclusionary populism focusing on racist anti-immigration discourses prevailed over inclusionary anti-austerity forms of populism, as the 2019 EP election showed. While the far-right non-affiliated sovereigntists and moderate eurosceptics gained 27 seats (compared to 2014), the European United Left/Nordic Green Alliance lost 14. With 207 seats out of 751, far-right populists are now in a position to wield significant leverage on the EU's political agenda, especially by blocking progressive socioeconomic agendas for a fair green transition, or institutional reform seeking to democratize the

Union. This is likely to happen, as they are likely to find allies among some radicalizing conservatives of the European People's Party.

Conclusion

This article aimed to review the important developments in the EU's socioeconomic governance in 2019, taking stock of where we stand ten years after the global financial crisis destabilized the European banking sector and, eventually, the eurozone as a whole. A number of arguments have been discussed, emanating from intense scholarly research and debates in political science. First, the Euro crisis was never a critical juncture bringing about a paradigmatic shift in the EU's socioeconomic governance. Rather, it has accelerated the reinforcement of existing structural features, especially by hardening fiscal discipline and subordinating social objectives to the imperatives of competitiveness. Second, ten years on, despite a seeming recovery, the austeritarian response to the crisis has left a legacy of increased social inequality, accentuating the divide between the wealthy core and the peripheries of Europe. Third, the EU's socioeconomic governance has been a battlefield for political forces pulling in different directions with social issues becoming increasingly salient over time. Fourth, the overdue far-reaching reforms for ensuring stabilization and democratization of the EMU have ended in a political deadlock. Fifth, while the EU seemed paralyzed, domestic political arenas have been profoundly reshaped by popular movements and the rise of populist parties (left and right). Yet ten years on from the crisis, exclusionary forms of populism have grown stronger than the more inclusionary movements across the EU.

Now the Covid-19 pandemic in 2020 has suddenly upset the constellation inherited from ten years of muddling through. The pandemic has starkly revealed the consequences of chronic underinvestment in health care as well as the limitations of fiscal discipline. Thus, the pandemic cannot be regarded as a fully symmetrical shock, as some countries (especially Italy and Spain) have experienced more significant infection rates and have very limited fiscal capacities and feeble economies to meet the challenge. In the face of this new driver of inequality within and between European societies, EU leaders have decided to suspend rules for fiscal discipline and discussions for a significant financial package for fighting the consequences of the pandemic are in process at the time of writing. To what extent decision-makers will fully be able to draw the lessons from the past nevertheless remains an open question.

Ultimately, Europeans face two main challenges when shaping 'the world after Covid-19' in a progressive – as opposed to socially regressive – fashion. The way they do so will be reflected in the reshuffling of the EU's multi-annual financial framework for 2021–7. The first challenge is to overcome misconceived beliefs about moral hazard and unlock the confrontation between debtor and creditor states. What is at stake is the capacity to garner the resources needed to ensure the resilience of economies and – green and social – investment. Their reflections should not only concern redistribution among member states but also put forward novel ideas about the EU's own resources (that is, the possibility of new European taxes). Second, fighting the consequences of the pandemic will have to be wisely articulated with the pre-existing agenda for a green deal promoted by the von der Leyen commission, which includes an important social policy component. Beyond the European Commission, a lot is expected from

Germany as it holds the presidency of the Council from July to December 2020. Will the German leadership be able to bridge the most crucial gaps between contrasting visions of the EU's socioeconomic agenda? With Brexit unresolved and migration issues looming (among others), expectations may be too high. In any event, current events have opened a window of opportunity for Europeans to overcome old resistances and embrace investment in a socially fair ecological transition. Without a positive agenda, collective inaction may pave the way for a major reactionary backlash.

References

Andor, L. (2017) 'The Impact of Eurozone Governance on Welfare Stability'. In Vandenbroucke, F., Barnard, C. and De Bare, G. (eds) *A European Social Union after the Crisis* (Cambridge: Cambridge University Press), pp. 143–59.

Arpe, J., Milio, S. and Stuchlik, A. (2015) 'Social Policy Reforms in the EU: A Cross-national Comparison'. Social Inclusion Monitor Europe (SIM) – Reform Barometer. Available online at: https://www.bertelsmann-stiftung.de/fileadmin/files/user_upload/Study_EZ_SIM_Europe_Reformbarometer_2015.pdf. Last accessed: 13 July 2018.

Blanchet, T., Chancel, L. and Gethin, A. (2019) 'Has the European Social Model Withstood the Rise in Inequalities?'. WID.world Issue Brief. 2019/2, Available online at: https://wid.world/document/european-inequality-wil-summary-2019-en-pdf/. Last accessed: 15 July 2020.

Blyth, M. (2013) *Austerity: The History of a Dangerous Idea* (Oxford: Oxford University Press).

Braun, B. (2018) 'Central Banking and the Infrastructural Power of Finance: The Case of ECB Support for Repo and Securitization Markets'. *Socio-Economic Review*, doi: 10.1093/ser/mwy008.

Copeland, P. and Daly, M. (2018) 'The European Semester and EU Social Policy'. *JCMS*, Vol. 56, No. 5, pp. 1001–18.

Council of the European Union. (2019) *Explainer on the euro area budgetary instrument.*

Crespy, A. (2016) *Welfare Markets in Europe. The Democratic Challenge of European Integration* (Basingstoke: Palgrave).

Crespy, A. and Menz, G. (2015) ''Introduction: The Pursuit of Social Europe in the Face of Crisis'. In Crespy, A. and Menz, G. (eds) *Social Policy and the Eurocrisis. Quo Vadis Social Europe* (Basingstoke: Palgrave), pp. 1–23.

Crespy, A. and Vanheuverzwijn, P. (2017) 'What 'Brussels' Means by Structural Reforms: Empty Signifier or Constructive Ambiguity?' *Comparative European Politics*, Vol. 17, pp. 92–111.

Crouch, C. (2011) *The Strange Non-death of Neo-liberalism* (Cambridge: Polity Press).

Della Porta, D. (2015) *Social Movements in Times of Austerity* (Cambridge: Polity Press).

Ferrera, M. (2017) 'The European Social Union: A Missing but Necessary "Political Good"'. In Vandenbroucke, F., Barnard, C. and De Bare, G. (eds) *A European Social Union after the Crisis* (Cambridge: Cambridge University Press), pp. 47–67.

Font, N., Graziano, P. and Tsakatika, M. (2019) 'Varieties of Inclusionary Populism? SYRIZA, Podemos and the Five Star Movement'. *Government and Opposition*. https://doi.org/10.1017/gov.2019.17.

Goncalves Raposo, I. (2019) 'The June Eurogroup Meeting: Reflections on BICC'. Bruegel Blogpost. Available online at: https://www.bruegel.org/2019/06/the-june-eurogroup-meeting-reflections-on-bicc. Last accessed: 28 February 2020.

Harmsen, R. (2005) 'L'Europe et les partis politiques nationaux: Les leçons d'un 'non-clivage'. *Revue internationale de politique comparée*, Vol. 12, No. 1, pp. 77–94.

Hennette, S., Piketty, T., Sacriste, G. and Vauchez, A. (2017) 'Treaty on the Democratization of the Economic and Social Government of the European Union ("T-Dem")'. Available online at: http://tdem.eu/en/treaty/. Last accessed: 6 March 2020.

Kotroyannos, D., Tzagkarakis, S. I. and Pappas, I. (2018) 'South European Populism as a Consequence of the Multidimensional Crisis? The Cases of SYRIZA, PODEMOS and M5S'. Available online at: https://nbn-resolving.org/urn:nbn:de:0168-ssoar-59933-3. Last accessed: 15 July 2020.

Kriesi, H., Grande, E., Lachat, R., Dolezal, M., Bornschier, S. and Frey, T. (2008) *West European Politics in the Age of Globalization* (Cambridge: Cambridge University Press).

Mair, P. (2000) 'The Limited Impact of Europe on National Party Systems'. *West European Politics*, Vol. 23, No. 4, pp. 27–51.

Mair, P. (2013) 'Smaghi versus the Parties: Representative Government and Institutional Constraints'. In Schäffer, A. and Streeck, W. (eds) *Politics in the Age of Austerity* (Oxford: Polity), pp. 143–68.

Makszin, K., Medve-Bálint, G. and Bohle, D. (2020) 'North and South, East and West: Is it Possible to Bridge the Gap?' In Coman, R., Crespy, A. and Schmidt, V.A. (eds) *Governance and Politics in the Post-crisis European Union* (Cambridge: Cambridge University Press), pp. 335–57.

Matthijs, M. and MacNamara, K. (2015) 'The Euro Crisis' Theory Effect: Northern Saints, Southern Sinners, and the Demise of the Eurobond'. *Journal of European Integration*, Vol. 37, No. 2, pp. 229–45.

Mudde, C. and Kaltwasser, R. (2013) 'Exclusionary vs. Inclusionary Populism: Comparing Contemporary Europe and Latin America'. *Government and Opposition*, Vol. 48, No. 2, pp. 147–174.

Network/Counterbalance, B. (2019) 'Not Worth Celebrating Yet? The Investment Plan for Europe – A Critical Analysis of the Pilot Phase of the "Juncker Plan"'. Available online at: https://bankwatch.org/wp-content/uploads/2019/09/EFSI-final.pdf. Last accessed: 29 February 2020.

Organization for Economic Cooperation and Development (2017) 'Understanding the Socio-economic Divide in Europe'. Background Report. Available online at: https://www.oecd.org/els/soc/cope-divide-europe-2017-background-report.pdf. Last accessed: 29 February 2020.

Papadopoulos, Y. and Piattoni, S. (2019) 'The European Semester: Democratic Weaknesses as Limits to Learning'. *European Policy Analysis*. doi: 10.1002/epa2.1060.

Pierret, L. (2019) 'The Political Use of the Term 'Moral Hazard': Evidence from Policymakers of the Eurozone'. *Bruges Political Research Papers*. 78, 78. Available online at: https://www.coleurope.eu/fr/research-paper/political-use-term-moral-hazard-evidence-policymakers-eurozone. Last accessed: 15 July 2020.

Piketty, T. (2018) 'La couleur de la justice fiscale', *Le Monde,* 11 December 2018.

Sangiovanni, A. (2013) 'Solidarity in the European Union'. *Oxford Journal of Legal Studies*, Vol. 33, No. 2, pp. 213–41.

Schild, J. and Howarth, D. (2020) 'Fiscal Capacity Building in the Eurozone: Germany between the Hanseatic League Countries and France'. Paper Presented at the International Workshop, 'Furthering or Fighting Core State Power Integration? The Post-Maastricht Ambiguities of German EU Policy', Berlin, 24–25 June 2019.

Schmidt, V.A. (2014) 'Speaking to the Markets or to the People? A Discursive Institutionalist Analysis of the EU's Sovereign Debt Crisis'. *British Journal of Politics and International Relations*, Vol. 16, No. 1, pp. 188–209.

Schmidt, V.A. and Thatcher, M. (eds) (2013) *Resilient Liberalism in Europe's Political Economy* (Cambridge: Cambridge University Press).

Schmitt-Beck, R. (2017) 'The 'Alternative für Deutschland in the Electorate': Between Single-issue and Right-wing Populist Party'. *German Politics*, Vol. 26,No. 1, pp. 124–48.

Seikel, D. and Truger, A. (2019) 'The Blocked Completion of the European Monetary Union'. Report. 52.

Spire, A. (2019) ''Reformuler la question sociale'. In Confavruex, J. (ed.) *Le fond de l'air est jaune. Comprendre une révolte inédite* (Paris: Seuil), pp. 91–8.

Sweeney, R. and Wilson, R. (2018) 'Cherishing All Equally 2019: Inequality in Europe and Ireland'. Available online at: https://www.feps-europe.eu/attachments/publications/cherishing %20all%20equally%202019.pdf. Last accessed: 15 July 2020.

Vandenbroucke, F., Barnard, C. and De Baere, G. (eds) (2016) *A European Social Union after the Crisis* (Cambridge: Cambridge University Press).

Vanheuverzwijn, P. and Crespy, A. (2018) 'Macro-economic Coordination and Elusive Ownership in the European Union'. *Public Adminstration*, Vol. 96, No. 3, pp. 578–93.

Zeitlin, J. and Vanhercke, B. (2017) 'Socializing the European Semester: EU Social and Economic Policy Co-Ordination in Crisis and Beyond'. *Journal of European Public Policy*, Vol. 25, No. 2, pp. 149–74.

JCMS 2020 Volume 58. Annual Review. pp. 147–159   DOI: 10.1111/jcms.13103

The Impact of Brexit on Black Women, Children and Citizenship

IYOLA SOLANKE
School of Law, University of Leeds, Leeds, UK

Introduction

2019 is an important moment for thinking about the relationship between the EU and its citizens. Throughout the Brexit countdowns between 2016 and 2020, attention was paid to the impact of Brexit on adult EU citizens in the UK and adult UK citizens in the EU. An intersectional approach to citizenship highlights, however, another group enjoying citizenship rights under EU law – non-migrant EU infant citizens whose parents are non-EU nationals, predominantly black women from Africa, Asia and the Caribbean. These rights arose from the ruling in the *Zambrano* case of 2009 (C-34/09), where the CJEU established two key rights: (1) EU citizenship rights for non-migrant Member State nationals; (2) the right to residence to non-EU nationals in order to care for their children holding national and EU citizenship.

The importance of EU law for these infant EU citizens and their non-EU parents (Zambrano families) was overlooked during the Brexit period. Their interests were not discussed in Brussels, even though the UK government had started to erode their rights long before Brexit. They became targets of the Conservative 'hostile environment' policy. Stigmatized by the intersection of their race, gender and immigration status, national immigration law was used to deprive them of welfare rights in 2012, long before the EU referendum. Zambrano families were not mentioned in the Withdrawal Agreement and no special consideration was made to their interests. Through political *inaction* in both the UK and EU they lost their residency rights once the UK left the EU. Only in 2019 were these non-EU parents given the possibility to apply for residency rights through the UK European Union Settlement Scheme. However, concern remains about how these applications will be processed and reviewed in the Home Office.

Reflection on the marginalization of Zambrano families is important for both UK and EU citizenship rights. At the time of writing the rights given in EU law to the non-EU parents of black British citizens will automatically disappear at the end of the transition period on 31 December 2020. This intersectional lens highlights first, the racial and gendered meaning of citizenship, second, how EU citizenship is intertwined with national immigration law, and third, the long-term detrimental effect of Brexit for infant black British citizens and their families.

Intersectional Discrimination in the 'Hostile Environment'

The concept of intersectional discrimination (Crenshaw, 1989) adopts a synergistic approach (Solanke, 2011) to discrimination. Set within critical race feminism (Wing, 1997), this intersectional approach insists that anti-discrimination law recognize that inequality occurs in a synergistic manner rather than in neat categories that can be separated from each other. Synergy emphasizes co-determination and interdependence, whereby the component elements work together to create something new. Just as oxygen and hydrogen produce water not 'oxydrogen', the synergy in intersectional discrimination creates a new subject – black women (Solanke, 2017). As originally conceived, it entwined race and gender in 'historical, social and political context' (Aylward, 1999) to highlight the experience of discrimination by black women workers (Degraffenreid, 1977) in the wake (Sharpe, 2016) of white patriarchal employment practices.

The concept of intersectional discrimination can be used to highlight the precarious position of black and migrant women in the EU, in particular to a group known as the 'Zambrano Carers', a name derived from the case (2011) decided by the Court of Justice of the EU (CJEU) concerning EU citizenship. This seminal case gave black and migrant women from *beyond* the EU an opportunity to gain secure residency in the Member States as mothers and carers of EU citizens. Official data suggests that 57 per cent of the mothers and carers in the UK who gained residency rights in this way have Nigerian, Jamaican or Ghanaian nationality; 94 per cent of Zambrano carers are lone parents and of these only 21 per cent are men (79 per cent are women). One can safely conclude from this data that the majority of Zambrano families in the UK comprise black mothers from beyond the EU bringing up black British children alone. The interests of these children and their mothers was not considered in the run up to Brexit.

The erosion of protection given in EU law began long before Brexit and the EU Referendum. The 'hostile environment' was originally introduced in 2010 by Teresa May while she was Home Secretary under the Conservative–Liberal Democrat Coalition government. Her stated aim was to force migrants without permission to remain in the UK to leave, by making life in the country unbearable for them. The subsequent Immigration Act 2014 introduced a range of restrictions on access to housing, bank accounts and driving licences. In addition, the Home Office mounted a number of high-profile campaigns, such as Operation Vaken in 2013 (Home Office, 2013), which saw advertising billboards on vans with the words: 'In the UK illegally? Go home or face arrest' being driven around parts of London (Sherwin, 2013) with high black and minority ethnic (BME) populations. These included billboard advertising, leaflets and random identity check conducted by border officials at London Underground stations in areas with BME communities, where only persons who did not look white were stopped (Wright and Withnall, 2013). Many of those stopped were not immigrants but British citizens (see Solanke, 2017). While the campaign was cancelled after high public outcry and the threat of legal action, the hostile environment continued to evolve with legal reforms such as the Zambrano Amendments. These were introduced to limit the impact of the Zambrano decision and deepen the hostile environment to immigrants in the UK – where the Zambrano decision created a right to remain in EU law, the Zambrano Amendments in national immigration law removed access to welfare to facilitate this.

This contribution begins with discussion of the Zambrano case and the response to it by legislators and the judiciary in the UK. This analysis will demonstrate that EU citizenship rights of baby black Europeans were being eroded long before the EU referendum in 2016. In the context of the 'hostile environment to immigrants', Brexit deprived mothers of the right to residency and their children of equal citizenship. This was achieved by a cynical judicial approach to the EU principle of the 'genuine enjoyment' of EU citizenship and the refusal to prioritise the best interests of the child in EU human rights law. 2019 was a crucial year for EU citizenship rights. The EU Settlement Scheme was created to protect the residency of EU citizens in the UK and was amended only at the last minute to include the rights of Zambrano mothers in order to comply with international obligations on child welfare. However, given the difficulties of this scheme, it is questionable whether it will be helpful in the long run.

The Zambrano Case

Mr. Zambrano arrived in Belgium with his wife and child on a visa but immediately applied for asylum due to political persecution in Colombia. His application was rejected but given the genuine danger of torture in Colombia, the family was allowed to remain in Belgium. Mr. Zambrano appealed the decision and during the following 12 years found stable employment. Despite not having a work permit, he found a secure job with a company, Plastoria, that for five years paid his social security and employment insurance contributions.

In this time, he had two more children who by virtue of Belgian law against statelessness became Belgian citizens, and thereby EU citizens. Consequently, when the Belgian authorities considered the refusal to grant him unemployment benefit as a result of his irregular status, the issue had to be looked at both under national social security law and within the prism of rights granted to EU citizens under Articles 20 and 21 TFEU. The key question was whether Mr. Zambrano could rely on the citizenship rights of his children to enjoy a derived right of residence in Belgium. Historically under EU law such rights could only be derived from migrant infants; in this case the two children had remained in the Member State of which they were national. Under traditional EU citizenship law, the absence of a cross-border element would make this a 'wholly internal' situation.

The Commission and all eight intervening Member States – including the UK – unanimously agreed that this was a 'wholly internal' situation and as such beyond the scope of EU law. However, Advocate General (AG) Sharpston argued that persons should not be treated in the same way as goods and services – in *Zambrano* she argued that people focused citizenship rights differ conceptually from the free movement rights of economic goods. Taking *Rottman* and *Chen*, 2004 (C-200/02) as a new starting point, she argued that once nationality is granted to persons,

> ... the children [Jessica and Diego] became citizens of the Union and entitled to exercise the rights conferred on them as citizens, concurrently with their rights as Belgian nationals. They have not yet moved outside their own Member State. Nor, following his naturalisation, had Dr. Rottman. If the parents do not have a derivative right of residence and are required to leave Belgium, the children will, in all probability, have to leave with them. That would, in practical terms, place Diego and Jessica in a position capable of causing them to lose the status conferred [by their citizenship of the Union] and the rights attaching thereto.

The question of deportation of a parent thus fell within the ambit of EU law because children – even non-migrant children – cannot exercise their rights as Union citizens (specifically, their rights to move and to reside in any Member State) fully and effectively without their parents.

The Grand Chamber of the CJEU found in favour of Mr. Zambrano directly under Article 20 TFEU. Importantly, the CJEU did not draw on the Citizenship Directive in their reasoning because the Zambrano family were not the 'beneficiaries' envisaged in Article 3(1), namely they were not 'Union citizens who move to or reside in a Member State other than that of which they are a national... '. Recalling the division of responsibilities between the Union and the Member States, the Grand Chamber repeated the bold mantra declared in *Grzelczyk*, 2001 (C194/99) that 'citizenship of the Union is intended to be the fundamental status of nationals of the Member States.' This declaration forms the crux of the reasoning, for immediately thereafter the Chamber decides:

> In those circumstances, Article 20 TFEU precludes national measures which have the effect of depriving citizens of the Union of the genuine enjoyment of the substance of the rights conferred by virtue of their status as citizens of the Union. A refusal to grant a right of residence to a third country national with dependent minor children in the Member State where those children are nationals and reside, and also a refusal to grant such a person a work permit, has such an effect. This effect was assumed because firstly, refusal of a right of residence to Mr. Zambrano would result in a situation where the Union citizen, namely the child, would be compelled to leave the EU with their parents. Refusal of a work permit would have the same impact: 'if a work permit were not granted to such a person, he would risk not having sufficient resources to provide for himself and his family, which would also result in the children, citizens of the Union, having to leave the territory of the Union'. Such circumstances would deny the infants any enjoyment of the 'substance of the rights conferred on them by virtue of their status as citizens of the Union'.

The Grand Chamber thus concluded that Article 20 TFEU precludes a Member State from refusing a third country national upon whom his minor children, who are European Union citizens, are dependent, a right of residence in the Member State of residence and nationality of those children, and from refusing to grant a work permit to that third country national, in so far as such decisions deprive those children of the genuine enjoyment of the substance of the rights attaching to the status of European Union citizen. The CJEU was unanimous in determining that the rights of EU citizenship could be accessed by an infant, even in their Member State of birth. The case therefore extended the boundaries of EU citizenship beyond the limits set out in the earlier case of *Chen*, 2004. It also extended derived rights to the carers of such non-migrant EU citizens, giving them residency rights under EU law regardless of their status under national law (Dereci, 2016). It is the latter extension of rights that proved to be a step too far for the British Conservative government.

EU Citizenship Law in the UK: The Response to *Zambrano*

The Legislative Response

The Zambrano case demonstrates that even while a Member State of the European Union, the UK found ways to undermine the effect of EU Law in the UK. The CJEU decision was given as the Conservative British government implemented its 'hostile environment' policy. In 2012, the government introduced reforms to Immigration Law that specifically targeted 'Zambrano mothers'. Specifically, the government decided that non-European parents whose children are British citizens should be treated as any other non-British/

EU national lacking a lawful right to reside. Law was used to create an *unequal* right of residence for Zambrano parents and carers by blocking automatic access to basic welfare, which is a consequence of the case.

The Legislative Response saw the introduction of three Regulations (SI 2012/2587, 2012; SI 2012/2612, 2012; SI 2012/2588, 2012) designed to specifically exclude anybody residing on the basis of *Zambrano* from rights to social assistance that they would otherwise have as lawfully resident persons. In 2012, at the same time that the EEA Regulations 2006 implementing Citizenship Directive, 2004/38 (European Council, 2004) were amended to give effect to the *Zambrano* decision, the Coalition government introduced the Immigration (European Economic Area) (Amendment) (No.2) Regulations 2012 (the 'Zambrano Amendments'). Since then, Zambrano carers – those in work and those out of work – have been banned from key mainstream housing and welfare benefits under national law. The 'Amendment Regulations' exclude them from income-related benefits including income support, jobseekers allowance, employment allowance, pension credit, housing benefit, council tax benefit, child benefit and child tax credit.

The Zambrano Amendments were intentionally designed to exclude Zambrano carers from key mainstream benefits. This exclusion may have contributed to the disproportionate impact of COVID-19 on Black and minority ethnic communities across the UK. The Amendments raise questions not only about the ethics of excluding working migrants from income-related benefits, but also about race and citizenship given their impact on the childhood experiences and integration of a new generation of black British/EU citizens. As a result these families are stigmatized, including the British children. In other words, they transformed the hostile environment to immigrants into a hostile environment for (black) British citizens, creating a second class citizenship in law demarcated by race. As a result, these children will not receive entitlements such as free school meals, school uniforms or travel passes regardless of whether their parent works or not. Black British children and their parents thus become dependent for their survival upon emergency funding provided by local authorities using limited emergency powers in Section 17 of the Children Act 1989. This may be an effective deterrent to the use of this lawful status – those eligible to gain a right to residency under *Zambrano*, may not use it if they will thereby be condemning themselves and their families to destitution – but it also effectively disenfranchises a social group already stigmatized and marginalized (EHRC, 2019). If the parents are unequal residents the children must as a corollary be unequal citizens, not only in childhood but also into adolescence and potentially throughout adulthood. The Amendments tell these children that their lives do not matter.

The Judicial Response

The blanket ban on access mainstream welfare, regardless of work, introduced by the Zambrano Amendments was challenged in court, with judges being asked whether 'genuine enjoyment' requires more than just skeleton welfare that may leave both mother and a British citizen infant on the brink of poverty and destitution. In other words, does a borderline and unstable existence equate to *compulsion* to leave? This is becoming an increasingly relevant question.

The Judicial Response was to ultimately support the Amendments as lawful in a series of cases, culminating in the Supreme Court decision in *HC*, 2013 (EWHC 3874; UKSC

73). In so doing, courts confirmed that the lives of these infant black British citizens do not matter – their best interests were not a primary concern. It is noteworthy that during the many years of deliberation on Zambrano Amendments, at no point was a question referred to the CJEU.

In one of the first cases, *Harrison*, 2012 (EWCA Civ 1736), Elias LJ introduced in the standard *dicta* for understanding the Zambrano principle. Dismissing a broad approach to the CJEU ruling, he stated:

> ... The right of residence is a right to reside in the territory of the EU. It is not a right to any particular quality or life or to any particular standard of living. Accordingly, there is no impediment to exercising the right to reside if residence remains possible as a matter of substance, albeit that the quality of life is diminished (paragraph 67).

The Harrison *dicta* was repeated in all challenges to the Zambrano amendments. *Sanneh*, 2013 (EWHC 793) concerned a woman who arrived in the UK from Gambia in 2006 on a student visa. In September 2009 she had a daughter, Awa, who became a British citizen through her father. Her visa expired in December 2009 and was not extended due to withdrawal of family financial support. Awa's father abandoned his new family and shortly after her birth Sanneh became Awa's sole carer and as a result she struggled financially. When Sanneh finally received the benefits wrongly paid to Awa's father, she had a monthly income of £477 made up of child benefit, child tax credit and child support. She supplemented her income with short term loans and irregular payments from Awa's father but could not cover all of her monthly expenditure. She and Awa lived on food parcels. In June 2011, as the Zambrano Amendments prohibited her from working, she applied for income support, but was refused. Her application in July 2011 for interim payments was also refused. Her situation deteriorated in 2012: in January she was evicted and had to move into emergency housing; in April her child tax credit was withdrawn; in August her child benefit was withdrawn. She was then granted income support from 14 September 2012. However, as she was granted permission to work on 1 September 2012, income support was withdrawn on 8 November 2012. In January 2013, the original decision was set aside and remade due to an error on a point of law made by the First Tier Tribunal.

Sanneh argued that the denial of the right to work and access to child benefits gave rise to a situation where she would be forced to leave the United Kingdom due to lack of means, and in the absence of an alternative carer she would have to take her daughter with her – she and her child would be compelled to leave EU territory. However, Sanneh lost because she coped too well. Following Elias J, Hickinbottom J stated that *Zambrano* carer cases rest upon evidence of *absolute compulsion* to leave in the absence of the claimed rights, in this case child benefits. Yet Sanneh demonstrated that she had been able to survive without them. He noted her 'management and human resources skills' and concluded that '... all of the evidence points to the Claimant being absolutely determined to stay in the United Kingdom, and there being no realistic possibility of her leaving because of financial circumstances ...' Thus, he ruled that 'there was no realistic prospect of the Claimant being compelled to leave the United Kingdom' (paragraph 102). Ironically, she failed the *Zambrano/Harrison* test of compulsion because she had managed to survive desperate and precarious conditions without benefits for four years. This cynical approach continued in *HC (*EWHC 3874*)* and *Hines* (EWCA Civ 660), even though these cases also concerned the best interests of the child.

The Best Interests of the Infant Black British Citizen?

The Courts have held that the substance of the *Zambrano* right to reside remains intact even if the Zambrano carer is left destitute and thus unable to care for their child who is a British citizen. Zambrano carers were left in no doubt that while they had a right to reside, they had no right to expect support to provide safe and secure lives for their British citizen child. In effect they were seen and treated as de facto 'benefit tourists' (see ICF GHK and Miliue, 2013). For their children who are British citizens and differ from other British citizens only because their primary carer is not an EU national, it means they have no right to the quality of life guaranteed to their fellow citizens. Judges have been unsympathetic to arguments calling for consideration of the best interest of the child, even where this involves domestic violence.

HC arrived in the UK from Algeria in 2008 on a six-month visitors' visa. In 2010 she married Mr. H, a British national of Egyptian origin and they had two children. In October 2012, before the birth of her second child, she fled the marital home due to domestic violence. She sought refuge with her sister in Oldham but could not stay there in the long term. As she was financially dependent upon her husband and had no resources of her own, she was forced to approach Oldham Council for assistance in November 2012. This was initially refused due to the Zambrano Amendments but eventually she was granted emergency housing, and sparse financial assistance under s.17 of the Children Act 1989 – from August 2013, she and her children were placed in interim housing in a two-bedroom accommodation and given £55 per week for food and £25.50 for bills.

HC challenged the legality of the ban on the basis that as the third country national parent of two British children resident in the UK, she should enjoy EU law rights to reside and work in the UK, derived from her children's rights to reside as EU citizens. As previously, Supperstone J found the blanket refusal of welfare benefits legal – it did not compel a Zambrano carer to leave the EU – and in response to the argument that Article 24 of the EU Charter called for the best interests of the child to be considered, he stated:

> there is no general requirement under EU law for Member States to provide parents with a particular level of support, regardless of their right to reside. The Defendants are, in my view, entitled to make legislation which properly reflects the rights of Zambrano carers and their children as a matter of EU law (EWHC 3874, 70).

Supperstone J referred regularly to *Sanneh*, citing in particular Hickinbottom's literal approach to the compulsion to leave. Compulsion would practically only arise through deportation or by 'force of economic necessity (for example by having insufficient resources to provide for his EU children because the state refuses him a work permit)' (paragraph 39). It did not arise from a ban on access to welfare benefits. He recognised no right to a particular quality of parenting as a Zambrano citizen, only an acknowledgement of its existence. Zambrano children, as stigmatized citizens, should not expect full enjoyment of the Marshallian trilogy of social, political and civil citizenship (Marshall, 1950). It is thus questionable whether partial enjoyment of citizenship is *genuine* enjoyment.

Vos went even further in Hines, 2014 (EWCA Civ 660) where he explicitly stated that the 'best interest of the child' was not a priority. Maureen Hines, a Jamaican citizen without permission to remain in the UK, was refused housing assistance despite being mother to a five-year old British boy, Brandon. Lambeth Council decided that even if the refusal caused Hines to leave the UK, Brandon's father, who had an EU right to permanent residence in the UK, could – and partially did – look after him. Hines unsuccessfully appealed Lambeth's decision but two specific questions went to the Court of Appeal, on citizenship and the best interests of the child.

The questions concerned the standard of review to be applied: should a higher level of review apply given the engagement of Article 20 TFEU? Secondly, what is the correct test when considering whether the removal of the mother jeopardized the continued residence of the EU citizen: the EU Charter 'best interests' of the child or the UK statutory test of practicality laid out in Regulation 15A (4A) (c) of the Immigration Regulations? Even if the latter, it was argued that as Regulation 15A (4A)(C) was introduced to implement EU law (the Zambrano principle), Lambeth's decision as per Art 51 CFR had to take into consideration EU human rights law, especially Articles 7 (respect for private and family life) and 24 (rights of the child) CFR. The correct question was therefore the best interests test that considered the fundamental rights of the child to have regular contact with her parents and enjoy family life.

Vos negated both questions. First, the relevance of Article 20 TFEU did not affect the intensity of the review and secondly, the engagement of Article 20 TFEU via Regulation 15A (4A)(C) did not call for a different test to be applied. He ruled that

> .... The reviewer was not obliged to consider Brandon's interests as paramount, though his interests were indeed to be taken into account as in fact happened (Hines EWCA Civ 660, 25).

Vos agreed that the removal of a parent would normally be against the best interests of the child and therefore clearly contrary to Article 24(3) of the EU CFR. However, he stated that the *Harrison* test meant that Brandon's welfare 'cannot be the paramount consideration because that would be flatly inconsistent with the statutory test' (Hines, EWCA Civ 660, 22) of whether he would be unable to reside in the UK if his mother left. Hines would only be entitled to housing assistance if refusal compelled Brandon to depart the United Kingdom. As Brandon's father was deemed to be 'responsible and caring' (Hines, EWCA Civ 660. 29). this would not be so – the boy could live with him. Thus, the substance of Brandon's EU right to residence was not impaired: he could in theory be cared for by his father, even if in practice this was not in his best interests due to his father's 12-hour shifts at work. His father was subsequently made redundant – putting his ability to *provide* for Brandon in question.

An appeal to *HC* UKSC 73, 2017 was heard by the Supreme Court in June 2017 (decision delivered in November 2017). The UKSC relied upon the post- *Zambrano* cases (*Dereci*, 2017 EUECJ C-165/14; S, Case C-304/14) and the *dicta* of Elias LJ in *Harrison* to support the conclusion that while the principle of residence was a narrow one based in EU law, entitlement to and levels of benefit were a matter for national law [9–15]. The CJEU decision in *Ymeraga* was called upon to confirm that the exercise of derived rights are not an implementation of EU law for the purposes of Article 51 CFR (*Ymreaga*, C-87/12, 41–43, 2013). Despite the absence of any strong evidence, in the hostile environment the UKSC supported the government's justifications for the Zambrano Amendments, and agreed that they fell within the wide margin of discretion allowed to national governments under both EU and ECHR law.

The UKSC focused on the immigration status of HC rather than her parental status or the status of her child. Sadly, British nationality did not improve the situation of the non-EU mother; rather non-EU nationality worsened the situation of the British child – the child was disenfranchised, becoming in effect a third country national like its mother. Only Supreme Court President Lady Hale focused on the rights of the child, making a link between the treatment of the mother and the life-experience of the British child. Her dissent centred the affected British infants:

> I have found this a very troubling case. It is not a case about adults' rights. It is a case about children's rights – specifically the right of these two very young British children to remain living in their own country and to have the support which they need in order to enable them to do so. Self-evidently they need the support of their mother in the shape of the care which she is able to give them. But they also need support in the shape of a place to live and enough to live on (paragraph 39).

She also stressed the distinction between Zambrano carers and other non-EU citizens:

> Yet *Zambrano* carers are not like any other third country nationals. They have British (or other EU citizen) children dependent upon them (paragraph 41).

Finally, she was also the only judge to raise the fundamental issue overlooked by the government in its relentless pursuit of hostility – 'how these children would be supported if the parent looking after them was unable to work, whether because of the demands of child care or for any other good reason' (paragraph 41).

Although she ultimately agreed with the majority that the situation of *Zambrano* carers and their children falls beyond EU social security law, Lady Hale saw a possibility that EU law was engaged. Having blocked the impact of the judgement with the Zambrano Amendments, Section 17 of the Children's Act (1989) was the administrative route by which the *Zambrano* principle in EU law was implemented domestically, EU human rights law, in particular Article 21 of the Charter – might be engaged. This is particularly important for the analysis presented here, as Article 21 CFR states:

> Any discrimination based on *any ground such as* sex, race, colour, ethnic or social origin, genetic features, language, religion or belief, political or any other opinion, membership of a national minority, property, birth, disability, age or sexual orientation shall be prohibited.Lady Hale suggested discrimination arose due to the arbitrary creation of two types of infant British citizens – one who is cared for by a parent who is a third country national with no recourse to public funding and another cared for by a non-Zambrano status parent with full entitlement to mainstream benefits and social assistance. The stigmatization of the former due to the accident of birth to a non-EU national parent would constitute discrimination.

Brexit Negotiations and the Withdrawal Agreement 2019

As mentioned in the Introduction, the rights given in EU law to the non-EU parents of black British citizens will disappear when the transposition period expires on 31

December 2020. As the 'hostile environment' was originally introduced by Teresa May while she was Home Secretary, it is unsurprising that as Prime Minister her government decided during Brexit not to 'goldplate'[1] the protection for Zambrano families set out in EU law (Home Office, 2018). During her tenure as Home Secretary, May had pushed for the restrictive approach to the Zambrano families: for example in *Yekini*, she argued for a compelling reason to explain why the father of an infant British citizen could not assume full parental responsibility for his care (*Yekini, EWHC*, 2014).

Brexit was used as an opportunity to strip the Zambrano status of any value. This was easy to do as given their marginalised status in society and lack of political voice, the situation of these families was ignored by politicians, the mainstream media and mainstream campaigns. Their status was not discussed during the Brexit negotiations or during ratification by the European Parliament. It was inevitable therefore that the rights of these mothers and children were not protected in the interim Joint Report of December 2017 or the final Withdrawal Agreement (WA) of October 2019.

Paragraph 9 of the Joint Report substantially retained pre-Brexit rights for migrant citizens after Brexit, setting out that EU citizenship rights can be enjoyed by

> Union citizens who in accordance with Union law legally reside in the UK, and UK nationals who in accordance with Union law legally reside in an EU27 Member State by the specified date, as well as their family members as defined by Directive, 2004/38/EC who are legally resident in the host State by the specified date, fall within the scope of the Withdrawal Agreement.

Paragraph 10 secures rights to non-discrimination on grounds of nationality only for these groups of Union citizens and their respective family members. Those who do not fall within these categories – non-migrant EU and UK citizens – have no access to such rights. Paragraph 14 explicitly states that,

> 'The right to be joined by family members not covered by paragraphs 12 and 13 after the specified date will be subject to national law'.

As the Zambrano infants are UK citizens residing in the UK, and therefore not migrant EU citizens, they do not fall under the Citizenship Directive. Neither the UK nor the EU specified what rights they will have. As concluded by the House of Commons Home Affairs Committee Report (2018, paragraph 21), this group was 'ignored during the first phase of negotiations'.

They were also ignored in the final stages of negotiations. The preamble of the WA mentions only Union citizens and UK nationals and their families who had 'exercised free movement rights' – again the infant UK nationals of Zambrano families are not covered by this as they have not exercised free movement rights. Chapter 1, Art 10–22, of the WA clarifies that its provisions only apply to migrant EU/UK citizens and their families. It was only in the dying embers of the May administration that there was a positive change in national policy: the EU Settlement Scheme (EUSS), which came into force in January 2019, was extended in June 2019 to these women whose residency is also dependent upon EU law (Home Office, 2020). This extension came about as a result of two specific duties

---

[1] Member States have discretion to provide more generous provisions in national law than that set out in EU law. This is known as 'gold-plating'.

in national and international law, involving the best interests of the child. First, Section 55 of the Borders, Citizenship and Immigration Act 2009 obliges the government to have regard to 'the need to safeguard and promote the welfare of a child under the age of 18 in the UK'. Second, Article 3 of the UN Convention on the Rights of the Child stipulates that the child's best interests must be a primary consideration in immigration cases.

In the EUSS, arrangements for Zambrano carers now mirror those for other EU nationals in the UK: settled status will be granted as long as the applicant can demonstrate compliance with the *Zambrano* requirements for a full five years. Even in the absence of compliance, an argument can be made for settled status if the person has acted as the primary carer of a British child for five consecutive years. However, it would be naïve to imagine the Home Office will look favourably upon their applications for settled status. The only option to improve their situation is a challenge to the Withdrawal Agreement, on the basis that the EU Commission breached the EU Charter by failing to provide for these mothers and their families in the Withdrawal Agreement. This is highly unlikely, given both Brexit fatigue and the COVID-19 pandemic.

Lady Hale was the only judge to raise the fundamental issue overlooked by the government in its relentless pursuit of hostility – 'how these children would be supported if the parent looking after them was unable to work, whether because of the demands of child care or for any other good reason.' (HC UKSC 73, 41). This question has implications for the UK but also more broadly for the idea of EU citizenship in a post-Brexit world.

Conclusion

Brexit has fulfilled the British government aim to deprive Zambrano carers – black and migrant women who are mothers to British citizen children, or carers to adult British nationals – of their right to residence in in the UK, as set out in EU law. However, this has also jeopardised the citizenship rights of those they look after. It is clear that no consideration was given to the impact of Brexit upon these children during the negotiation phase. The rights of these citizens were also not the focus of any campaigns or discussions during or after Brexit.

The loss of these rights could have been avoided if the EU had paid attention to all of EU citizenship law and the rights of the child set out in EU human rights law: Article 24 CFR says that:

> 1. Children shall have the right to such protection and care as is necessary for their well-being. They may express their views freely. Such views shall be taken into consideration on matters which concern them in accordance with their age and maturity. 2. In all actions relating to children, whether taken by public authorities or private institutions, the child's best interests must be a primary consideration. 3. Every child shall have the right to maintain on a regular basis a personal relationship and direct contact with both his or her parents, unless that is contrary to his or her interests.

However, given the judicial deference to the legislator, it is perhaps unsurprising that the EU legislator also ignored these infant citizens. By limiting negotiations to the Citizenship Directive alone, the EU negotiators in the Commission have arguably breached EU law and effectively helped the British government to deepen and extend the hostile environment in the UK. What does this tell us about the direction of travel – in the next phase, will the EU negotiator stand up for citizenship or indeed any other rights to be lost through Brexit?

COVID-19 has answered the question raised by Lady Hale on support for the children if the parent is unable to work – if nearly 25% of black mothers struggle to feed their children (compared to 19% of white mothers), the situation will be even worse for Zambrano mothers with no recourse to basic welfare (Fawcett Society, 2020). Access to the EUSS has changed little – as before Brexit, the Zambrano mothers and their British children remain in a precarious position. It is questionable whether this action of an EU institution is compatible with EU human rights law, as set down in the EU Charter of Fundamental Rights. In the absence of legal action before the CJEU to challenge the Withdrawal Agreement, it is unlikely that there will be any justice for the Zambrano families. However, even without the COVID 19 pandemic sweeping the globe, such action is hard to imagine.

References

Aylward, C. A. (1999) 'An Intersectional Approach to Discrimination. Addressing Multiple Grounds in Human Rights Claims'. Discussion Paper, Ontario Human Rights Commission.

Catherine Zhu and Man Levette Chen v Secretary of State for the Home Department (2004) 'Case C-200/02, ECR I-9925'.

Children's Act 1989 c.41 https://www.legislation.gov.uk/ukpga/1989/41/contents

Crenshaw, K. (1989) 'Demarginalising the Intersection of Race and Sex: A Black Feminist Critique of Antidiscrimination Doctrine, Feminist Theory and Antiracial Politics'. *University of Chicago Legal Forum*, Iss. 1, Art. 8.

DeGraffenreid v. General Motors Assembly Division, St. Louis (1977) '558 F.2d 480, 8th Cir'.

Dereci, Rendón Marin v Administración del Estado (Judgment: Citizenship of the Union) (2016) 'EUECJ C- 165/14; (2017) QB 495'.

European Council (2004) 'Directive 2004/38/EC of the European Parliament and of the Council of 29 April 2004 on the right of citizens of the Union and their family members to move and reside freely within the territory of the Member States amending Regulation (EEC) No 1612/68 and repealing Directives 64/221/EEC, 68/360/EEC, 72/194/EEC, 73/148/EEC, 75/34/EEC, 75/35/EEC, 90/364/EEC, 90/365/EEC and 93/96/EEC (Text with EEA relevance)'.

EHRC (2019) Is Britain Fairer? 2018 Report. https://www.equalityhumanrights.com/en/britain-fairer

Fawcett Society (2020) s. https://www.fawcettsociety.org.uk/news/impact-on-bame-women-un-equal-pressures-at-work-and-home

Harrison v. Secretary of State for the Home Department (2012) 'EWCA Civ 1736'.

HC v Secretary of State for Work and Pensions (2013) 'EWHC 3874 (Admin)'.

Hines v London Borough of Lambeth (2014) 'EWCA Civ 660'.

HM Government (2019) Agreement on the Withdrawal of the United Kingdom of Great Britain and Northern Ireland from the European Union and European Atomic Energy Community. 19 October 2019. https://www.gov.uk/government/publications/new-withdrawal-agreement-and-political-declaration

Home Office (2013) Operation Vaken: Evaluation Report. https://assets.publishing.service.gov.uk/government/uploads/system/uploads/attachment_data/file/254411/Operation_Vaken_Evaluation_Report.pdf

Home Office (2020) EU Settlement Scheme: A Person with a Zambrano right to reside. Version 3.0. https://assets.publishing.service.gov.uk/government/uploads/system/uploads/attachment_data/file/865751/eu-settlement-scheme-person-with-a-zambrano-right-to-reside-v3.0-gov-uk.pdf

House of Commons Home Affairs Committee (2018) 'Home Office Delivery of Brexit; Immigration' 3rd Report of Session 2017-19 https://publications.parliament.uk/pa/cm201719/cmselect/cmhaff/421/421.pdf

ICF GHK and Miliue (2013) A fact finding analysis on the impact on the Member States' social security systems of the entitlements of non-active intra-EU migrants to special non-contributory cash benefits and healthcare granted on the basis of residence. Available at: https://ec.europa.eu/employment_social/empl_portal/facebook/20131014%20GHK%20study%20web_EU%20migration.pdf

Joint Report from the Negotiators of the EU and UK, 8 December 2017, Available at: https://assets.publishing.service.gov.uk/government/uploads/system/uploads/attachment_data/file/665869/Joint_report_on_progress_during_phase_1_of_negotiations_under_Article_50_TEU_on_the_United_Kingdom_s_orderly_withdrawal_from_the_European_Union.pdf

Marshall, T.H. (1950) *Citizenship and Social Class* (London: Pluto Press).

R (on the application of HC) (Appellant) v Secretary of State for Work and Pensions and others (Respondents) (2017) 'UKSC 73'.

Rudy Grzelczyk v Centre public d'aide sociale d'Ottignies-Louvain-la-Neuve (2001) 'C 184/99'.

Ruiz Zambrano v. Office national de l'emploi (2011) 'Case C-34/09, EU:C:2011:124'.

S v Secretary of State for the Home Department (Case C-304/14) (2017) 'QB 558; (2017) 2 WLR 180'.

Sanneh v Home Secretary for Work and Pensions (2013) 'EWHC 793 (Admin)'.

Sharpe, C. (2016) *In the Wake. On Blackness and Being* (Durham, NC: Duke University Press).

Sherwin, A. (2013) 'Controversial 'Go Home' Vans Persuaded Just 11 Illegal Immigrants to Leave Britain'. *The Independent*, 31 October 2013. https://www.independent.co.uk/news/uk/politics/controversial-go-home-vans-persuaded-just-11-illegal-immigrants-to-leave-britain-8916287.html

Solanke, I. (2011) 'Infusing the Silos in the Equality Act 2010 with Synergy'. *Industrial Law Journal*, Vol 40, pp. 336–58.

Solanke, I. (2017) *Discrimination as Stigma: A Theory of Anti-Discrimination Law* (Oxford: Hart).

The Allocation of Housing and Homelessness (Eligibility) (England) (Amendment) Regulations (2012) 'SI 2012/2588'.

The Child Benefit and Child Tax Credit (Miscellaneous Amendments) Regulations 2012 (SI 2012/2612)

The Social Security (Habitual Residence) (Amendment) Regulations (2012) 'SI 2012/2587'.

Wing, A.K. (1997) *Critical Race Feminism. A Reader* (New York: New York University Press).

Wright, O. and Withnall, A. (2013) 'Doreen Lawrence Pledges to Condemn "Racial Profiling" Spot Checks in the House of Lords'. *The Independent*, 2 August 2013. http://www.independent.co.uk/news/uk/politics/exclusive-doreen-lawrence-pledges-to-condemn-racial-profiling-spot-checks-in-the-house-of-lords-8742754.html.

Yekini, R. (2014) (on the Application of) v London Borough of Southwark EWHC 2096 (Admin).

Ymeraga v Ministre du Travail, de l'Emploi et de l'Immigration (Case C-87/12) (2013) '3 CMLR 33'.

JCMS 2020 Volume 58. Annual Review. pp. 160–172   DOI: 10.1111/jcms.13070

A Decade of Crisis in the European Union: Lessons from Greece*

ALEXIA KATSANIDOU[1] and ZOE LEFKOFRIDI[2]
[1]GESIS – Leibniz Institute for the Social Sciences & University of Cologne, Cologne [2]University of Salzburg, Sazburg

Introduction: How Greece Became the Black Sheep of the Eurozone

In 2004 few could imagine Greece on the brink of state bankruptcy. Greece featured in the global news as the proudly successful host of the Olympic Games, it had successfully joined the Euro and was enjoying economic growth. This euphoria would end with the global financial crisis that followed the 2008 Lehman Brothers' collapse.

When the private rating agency Standard & Poor's downgraded Greek government bonds to junk status in 2010 the eurozone was ill-prepared to deal with it. Eurozone membership had given countries with high inflation records, like Greece, the opportunity to borrow at a favourable interest rate to fund their current account deficits. Eurozone members initially perceived Greece's troubles not as 'European' but as 'domestic' (Lefkofridi and Schmitter, 2015). The Greek crisis was diagnosed as being caused by domestic factors, such as low competitiveness, low revenues, high government spending and rent-seeking (Axt, 2010). Dismissing both the role played by governments and banks in countries other than Greece and the global context (Flassbeck, 2012; Krugman, 2012), discussions raged about lending to 'lazy' and 'corrupt' Greeks, who had been living 'beyond their means' (Endres, 2010; Jonker-Hoffrén, 2013).

When market confidence in the bonds of other eurozone members (Irish, Italian, Portuguese and Spanish) started declining as well, these countries were quick to reassure both markets and their eurozone partners that they were not 'another Greece' (Wachman, 2010). In this context, country differences were reduced to 'cultural characteristics and habits', as reflected in stereotypes of laziness, non-productivity, corruption, wasteful spending and lying (Van Vossole, 2016). A new acronym for a group of troubled countries – Portugal, Ireland, Italy, Greece and Spain – entered public discourse: 'PIIGS'. In the meantime, a huge market of credit default swaps had developed, in which speculators treated sovereign public debt as if it were equivalent to private corporate debt. In denial of their interdependence that necessitated solidarity, eurozone leaders opted to attribute blame to minimize electoral costs at home. By 2011, the eurozone had become deeply divided and the Euro – the second strongest currency in the world – fell hostage to the domestic politics of its member states.

A potential Greek bankruptcy was dangerous for the European banks that held most of the Greek debt, which would then need to be bailed out with taxpayers' money. Given power asymmetries, however, non-indebted eurozone members had more space for

* The authors would like to thank Yevhen Voronin for his invaluable help as research assistant at GESIS and the enriching feedback of the editors of the Annual Review.

manoeuvre and a higher capacity to exercise pressure at the EU-level negotiations (Schimmelfennig, 2015). Greece's exit from the eurozone was portrayed as a worse choice than surrendering sovereignty and, at the same time, as one that would incur heavy economic losses. Bailout deals were thus presented as an act of solidarity towards crisis-ridden countries, but in fact they placed most of the financial burden for saving European banks on the public budgets of debtor countries like Greece. For all countries in need of financial help, including Greece, responsibility – as defined by the creditors – was the condition for receiving the expected pay-offs (loans). Financial help was offered at very high interest rates (thus generating high profits in creditor countries) and made the release of each portion of the loan conditional on the implementation of very concrete domestic market reforms and harsh austerity measures. By signing memoranda of understanding (MoUs), indebted countries' governments surrendered their sovereignty and hence severely constrained their own – and their successors' – repertoire of policy action (Alonso, 2014). This loss of sovereignty was legitimized by moral arguments about the misbehaviour of the indebted countries and their populations (Van Vossole, 2016).

The duration of this extraordinary period in modern Greek history can be clearly signposted by two events milestones. The crisis started with the dramatic appeal of the Greek Prime Minister George Papandreou (of the Panhellenic Socialist Movement [PASOK]) for financial rescue in April 2010 from Kastellorizo, the most remote Greek island facing the Turkish coast. This symbolized Greece's vulnerability at its eastern borders and highlighted the security dimension of a potential economic failure (and consequently, international isolation). The alleged end of this crisis was officially marked with the announcement of Prime Minister Kyriakos Mitsotakis (New Democracy [ND]) about the closure of the International Monetary Fund's (IMF) offices in Athens. The assumption in the media was that after reaching this milestone Greece is now back to normality.

The question is how much truth the assumption contains. According to IMF's Poul Thomsen (2019) ten years later, the economic outcome of the MoU therapy has been worse than anticipated: GDP per capita is still 22 per cent below the pre-crisis level, and continued to drop until 2015 as a result of the MoUs, a treatment hardly better than the malady itself. It is expected to take another 15 years, until 2034, for Greece to return to pre-crisis levels.[1] What are the consequences for society and politics and what are the lessons to be learned?

I. The Social Impact of Austerity Solutions to the Crisis

The motto of the crisis was 'there is no alternative' to austerity. The application of this doctrine to Greece meant radical cuts in public spending, the significant deterioration of social services and the re-shaping of care (Vaiou, 2016). In the case of health care, the MoU-induced changes included the reduction of public health care provision combined with a rise in the cost of services, thus impacting on access, equity and service quality (Petmesidou, 2019). This new reality affected disproportionally vulnerable social groups that rely on state services; namely, the poor, women, migrants, children, the elderly and

---

[1]This calculation is based on the assumption that no other major crisis would hit the country – an assumption currently challenged by the Covid-19 pandemic.

people with special needs (Kokaliari, 2018; Rotarou and Sakellariou, 2019). To illustrate, the relative gap in access to care between the richest and poorest population groups increased almost tenfold (Karanikolos and Kentikelenis, 2016). The elderly among the poor have shifted towards less healthy behaviour and score worse on a lifestyle health determinant index (Foscolou *et al.,* 2017).

Austerity-based labour market reforms, such a reduction in salaries and the minimum wage, the weakening of trade unions and of labour protection and the violations of trade union and collective bargaining rights, led to the deterioration of working and living conditions (International Labour Organization, 2012; Papadopoulos, 2019). Both men and women sought and accepted work in the informal sector for undeclared income and pay (Papageorgiou and Petousi, 2018, p. 155). It should be noted that in Greece, despite women's increasing participation in the labour force, their work tends to be perceived as secondary (auxiliary) to that of men, who are expected to be the major breadwinner (Karamessini, 2013). One could thus argue that the impact of the crisis has been more severe for men, who occupied a privileged position in the labour market and tried to keep their jobs at any cost (such as through wage reductions) as the lack of employment signifies they have failed to fulfil their role (Papageorgiou and Petousi, 2018, pp. 155–6). As job precarity and job loss became the new norm they were accompanied by an upward trend in attempted suicides in the Greek capital, where almost half of the population resides (Stavrianakos *et al.,* 2014). Besides depression and anxiety, violence in the cities rose as well, including violations of women's fundamental rights (Kokaliari, 2018; Vaiou, 2016).

At the time of writing, Greece has the highest unemployment rate per capita in the EU, followed by Spain and Italy. The impact of the crisis on employment has been not only tremendous but also persistent, affecting all age groups. Young people, however, and especially those with low individual educational capital and a low family income have been the hardest hit by the crisis (Papadakis *et al.,* 2020). Lack of prospects and fruitless job-seeking, in turn, have decreased the trust of young people in political institutions, thus increasing their political alienation (Papadakis *et al.,* 2015, p. 67).

To survive, the indebted Greek state still provides some social services but demands very high taxes to finance the debt. In turn, high unemployment renders taxes unaffordable. Greeks nowadays even prefer to decline real estate inheritance – in a break from the tradition of providing social and economic security for their children: the bricks and mortar that once represented kinship and roots now signify a burden (Knight, 2018, p. 31). The desire for disinheritance not only disrupts an established cultural order but it also leads to the redistribution of land and property from households to foreign and Greek investors. As a result, the numbers of have-nots increase, and so does the gap between the poor and the wealthy. This, in turn, has political repercussions.

II. The Political Dimension of the Crisis

In Greece, the two-party competition for the government has been nurtured by a complex electoral system called reinforced proportional representation (PR). This name is misleading because what the Greek system 'reinforces' is not proportionality but big parties. By granting a generous bonus to the party that comes first in the votes (50 out of 300 seats), the system manufactures majorities that have consistently produced single-party cabinets since the establishment of the Third Hellenic Republic in 1974. Thanks to this law, two major Greek parties alternated in power up until the crisis: the ND, a centre-right christian democratic party, and PASOK, a centre-left social democratic party. The two parties' combined share of the vote has been about 80 per cent throughout the 30-year period preceding the crisis. All other parties remain in permanent opposition, as reinforced PR renders them utterly irrelevant for forming a government.

At the beginning of the economic crisis in 2009 this firmly rooted party system seemed robust and was able to absorb the first signs of discontent. It would, however, be shaken by the earthquake elections of 2012 (Teperoglou and Tsatsanis, 2014), which generated increasing levels of volatility and the fragmentation of the party system. New parties and splinters from established organizations tried to voice popular opposition to austerity, thus giving voters the opportunity to throw the 'rascals out' (Nezi, 2012). Though the essence of the Greek electoral rules (the reinforcement of big parties) remained unchanged from 2009–19, we observed a complete de-alignment of voters that is breaking down the party system and changing the traditions of government formation (Verney, 2014). After a technocratic government and two elections (May and June 2012), in January 2015, Greek voters brought to power the Coalition of the Radical Left (Syriza), a formerly marginal alliance of small, radical left organizations (Lefkofridi and Nezi, 2019). As seen in Figure 1, the crisis therefore tells a story of de-alignment and realignment and of the reshaping of the political space for parties and voters. This mirrors political instability at the government level: during the period 2009–19 the country was ruled by as many as nine different governments, which included six elected and three non-elected cabinets.

Figure 1: Party Performance, Electoral Volatility and Effective Number of Parties in Greece 2009–19.

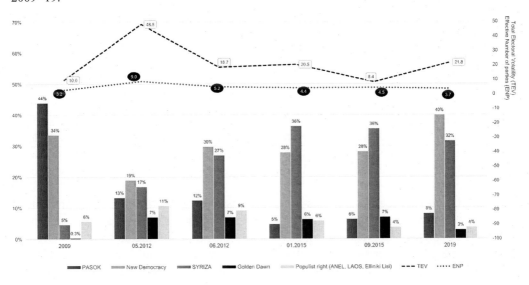

III. A New Division Line?

Historically, the key division in Greek politics was mainly along the left–right dimension, which was flexible in its meaning but stable as the strongest predictor of voter choice (Freire and Lobo, 2005). This changed with the signing of the MoU and the austerity measures imposed. At the beginning of the crisis, like the leaders at the EU level, who failed to agree on a *European* course of action, the leaders of established Greek parties failed to reach consensus on the *national* course of action; namely, to unify behind the MoU's programme or agree on an alternative path (Gemenis and Nezi, 2015). Unlike Portugal or Ireland (Mair, 2013), the major players of the Greek political scene, PASOK and ND, initially represented opposing sides of the MoU debate, enhancing its politicization. PASOK chose the route of accepting MoU and austerity, which inevitably alienated large parts of its constituency.

Though the MoU's spirit resonated well with large parts of ND's ideology, its leader chose to oppose it, even ousting the single ND deputy who deviated from the official anti-MOU line in 2010. By avoiding being classified as in favour of MoU it sought to optimize votes in the upcoming election, which is the path to executive power in disproportional electoral systems (Lefkofridi and Nezi, 2019). PASOK's PM George Papandreou's 2011 announcement of his plan to hold a referendum on the bilateral loan agreement between Greece and its lenders led to the fall of his government, followed by technocratic and caretaker cabinets. Even though ND officially supported Papademos' technocratic government of 'national unity' (11 November 2011–16 May 2012), ND leader Samaras continued to employ his fierce anti-MoU rhetoric.

However, when Prime Minister Papademos negotiated the second MoU in February 2012, Samaras committed to implementing it (European Commission, 2012). This was after external pressure to show 'responsibility' (as defined by the creditors), inter alia, from his partners in the European People's Party, with whom he would have to negotiate to win the election. His U-turn on the issue of MoU was sealed by the ousting of 21 deputies who diverged from the official, now pro-MoU, line.

PASOK's demise and ND's compromise created an optimal opportunity structure for new challengers. Support for or opposition to the MoU was by 2012 the most prominent division in the elections (Dinas and Rori, 2013). This was reinforced by the fact that economic issues could no longer function as valence issues – economic voting in the traditional sense simply could not function as no voters offered a positive sociotropic evaluation of the economy and took a stand on the issue (Nezi and Katsanidou, 2014). Among political parties, support for the MoU was not structured along the left–right dimension, and a new cross-cutting division became salient (Gemenis and Nezi, 2015). This dimension captured positions towards economic policies and reforms and correlated very strongly with pro or anti-EU positions (Katsanidou and Otjes, 2015). This created a new political space were both left and right-wing parties could position themselves for or against the MoU.

For left anti-MoU parties such as Syriza, the issue of austerity was most prominent. For right-wing anti-MoU parties, such as ANEL (Independent Greeks, a patriotic spinoff from ND (Gemenis and Nezi, 2015), sovereignty played a significant role. PASOK was attacked on both sides for signing the first MoU. By positioning itself as a pro-MoU party it had not only surrendered Greek sovereignty but also its raison d' être as a leftist party.

© 2020 The Authors. JCMS: Journal of Common Market Studies published by University Association for Contemporary European Studies and John Wiley & Sons Ltd

In contrast, anti-MoU parties profited electorally from their positions, as PASOK and (eventually also) ND were pro-EU and pro-MoU (Vasilopoulou, 2018). By participating actively in the demonstrations against both PASOK's (2010–12) and ND's (2012–15) MoUs (Tsakatika and Eleftheriou, 2013), Syriza became the authoritative voice of voter discontent with established parties and MoUs, thus meeting the voters demands spot on (Tsakatika, 2016).

The powerful bipartisanism of PASOK and ND crumbled as a result of the crisis for two main reasons. On the one hand, PASOK and ND, which had governed alternately since the restoration of the Hellenic Republic, were linked to voters through party patronage. MoU constraints left little margin for manoeuvre and there was almost nothing left they could offer to voters, which broke their patronage links (Afonso, 2013). On the other hand, the clarity of responsibility provided in disproportional systems with single-party governments makes the attribution of blame easier, thus making the government more vulnerable to challengers. The party that signed the first MoU (PASOK) was seen as the main culprit for the crisis and its management (Capelos and Exadaktylos, 2017). The way the crisis was handled by governing political parties and their challengers intensified three phenomena: the rise of the extreme right, euroscepticism and populism.

IV. The Extreme Right in Greece: From Zero to Hero and Back?

The way the eurozone crisis was handled at the EU level generated unique opportunities for political entrepreneurs all around Europe. In particular, the salience of cultural arguments and nation-bashing based on cultural stereotypes (Van Vossole, 2016) presented unique opportunities for entrepreneurs on the right-wing pole of the political spectrum.

In the Greek case, the failure of mainstream parties to absorb the divisions led to a new dimension of contestation, whereby opposition was articulated in both economic (austerity) and cultural (national identity) terms. Importantly, the electoral rise of the marginal racist organization Golden Dawn began alongside the economic crisis in the country's biggest urban centre, Athens. Utilizing the drop in living standards and the high concentration of irregular Afro-Asian immigrants in certain Athenian neighbourhoods, it first gained local support in the 2010 municipal elections (Dinas et al., 2016).

Golden Dawn's success varied across Greece, mainly concentrating on areas with high unemployment, immigrants and income inequalities (Georgiadou et al., 2018). From attracting almost zero per cent of the national vote share in 2009 Golden Dawn had risen to 7 per cent by May 2012 and managed to gain 18 seats in a parliament of 300. It preserved this share until 2015, but in 2019 it won only 2.9 per cent of the vote, thus falling short of the 3 per cent threshold. However, another far-right party called the Elliniki Lisi (Greek Solution) secured 3.7 per cent of the national vote and 10 parliamentary seats. Support for such clearly nationalist parties, in turn, raises questions about Greeks' attitudes towards the EU.

V. Euroscepticism

Greece used to be one of the most europhile countries in the EU. This changed during the crisis years. The significant eurosceptic shift in public opinion was mainly framed through the prism of soft euroscepticism, rejecting economic EU policies and the interference of the EU in national politics (Vasilopoulou, 2018). A significant rise in the eurosceptic party vote makes clear that the EU became also a significant electoral a target for blame (Verney, 2015).

Yet euroscepticism in Greece remains soft in character: Greeks' support for eurozone membership remained relatively high throughout the economic crisis (Karyotis and Rüdig 2015). The Greek population is pragmatic when it comes to eurozone and EU membership (Clements *et al.,* 2014), mainly from fear of international isolation and due to the geopolitical insecurity generated by its location at the border between West and East. As euroscepticism was gaining ground, pro-EU sentiments also became more directly politicized. For instance, a new centrist pro-EU party, Potami, representing the educated, liberal and pro-EU middle classes, emerged. The appearance of political parties on both sides of the EU dimension, in turn, increased its electoral relevance.

Amidst political instability, global markets and European partners thus broke the taboo about exiting the EU and openly spoke about a potential Grexit. In the course of the crisis, undertaking economic austerity became a condition for EU membership (Lefkofridi and Nezi, 2019). This strategy deflated the tension faced by mainstream parties (PASOK and ND) that had signed MoUs and were under pressure by their creditors to implement them. While their own supporters were both pro-EU and pro-MoU, the broader public was, until January 2015, pro-EU but anti-MoU.[2] The tension was caused by the disproportional electoral rules that compelled them to appeal to the electorate at large. If failure to comply with austerity (which was the dominant interpretation of responsible policy) was defined as incompatible with EU membership, PASOK's and ND's submission to MoUs would be vindicated. Even better, their key opponent, Syriza, would be disadvantaged.

Making austerity a prerequisite for EU membership heightened latent divisions within Syriza, where a non-negligible fraction of supporters denounced austerity so vigorously that they would leave the EU than submit (Lefkofridi and Nezi, 2019). The revival of the idea of a referendum on the bailout conditions was PM Tsipras' solution of last resort when he saw that preserving EU membership and opposing austerity was becoming increasingly impossible in the absence of cash to run the state.

The referendum of 5 July 2015 resulted in renouncing the MoU terms. This obliged the EU to show how much democracy it was willing to tolerate (or which of its *demoi* mattered more than others). At the same time, divisions among Syriza supporters and politicians on eurozone membership and its long internal conflict towards the EU, which had been swept under the carpet, came to the fore. The post-2015 referendum capitulation of Syriza's anti-MoU stance signified its willingness to remain in power. Tsipras sought to appeal to the broader public's wish to remain in the EU instead of catering to a smaller segment of pro-Grexit voters (Lefkofridi and Nezi, 2019). Tsipras solved the internal party conflict using a snap election (September 2015) to expel rebels from both his cabinet and the party. Indeed, most voters rewarded Syriza for the effort in negotiations with creditors, irrespective of the outcome (Katsanidou and Reinl, 2020; Tsatsanis and Teperoglou, 2016). In the eyes of many Greek voters the referendum provided evidence

---

[2]Lefkofridi and Nezi (2019) show that during the period 2012–15 consistent support for austerity was expressed mainly by supporters of governing parties (PASOK and ND). During the same period, the mean voter was consistently against the MoU until January 2015. However, in September 2015 the mean voter had moved to the pro-MoU camp.

that Syriza had fought sincerely for their interests and (unlike PASOK and ND) did all it could to secure better than its predecessors conditions and avoid austerity.

Though Greeks never wanted to leave the EU, they were – and remain – angry with the way the EU, especially Germany, and their own governments managed the crisis and with the imposition of austerity measures. Greek euroscepticism during the crisis connects to broader clashes between the people and the elites (Michailidou, 2017), to which we now turn.

VI. The Greek Crisis Version of Populism

The Greek political system as a whole has long been characterized by the presence of populism (Pappas, 2013). Discourse analysis approaches have demonstrated that, during the lifespan of the Third Greek Republic, the populism/anti-populism divide was perpetually salient and become reactivated or even dominant under crisis conditions (Stavrakakis and Katsambekis, 2019).

True to their populist tradition, mainstream party politicians reacted with a blame-shifting populist rhetoric as soon as the crisis hit (Vasilopoulou *et al.,* 2014). This initial reaction led during the crisis to a new division, which was also observed in other EU member states (Karremans and Lefkofridi, 2020): the challengers utilized this division by framing populist mainstream parties as systemic (establishment) and themselves as the true expression of the people by positioning themselves against the responsible mainstream and the only real anti-MoU forces, formed by the parties PASOK and ND.

Greece's new version of the populist/anti-populist discursive cleavage was thus framed as a division between the parties and voters who accepted the necessity of radical restructuring reforms, and those who preferred to stick to the existing state of affairs (Pappas, 2016). The empirical crystallization of this new division line was a strange coalition of left (Syriza) and right (ANEL) anti-MoU parties that resumed executive power in January 2015.

The coalition, dubbed SyrizaNEL addressed populists on both sides of the spectrum by promising to break with the austerity policies and offering alternative scenarios for managing the crisis, where sovereignty would not be as compromised as it had been by ND and PASOK. On the public level, populist attitudes are associated with voters with a low income and low education, euroscepticism and opposition to economic liberalism on both sides of the spectrum. The association with anti-immigrant and anti-democratic attitudes holds only for right-wing populists (Tsatsanis *et al.,* 2018).

In this context, Syriza's discourse was a distinct articulation of left-wing populism (Stavrakakis and Katsambekis, 2014), which included the unrealistic expectation that Russia and China would provide the necessary funds (Mudde, 2017). Though these alternatives would bring Greece in direct confrontation with the country's foreign creditors, many Greek citizens who shared little of Syriza's ideology were drawn to its promises. Indeed, the ideological homogeneity of Syriza voters at the 2015 election was very low (Andreadis and Stavrakakis, 2017). The element that connected them to Syriza was the sentiment that this party represented their interests towards foreign creditors, and that it was 'fighting for them' (Katsanidou and Reinl, 2020). Its coalition with a flag-waving right-wing party enhanced its image of patriotic resistance. That link broke when the anti-austerity issues and divisions that had brought Syriza to power in 2015 were no longer relevant (Rori, 2020) and new ways to connect Syriza to its voters now needed to be forged.

VII. A New Equilibrium for Post-MoU Greece

Taking stock of the impact of the crisis, we see that austerity has had severe consequences on the social fabric. The asymmetry in the distribution of the negative consequences of the MoU therapy for various population groups helps us understand the political turbulence that Greece has experienced during the last decade. No doubt, the crisis opened up windows of opportunity for institutional change, including changes in electoral rules. Changing the rules of the game could help transform the Greek political party landscape towards more cooperation and consensus (Lijphart, 2012); elements sorely needed in a country with serious financial and economic problems.

While in government, Syriza brought to parliament a proposal for simple PR, given that the last time a simple PR system had been used in Greece was 1989. Though the simple PR law passed (179/281 votes) in July 2016, it failed to reach the threshold (200 votes out of 300 parliamentary votes in total) for its immediate implementation and could be applied only to the election after next (in 2023). The July 2019 election was thus conducted under the old law. ND, reaping the benefits of popular dissatisfaction with Syriza and electoral disproportionality, achieved the parliamentary majority necessary for a single party cabinet. Indeed, negative sentiments toward Syriza's failures in government were more prominent than enthusiasm for ND. Crucially, abstention remained at high levels (43.3% in the September 2015 election and 42% in 2019) despite compulsory voting. ND attracted voters from all camps (from left-wing Syriza to the neo-nazi Golden Dawn[3]), who wished to kick Syriza out. Thanks to the disproportional electoral law, small yet prominent party formations of the crisis era, such as the centrist pro-European Potami and the Centre Union, the patriotic right-wing ANEL and the Golden Dawn, vanished from the Greek political map.

Does this mean that Greece has now returned to normal politics after the last election? Or is it still engulfed in the difficult phase in which every party in office is doomed to suffer heavy defeats at the next election? Evidence of the crisis' stark consequences for the political system helps us appreciate the present situation and project into the future. The volatile electoral behaviour and party system fragmentation generated by the crisis seems to have been tamed – not only because of EU constrains but also because the domestic (disproportional) rules of the game remained unchanged (Lefkofridi and Nezi, 2019). In the last two elections (in September 2015 and July 2019), a majority of Greeks supported, as they had always done, the two biggest parties. Yet, this time Syriza had replaced PASOK as the key competitor of ND. Despite losing power in 2019, Syriza emerged a winner from the crisis as it went a long way from being a small niche party of the left into being one of the two pillars of the Greek two-party system, thus consolidating a central place in Greek politics. Though it has seemingly been restored, traditional two-party competition for executive power is still vulnerable. Greek party politics remains adversarial

---

[3]The 2019 election put an end to the electoral ambitions of Golden Dawn. The party was on trial for a long time, accused of being a criminal organization, and some of its members were accused of the murder of a rap musician propagating anti-racism messages. The electoral constituency of Golden Dawn was absorbed either by ND or the new nationalistic right-wing party Elliniki Lisi.

and very polarized. That said, unity and consensus are (still) lacking not only in Greece by also in its operating environment, the EU.

The Greek crisis teaches us three major lessons for Europe and its future. First, the power asymmetry between creditor and debtor states demonstrates the inequality of the *demoi* of the different member states. Given that democracy is a fundamental value of the Union, such selective understanding is problematic, to say the least. Second, the crisis was a lost opportunity for further integration and solidarity. European solidarity was absent until the realization that without concerted action the Euro boat would sink and, even then, solidarity was only reciprocal and shaped much to benefit the creditor countries. Lack of willingness to support a fellow member in need was manifested again during the refugee crisis. At the time of writing, the Covid-19 pandemic again tests the willingness of EU member states to act in solidarity and in pursuit of common European goals. Despite an effort to communicate otherwise, hopes for European solidarity and concerted action towards common goals have proven thus far to be an illusion. Last but not least, the pandemic is causing an economic recession and depending on which instruments the EU will adopt, the possibility of having to accept new MoUs for Greece and other countries is not very remote. In the attempt to teach Greece to live with balanced budgets, the MoUs signed during the eurozone crisis focused too much on quickly implementable measures like cuts and tax increases and failed to introduce much needed structural reforms (towards a more efficient, functional and transparent administration). Besides its (failed) outcome, we highlight the fact that the bitter medicine of austerity was legitimized by cultural stereotypes, which gave rise to nationalism and racism – exactly what tore Europe apart in the Second World War. The repetition of history would prove fatal for the Union, given that the Covid-19-induced recession is likely to hit creditors and debtors alike, but the consequences follow an asymmetric pattern (just as in the eurozone crisis). This necessitates a rethinking of the Union, one that would fill the concept of solidarity with practical meaning, and the Greek crisis has a lot to teach those who listen.

References

Afonso, A. (2013) 'Why Portuguese Parties Have Survived Austerity, Whereas Greek Parties Failed'. LSE European Politics and Policy (EUROPP) Blog. Available online at https://blogs.lse.ac.uk/europpblog/2013/07/29/why-portuguese-parties-have-survived-austerity-where-greek-parties-failed/

Alonso, S. (2014) 'You Can Vote But You Cannot Choose': Democracy and the Sovereign Debt Crisis in the Eurozone. Working Paper. Instituto Carlos III de Madrid. Available online at: https://e-archivo.uc3m.es/handle/10016/18315

Andreadis, I. and Stavrakakis, Y. (2017) 'European Populist Parties in Government: How Well Are Voters Represented? Evidence from Greece'. *Swiss Political Science Review*, Vol. 23, No. 4, pp. 485–508.

Axt, H.-J. (2010) 'Verschuldung in Griechenland: Ursachen einer hausgemachten Krise und Folgen für den Euro-Raum'. Vol. Sudost Europa, 58, No. 4, pp. 542–67.

Capelos, T. and Exadaktylos, T. (2017) 'Feeling the Pulse of the Greek Debt Crisis: Affect on the Web of Blame'. *National Identities*, Vol. 19, No. 1, pp. 73–90.

Clements, B., Nanou, K. and Verney, S. (2014) "We No Longer Love You, But We Don't Want To Leave You': The Eurozone Crisis and Popular Euroscepticism in Greece'. *Journal of European Integration*, Vol. 36, No. 3, pp. 247–65.

Dinas, E., Georgiadou, V., Konstantinidis, I. and Rori, L. (2016) 'From Dusk to Dawn: Political Opportunities and Party Success of Right-wing Extremism'. *Party Politics*, 22(1), 80–92. https://ruomo.lib.uom.gr/bitstream/7000/532/7/dusk_to_down.pdf

Dinas, E. and Rori, L. (2013) 'The 2012 Greek Parliamentary Elections: Fear and Loathing in the Polls'. *West European Politics*, Vol. 36, No. 1, pp. 270–82.

Endres, A. (2010) 'Haushaltskrise: Griechen gefährden ein hilfloses Euroland'. *Die Zeit*. Available online at: https://www.zeit.de/wirtschaft/geldanlage/2010-02/griechenland-furcht

European Commission (2012) 'Memorandum of Understanding Between the European Commission Acting on Behalf of the Euro Area Members States, and the Hellenic Republic'. Available online at: http://ec.europa.eu/economy_finance/eu_borrower/mou/2012-03-01-greece-mou_en.pdf. Las accessed May 9 2017.

Flassbeck, H. (2012) *Zehn Mythen der Krise* (Berlin: Suhrkamp).

Foscolou, A., Tyrovolas, S., Soulis, G. *et al.* (2017) 'The Impact of the Financial Crisis on Lifestyle Health Determinants among Older Adults Living in the Mediterranean Region: The Multinational MEDIS Study (2005-2015)'. *Journal of Preventive Medicine and Public Health*, Vol. 50, No. 1, pp. 1–9.

Freire, A. and Lobo, M.C. (2005) 'Economics, Ideology and Vote: Southern Europe, 1985–2000'. *European Journal of Political Research*, Vol. 44, No. 4, pp. 493–518.

Gemenis, K. and Nezi, R. (2015) 'Government–Opposition Dynamics during the Economic Crisis in Greece'. *Journal of Legislative Studies*, Vol. 21, No. 1, pp. 14–34.

Georgiadou, V., Rori, L. and Roumanias, C. (2018) 'Mapping the European Far Right in the 21st Century: A Meso-level Analysis'. *Electoral Studies*, Vol. 54, pp. 103–15.

International Labour Office (2012) '365th Report of the Committee on Freedom of Association'. Available online at: http://www.ilo.org/gb/GBSessions/previous-sessions/GB316/ins/WCMS_193260/lang–en/index.htm. Last accessed 2 June 2020.

Jonker-Hoffrén, P. (2013) 'Finland: A Tough Nordic Accountant that is Caught up by Reality'. London: London School of Economics and Political Science. Available online at: http://eprints.lse.ac.uk/78317/. Last accessed 2 June 2020.

Karamessini, M. (2013) 'Structural Crisis and Adjustment in Greece'. *In Karamessini M and Rubery J. (eds) Women and Austerity: The Economic Crisis and the Future for Gender Equality* (London: Routledge), pp. 164–85.

Karanikolos, M. and Kentikelenis, A. (2016) 'Health Inequalities after Austerity in Greece'. *International Journal for Equity in Health*, Vol. 15, No. 1.

Karremans, J. and Lefkofridi, Z. (2020) 'Responsive versus Responsible? Party Democracy in Times of Crisis'. *Party Politics*, Vol. 26, No. 3, pp. 271–9.

Karyotis, G & Rüdig, W (2015) Blame and Punishment? The Electoral Politics of Extreme Austerity in Greece. *Political Studies*, 63(1), 2–24.

Katsanidou, A., and Otjes, S. (2015) 'Mapping the Greek Party System after the 2015 Elections: How the Economy and Europe Have Merged into a Single Issue'. LSE European Politics and Policy Blog. Available online at https://blogs.lse.ac.uk/europpblog/2015/02/25/mapping-the-greek-party-system-after-the-2015-elections-how-the-economy-and-europe-have-merged-into-a-single-issue/. Last accessed 2 June 2020.

Katsanidou, A. and Reinl, A.-K. (2020) 'Populists in Government: Voter Defection and Party Resilience'. *Representations*. doi: 10.1080/00344893.2019.1700153.

Knight, D.M. (2018) 'The Desire for Disinheritance in Austerity Greece'. *Focaal*, Vol. 2018, No. 80, pp. 30–42.

Kokaliari, E. (2018) 'Quality of Life, Anxiety, Depression, and Stress among Adults in Greece Following the Global Financial Crisis'. *International Social Work*, Vol. 61, No. 3, pp. 410–24.

Krugman, P. (2012) 'Euro Update: The Perils of Pointless Pain'. New York Times https://krugman.blogs.nytimes.com/2012/09/26/euro-update-the-perils-of-pointless-pain/

Lefkofridi, Z. and Nezi, R. (2019) 'Responsibility versus Responsiveness ... to Whom? A Theory of Party Behavior'. *Party Politics*, Vol. 26, No. 3, pp. 334–46.

Lefkofridi, Z. and Schmitter, P.C. (2015) 'Transcending or Descending? European Integration in Times of Crisis'. *European Political Science Review*, Vol. 7, No. 1, pp. 3–22.

Lijphart, A. (2012) *Patterns of Democracy: Government Forms and Performance in Thirty-six Countries* (New Haven, CT: Yale University Press).

Mair, P. (2013) 'Smaghi versus the Parties: Representative Government and Institutional Constraints'. In Streeck, W. and Schafer, A. (eds) *Politics in the Age of Austerity* (Cambridge: Polity Press), pp. 143–68.

Michailidou, A. (2017) ''The Germans are Back': Euroscepticism and Anti-Germanism in Crisis-stricken Greece'. *National Identities*, Vol. 19, No. 1, pp. 91–108.

Mudde, C. (2017) *Syriza: The Failure of the Populist Promise* (Cham: Palgrave Macmillan).

Nezi, R. (2012) 'Economic Voting under the Economic Crisis: Evidence from Greece'. *Electoral Studies*, Vol. 31, No. 3, pp. 498–505.

Nezi, R. and Katsanidou, A. (2014) 'From Valence to Position: Economic Voting in Extraordinary Conditions'. *Acta Politica*, Vol. 49, pp. 413–30.

Papadakis, N., Amanaki, E., Drakaki, M. and Saridaki, S. (2020) 'Employment/Unemployment, Education and Poverty in the Greek Youth, within the EU Context'. *International Journal of Educational Research*, Vol. 99. doi 10.1016/j.ijer.2019.101503.

Papadakis, N., Kyridis, A. and Papargyris, A. (2015) 'Searching for Absents: The State of Things for the NEETs (Young People Not in Education, Employment or Training) in Greece. An overview'. *Journal of Sociological Research*, Vol. 6, No. 1, pp. 44–75.

Papadopoulos, N.A. (2019) 'Austerity-based Labour Market Reforms in Greece vs Fundamental Rights in the Aftermath of the European Debt Crisis: An Analysis of Supranational & National Bodies' Jurisprudence'. *European Public Law, Vol 26, no. 2 (Forthcoming)*.

Papageorgiou, Y. and Petousi, V. (2018) 'Gender Resilience in Times of Economic Crisis: Findings from Greece'. *Partecipazione e Conflitto*, Vol. 11, No. 1, pp. 145–74.

Pappas, T.S. (2013) 'Why Greece Failed'. *Journal of Democracy*, Vol. 24, No. 2, pp. 31–45.

Pappas, T.S. (2016) 'Modern Populism: Research Advances, Conceptual and Methodological Pitfalls, and the Minimal Definition'. In Thompson, W. (ed.) *Oxford Research Encyclopedia of Politics* (Oxford: Oxford University Press, 1–27. https://oxfordre.com/politics/view/10.1093/acrefore/9780190228637.001.0001/acrefore-9780190228637-e-17.

Petmesidou, M. (2019) 'Challenges to Healthcare Reform in Crisis-hit Greece'. *E-cadernos CES*, Vol. 31, pp. 19–42. doi.org/10.4000/eces.4127.

Rori, L. (2020) 'The 2019 Greek Parliamentary Election: Retour à la Normale'. *West European Politics*, Vol. 43, No. 4, pp. 1023–37.

Rotarou, E.S. and Sakellariou, D. (2019) 'Access to Health Care in an Age of Austerity: Disabled People's Unmet Needs in Greece'. *Critical Public Health*, Vol. 29, No. 1, pp. 48–60.

Schimmelfennig, F. (2015) 'Liberal Intergovernmentalism and the Euro Area Crisis'. *Journal of European Public Policy*, Vol. 22, No. 2, pp. 177–95.

Stavrakakis, Y. and Katsambekis, G. (2014) 'Left-wing Populism in the European Periphery: The Case of Syriza'. *Journal of Political Ideologies*, Vol. 19, No. 2, pp. 119–42.

Stavrakakis, Y. and Katsambekis, G. (2019) 'The Populism/Anti-populism Frontier and its Mediation in Crisis-ridden Greece: From Discursive Divide to Emerging Cleavage?' *European Political Science*, Vol. 18, No. 1, pp. 37–52.

Stavrianakos, K., Kontaxakis, V., Moussas, G., Paplos, K., Papaslanis, T., Havaki-Kontaxaki, B. and Papadimitriou, G. (2014) 'Attempted Suicide During the Financial Crisis in Athens'. *Psychiatrike= Psychiatriki*, Vol. 25, No. 2, pp. 104–10.

Teperoglou, E. and Tsatsanis, E. (2014) 'Dealignment, De-legitimation and the Implosion of the Two-party system in Greece: The Earthquake Election of 6 May 2012'. *Journal of Elections, Public Opinion & Parties*, Vol. 24, No. 2, pp. 222–42.

Thomsen, P. (2019) 'The IMF and the Greek Crisis: Myths and Realities'. IMF. Retrieved 26 February 2020, from https://www.imf.org/en/News/Articles/2019/10/01/sp093019-The-IMF-and-the-Greek-Crisis-Myths-and-Realities

Tsakatika, M. (2016) 'Syriza's Electoral Rise in Greece: Protest, Trust and the Art of Political Manipulation'. *South European Society and Politics*, Vol. 21, No. 4, pp. 519–40.

Tsakatika, M. and Eleftheriou, C. (2013) 'The Radical Left's Turn Towards Civil Society in Greece: One strategy, two paths'. *South European Society and Politics*, Vol. 18, No. 1, pp. 81–99.

Tsatsanis, E., Andreadis, I. and Teperoglou, E. (2018) 'Populism from Below: Socio-economic and Ideological Correlates of Mass Attitudes in Greece'. *South European Society and Politics*, Vol. 23, No. 4, pp. 429–50.

Tsatsanis, E. and Teperoglou, E. (2016) 'Realignment under Stress: The July 2015 Referendum and the September Parliamentary Election in Greece'. *South European Society and Politics*, Vol. 21, No. 4, pp. 427–50.

Vaiou, D. (2016) 'Tracing Aspects of the Greek Crisis in Athens: Putting Women in the Picture'. *European Urban and Regional Studies*, Vol. 23, No. 3, pp. 220–30.

Van Vossole, J. (2016) 'Framing PIGS: Patterns of Racism and Neocolonialism in the Euro crisis'. *Patterns of Prejudice*, Vol. 50, No. 1, pp. 1–20.

Vasilopoulou, S. (2018) 'The Party Politics of Euroscepticism in Times of Crisis: The Case of Greece'. *Politics*, Vol. 38, No. 3, pp. 311–26.

Vasilopoulou, S., Halikiopoulou, D. and Exadaktylos, T. (2014) 'Greece in Crisis: Austerity, Populism and the Politics of Blame'. *JCMS*, Vol. 52, No. 2, pp. 388–402.

Verney, S. (2014) ''Broken and Can't be Fixed': The Impact of the Economic Crisis on the Greek Party System'. *International Spectator*, Vol. 49, No. 1, pp. 18–35.

Verney, S. (2015) 'Waking the 'Sleeping Giant' or Expressing Domestic Dissent? Mainstreaming Euroscepticism in Crisis-stricken Greece'. *International Political Science Review*, Vol. 36, No. 3, pp. 279–95.

Wachman, R. (2010, April 29) 'Santander Boss Dismisses Fears of Debt Crisis in Spain'. *The Guardian*. Available online at: https://www.theguardian.com/business/2010/apr/29/santander-debt-crisis-spain-greece. Last accessed 2 June 2020.

JCMS 2020 Volume 58. Annual Review. pp. 173–186   DOI: 10.1111/jcms.13082

Mainstreaming Gender and Climate Change to Achieve a Just Transition to a Climate-Neutral Europe

GILL ALLWOOD
Nottingham Trent University, Nottingham

In November 2019 the European Parliament (2019/2930(RSP)) declared a climate and environmental emergency, calling for urgent and concrete action. The year 2019 was Europe's hottest year on record (Copernicus Climate Change Service, 2019), and the Intergovernmental Panel on Climate Change (2018, p. v) reported that 'emissions of greenhouse gases due to human activities, the root cause of global warming, continue to increase, year after year'. Swedish teenage climate activist Greta Thunberg inspired and led a worldwide school strike movement, and mass protests dominated by young women took place around the world (Wahlström *et al.,* 2019). The European Parliament resolution of 14 March 2019 (2019/2582(RSP)) 'welcomes the fact that people across Europe, in particular younger generations, are becoming increasingly active in demonstrating for climate justice'. At the institutional level 2019 was a year of renewal, with the European Parliament elections in May, the adoption of a new Council strategy in June and the appointment of a new Commission in December. Climate change was a priority for all these institutional actors. The Council strategy 2019–24, for example, insists on the urgent need to build a 'climate-neutral, green, fair and social Europe'. The new President of the Commission Ursula von der Leyen announced her intention to see Europe become the first climate-neutral continent by 2050.

Climate change arrived on the EU agenda in the 1980s, emerging out of environmental policy, which was already established as an area that required transnational action. Throughout the 1990s and early 2000s the climate ambition of the EU exceeded its ability to agree on, and implement, effective actions (Dupont and Oberthür, 2015). When the USA withdrew from the Kyoto protocol in 2001 the EU took on a global leadership role and has continued to construct an identity as a global actor around the issue of climate change (Jordan *et al.,* 2010). This had economic motivations (to avoid being undercut by exporters with lower environmental standards) but was also part of the post-Maastricht efforts to increase the EU's global actorness. The past decade has seen climate change gain prominence and take centre stage. In 2009 the landmark climate and energy framework (COM(2014)15 final) introduced targets for greenhouse gas emissions, energy efficiency and renewable energy. Within the European Commission climate action gained its own Directorate General, DG CLIMA. This was an important part of the process of institutionalizing climate change. The issue of climate change continued to rise up the EU and the global agenda, and there was a strong dynamic between the two. The Lisbon Treaty (2007) gave the EU competence to conclude international environmental agreements. The EU, along with its member states, is a party to the United Nations

Convention on Climate Change (UNFCCC) and plays a key role in trying to reach agreement on global targets (Biedenkopf and Dupont, 2013; Oberthür and Groen, 2018).

It is in this context that the EU emerged as an influential player in the 2015 Paris Agreement, the first climate agreement to be universal and legally binding. International targets and monitoring and reporting have acted as an impetus for action on the part of the EU and many, although not all, its member states (Dupont, 2019). The European Green Deal (2019), drafted against the background of the Intergovernmental Panel on Climate Change (2018) report on the predicted impact of a global temperature rise of 1.5°C, further highlights the way that the issue of climate change has become part of the institutional fabric of the EU. Reinforcing the EU's commitments under the Paris agreement, as well as the UN's 2030 Agenda, with its Sustainable Development Goals (SDGs) (2015), it provides a framework in which the EU can try to assert leadership and mould its own efforts towards a sustainability that 'leaves no-one behind'. The Council's conclusions on climate diplomacy of 18 February 2019 describe 2019 as the year of pushing further convergence between the SDGs and the climate agenda.

The initial focus of EU climate policy was climate change mitigation. This refers to strategies for reducing climate change, largely through the reduction of greenhouse gas emissions. Key policy frameworks are the Climate and energy package and the Environmental Action Programme, which provides an overarching framework for all environmental and climate policy. The European Green Deal (COM(2019)640 final), proposed by the new Commission in 2019, sets out a strategy to achieve net-zero greenhouse gas emissions by 2050 while sustaining economic growth, and promises to enshrine this in legislation, with the first climate laws due to be proposed in 2020.

Since 2013, internal EU climate policy has also included an adaptation strategy, in recognition of the fact that climate change is having an impact within the EU, as well as, more obviously, elsewhere. While climate change mitigation is more readily framed as an issue to be dealt with at the EU level, adaptation to the effects of climate change appeared, until recently, to require local responses or to be of concern only in the countries that are most severely hit by the impact of climate change, and are concentrated in the global south. The floods and heat waves of the early 2000s raised awareness of the impact of climate change within the EU and of its cross-border nature (Rayner and Jordan, 2010), prompting the adoption of an EU adaptation strategy (COM(2013)216). Member states are encouraged to produce national adaptation strategies, setting out, for example, how they will climate-proof their transport, energy and agriculture sectors, and protect their populations from flooding, droughts and heat waves.

Adaptation has a longer history as part of EU external relations. The visible impact of climate change in developing countries, and the use of development aid for adaptation purposes, mean that climate change has been prominent in EU development policy. A Commission communication in 2003 (COM(2003)85 final) declared that climate change was a problem for development, as well as an environmental problem. Since the Lisbon treaty (2007), however, climate change has been substantially reframed on the external agenda, replacing a development frame with one much more closely related to migration and security (Youngs, 2014). Development policy is expected to align with the Union's strategic priorities, set out in the Global Strategy (2016), which is the overarching statement of EU foreign policy and that frames climate change as a security threat and a root cause of migration (Global Strategy, 2016, p. 27).

This article will focus on two aspects of recent EU climate policy. The first is not new, but is important. It is the recognition that climate change, like other cross-cutting issues, cannot be addressed in isolation. It is inextricably connected to key areas of EU activity, including energy, transport and agriculture. Climate objectives need to be integrated into all areas of policymaking. This is referred to as climate mainstreaming and has been embraced by EU policymakers as a desirable practice. It has obvious parallels with gender mainstreaming, but, as this article shows, is itself gender blind, and this is problematic. The second aspect of recent EU climate policy on which this article focuses is new. It is the growing presence of statements about the need for a 'just transition' to a climate-neutral economy, one which 'puts people first' and ensures that 'no-one is left behind'. I argue that embedding a gender lens in these two aspects of EU climate policy makes a valuable contribution to efforts to create a sustainable and just future.

I. What Does Gender Have to Do with Climate Change?

On the surface, it may seem that climate change affects everyone equally. As British Conservative MEP and member of the European Parliament Committee on Women's Rights and Gender Equality, Marina Yannakoudakis, said, 'The climate is the same for males and females, so far as I know. When it rains we all get wet' (BBC News, 2012). However, gender, development and environment scholars have produced a large volume of literature demonstrating that climate change is, indeed, gendered. The early contributions to this literature argued that structural inequalities in the global political economy and within societies increase women's vulnerability to the impact of climate change (Agrawala and Crick, 2009; Alston, 2013; Brody *et al.,* 2008; Skinner, 2011). They argued that climate change has a particularly detrimental effect on the poorest countries and, within them, on the poorest parts of the population. As women constitute a large proportion of the poorest in society, they will be amongst the hardest hit and the least well positioned socially, legally and economically, to respond (Morrow, 2017). There is evidence to support the argument that women's vulnerability to the effects of climate change is increased in relation to men's by their relative disadvantage in terms of access to resources, land ownership, education and caring responsibilities (Dankelman, 2010). However, there is also a crucial insistence in the literature that women cannot be perceived as helpless victims of climate change (MacGregor, 2017).

A second strand of the early gender and climate change literature emphasized women's agency and specific skills and knowledge which, it was argued, made them potentially useful actors in climate change adaptation. As food producers, for example, they were well placed to adapt agricultural techniques to changing environmental conditions. It was also argued that, as energy users in the home, they could play a role in climate change mitigation by adopting new forms of cooking stoves, for example. The gendered impact of climate change and women's role as climate actors are not confined to the global south, and researchers have demonstrated these links in rich industrialized countries, including EU member states (Tschakert and Machado, 2012, p. 278). They have shown that there are gendered differences in the causes of climate change, including transport and energy use. They have exposed gendered differences in vulnerability to the effects of climate events, such as heat waves and floods, and they have discovered gendered differences in attitudes towards climate change and towards the need to adopt mitigation and adaptation measures.

Drawing on Buckingham and Le Masson (2017, pp. 2–3), gender is understood here to 'comprise relations between women and men, and between and among different groups of women and men, not to mention between different conceptualisations of masculinity and femininity, which can each be practised by either, and both, women and men'. Gender inequalities intersect with other structural inequalities including class, race/ethnicity, physical ability, sexuality, region and age (Collins and Bilge, 2016). Gender is one of many axes of power that have an impact on the lives of groups and individuals. Its pervasiveness as a marker of difference and inequality makes it worthy of attention, in its intersections with other structural inequalities.

An intersectional analytical lens has been used by feminist scholars to make important contributions to our understanding of the impact of climate change and responses to it (Djoudi *et al.,* 2016; Kaijser and Kronsell, 2014; MacGregor, 2014; Nagel, 2012, 2016; Sultana, 2014; Tschakert and Machado, 2012). Intersectionality can help us understand individual and group-based differences in relation to climate change. Rather than designating women as vulnerable victims of climate change, an intersectional approach demonstrates that social structures based on characteristics such as gender, socioeconomic status, ethnicity, nationality, health, sexual orientation, age and place influence the responsibility, vulnerability and decision-making power of individuals and groups. For example, research on Sweden and the EU (Kaijser and Kronsell, 2014; Kronsell, 2013; Magnusdottir and Kronsell, 2016) shows that there are gendered differences in energy consumption and transportation, but that gender is not the only relevant factor. Class sometimes matters more than gender; women are not a homogenous group and there are considerable differences within the global north and the global south. Magnusdottir and Kronsell (2016, p. 66), for example, argue that, 'Well-educated, female climate experts most likely have less in common with low-income working class women across Europe than with their male colleagues at the Commission and this applies to their climate impact as well as climate vulnerability'. An intersectional approach leads us to ask which inequalities matter in each case (Kaijser and Kronsell, 2014, p. 422).

Scholars and activists have pointed out that women's presence in climate decision-making is poor, and some have called for this to be rectified (Women's Environment and Development Organization, 2018). There is some evidence that women in climate decision-making make a difference. For example, Magnusdottir and Kronsell (2015) show that carbon emissions are lower in countries where women have higher political status. These findings support the argument that women should be included in climate decision-making because they bring different perspectives, knowledge and experience, which would lead to different policy outputs.

However, not all agree that there is a direct positive correlation between the presence of women in climate decision-making and gender-sensitive policy outputs. In a later study, Magnusdottir and Kronsell (2016) find that a critical mass of women policymakers does not automatically result in gender-sensitive climate policy. Their study finds that, even in the most gender-sensitive European countries, gender differences in material conditions and in attitudes towards climate issues were completely invisible and excluded from climate policy texts. Policy-makers were largely unaware of the relevance of gender differences and how to consider them in relation to climate policymaking, regardless of

© 2020 The Authors. JCMS: Journal of Common Market Studies published by University Association for Contemporary European Studies and John Wiley & Sons Ltd

the gender balance of the institutions where climate policy is made (Kronsell, 2015, p. 77). This is not to say that women and men should not be equally represented in all sites of decision-making, but this would be on grounds of equality and justice, rather than substantive policy change. This is part of a much larger feminist debate on the extent to which women in decision-making make a difference to gendered outcomes (Franceschet *et al.,* 2012).

In summary, climate change is gendered, as a result of the deeply entrenched gender inequalities that exist in all societies. Policies that ignore gender inequalities risk perpetuating or even exacerbating them. Feminist international relations scholar, Cynthia Enloe, never ceases to encourage us to 'ask the gender question' (2004, p. 94). This does not mean simply looking at women. It means asking which women (and which men)? Which differences make a difference? We need to investigate and address gender inequalities in relation to climate change that can often leave women more vulnerable to its impact without suggesting that this vulnerability is innate or the same for all women. Taking a gender lens to climate change enables us to ask where and how gender matters. This is a first step to achieving gender justice in relation to climate change.

II. Mainstreaming Climate Change, Mainstreaming Gender

There is a long-standing and widespread recognition in EU policymaking that some objectives cannot be reached by treating them as stand-alone goals, but that they need to be woven into all areas, and at all stages, of decision-making. Gender mainstreaming and environmental policy integration are two examples of this and both are treaty-based obligations. This means that gender equality and environmental objectives must be 'mainstreamed' or 'integrated' into all areas of EU policymaking, including sectors where they are not immediately obvious. In the case of gender equality, for example, this might include foreign and security, agriculture or industry. Mainstreaming also requires that the cross-cutting issue (gender or environment) be considered at all stages of the policymaking process, from definition of the issue and problem framing to implementation, monitoring and evaluation. Calls for climate mainstreaming are increasingly common in EU policy documents (Dupont, 2016).

There is an extensive body of literature on gender mainstreaming, and much of it focuses on why mainstreaming has failed to realize its radical potential (Allwood, 2013; Guerrina and Wright, 2016; Rao *et al.,* 2016). Many authors draw attention to the contradiction between gender mainstreaming as a transformative, agenda-setting idea with radical feminist potential and gender mainstreaming as an integrationist policy practice (Arora-Jonsson and Sijapati, 2018; Chappell and Guerrina, 2020, p. 17; Porter and Sweetman, 2005).

In its integrationist form, gender mainstreaming is incorporated as a policy tool into structures, processes and norms that remain otherwise unchanged. 'Gender' in this form of gender mainstreaming lacks the meanings it carries in feminist and gender theory, in particular its underlying conceptions of power and intersecting inequalities (Zalewski, 2010). Instead, it refers to undifferentiated categories of men and women, and is often shorthand for policies targeted at women or is an excuse to discontinue such policies (Stratigaki, 2005). The integrationist form often consists of a set of tools and procedures, along with detailed instructions for their implementation and for the measurement of their success (Meier and Celis, 2011; Woodward, 2008), hence the frequent assertion that gender mainstreaming has become a box-ticking exercise, devoid of any substantive content (Rao *et al.,* 2016, pp. 76–7).

The transformative form, in contrast, has its roots in feminist theories of gender and was originally proposed as a way of radically transforming policy approaches to gender inequalities. Instead of addressing gender inequality as a separate policy issue, gender mainstreaming brought a commitment to achieving gender equality in all policy areas, including those previously perceived to be gender neutral. It aimed to address gender at all stages of policymaking, so that policies would be designed with the goal of gender equality already contained within them, rather than remedial action being taken once they had already been formulated or implemented (Acker, 1990; Connell, 2006; Daly, 2005).

Studies of gender mainstreaming and other forms of policy coordination, including climate mainstreaming, have identified obstacles to their success (De Roeck *et al.,* 2018). Kok and de Coninck's (2007) study of climate change mainstreaming, for example, shows that organisational structures were not designed for cooperation, coordination and joint decision-making on different levels. There are power imbalances among Commission DGs; different configurations of the Council of Ministers and among the Council, the European Parliament and the Commission. The European Parliament, and in particular its various committees on the environment, development and gender equality, have together been increasingly active in advocating the mainstreaming of these issues throughout all European Parliament decision-making, but the Parliament can be squeezed out of forms of decision-making dominated by intergovernmentalism, and this applies to most of the Union's climate change policies. Power imbalances and inter-institutional rivalries make it difficult for issues such as environmental protection to impinge on policies shored up by powerful economic interests such as trade and agriculture. Gupta and van der Grijp (2010) specifically identify institutional resistance, often based on powerful economic interests, as the main obstacle to mainstreaming climate change. Specifically, mainstreaming this cross-cutting issue is seen as threatening the status quo and unsettling the vested interests of industry and the energy lobby. Resistance is therefore strong. Any policy competition or struggle for scarce resources will expose these imbalances, and rhetorical commitment to mainstreaming may lack underlying substance, particularly in times of economic crisis.

Mainstreaming is widely embraced in EU policy documents and has grown to encompass a range of new imperatives, from climate change to migration and security. There are also calls for these cross-cutting issues to be mainstreamed in combination, and not just singly. EU policy documents increasingly use the term 'nexus' to describe the intersection between two or more policy areas (Carbone, 2013; De Roeck *et al.,* 2018; Furness and Gänzle, 2017; Lavenex and Kunz, 2009). Climate change is placed in a series of nexuses, including climate security and climate migration. The Council conclusions on climate diplomacy of 26 February 2018 'resolve [...] to further mainstream the nexus between climate change and security in political dialogue, conflict prevention, development and humanitarian action and disaster risk strategies'. While this statement is an important recognition that policy issues are intersecting and cannot be addressed in isolation from each other, it raises substantial questions about how gender can be mainstreamed throughout other cross-cutting issues. Not only are climate change, migration and other cross-cutting issues to be mainstreamed, but so must be the nexus between them. This raises questions about the practicalities of addressing complex webs of intersecting issues, especially when some of them are accorded priority status. It also creates a context in which the mainstreaming of gender becomes even more challenging (Allwood, 2019). The literature on horizontal policy coordination and policy nexuses suggests that successful policy coherence requires a strong, shared vision that acts as a strategic goal and maintains focus on the objective, and not on the procedural tools and instruments.

The substantial literature shows that, despite repeated rhetorical commitments by EU actors, gender mainstreaming is still absent from key policy areas and is often treated as procedural, rather than substantive (Meier and Celis, 2011). From the literature on nexuses and policy integration, environmental policy integration and gender mainstreaming, we know that institutional power relations persist and the more powerful actors can ensure that mainstreaming or policy integration acts in their favour. Power relations between the policymaking institutions give precedence to certain policy objectives, whether economic competitiveness or security. As policymakers increasingly refer to cross-cutting issues and to policy nexuses, we need a way to understand and improve how they intersect.

III. Gender and EU Climate Policy

Taking a gender lens to EU climate policy reveals, firstly, that much of it remains resolutely gender blind. The European Green Deal (COM(2019)640 final) makes no mention of gender/women/men (although it states that the SDGs will be at the heart of the EU's policymaking action); the climate and energy framework (COM(2014)15 final) makes no mention of gender/women/men; A Clean Planet for All (COM(2018)773 final) makes no mention of gender/women/men; the Environmental Action Programme (1386/2014/EU) makes one mention of pregnant women as a vulnerable group. This is despite the fact that gender mainstreaming is a treaty obligation; that a framework for EU gender equality policy and gender mainstreaming is set out in the Gender Equality Strategy (COM(2020)152 final) and a framework for integrating gender equality into all external action is set out in the Gender Action Plan (GAPII); and that the EU is committed to the SDGs (2015) and to the UNFCCC's Gender Action Plan (2019).

Impact assessments are a tool to consider the potential impact of proposed actions and are a key component of the EU's gender mainstreaming toolkit. The Commission's impact assessments incorporate three dimensions: the potential economic, social and environmental consequences of the proposed initiative. Gender-related impacts are addressed under social issues. According to the EC guidance on social impact assessment, the following questions have to be asked: does the option have a different impact on women and men? Does the option promote equality between women and men? (EIGE, 2017). However, impact assessments are not always carried out, and when they are gender is often ignored. For example, the impact assessment accompanying the Environmental Action Programme (SWD/2012/0398) does not contain a single reference to gender, nor does the in-depth analysis (2018) accompanying the Commission communication 'A Clean Planet for All', or the impact assessment (SWD(2014) 15 final) accompanying the climate and energy framework proposal.

Elements of gender awareness in relation to climate change exist in fragments of EU policy, but they lack coherence. The Gender Equality Strategy 2020–5 has a short section on climate change that points out some of the ways in which climate change is gendered and states that, 'addressing the gender dimension can therefore have a key role in leveraging the full potential of these policies', but it gives no detail about how this will be done. GAPII refers to climate issues twice, both in relation to women's participation in climate decision-making. However, the relevant objective, 'Equal rights enjoyed by women to participate in and influence decision-making processes on climate and environmental issues', is the one least often included in the implementation reports submitted to the European Commission by the EU Delegations, member state governments and the European external action service.

EU institutions still tend to frame gender equality as 'equality between men and women', ignoring the heterogeneity of these two categories, the power relations within, as well as between, them, and the intersection of other structural inequalities with gender. There are institutional pockets in which a more nuanced gender analysis emerges. The Gender Equality Strategy (2020–5) makes some move away from a focus on equality between women and men. It states that the Gender Equality Strategy will aim to achieve 'a Europe where women and men, girls and boys, in all their diversity, are equal [...] The Commission will enhance gender mainstreaming by systematically including a gender perspective in all stages of policy design in all EU policy areas, internal and external. The Strategy will be implemented using intersectionality as a cross-cutting principle' (p. 2). Although there is no detail about how this will be done, the recognition of intersectionality is an important step away from equating gender equality solely with a men-women binary.

The only EU institution that has paid significant attention to the relation between gender and climate change is the European Parliament, which has produced a number of relevant reports and resolutions. Some focus solely on women and adaptation in the global south (2018/2086(INI)), but others contain sophisticated gender analyses of climate issues and responses (2012/2197(INI)). For example, the European Parliament resolution of 20 April 2012 (2012/2197(INI)), based on a report by the French Green MEP, Nicole Kiil-Nielsen, states that 'there will not be any climate justice without true gender equality'. This is a stark declaration of the inseparable nature of gender justice and climate justice. It predates the SDGs, but shares with them the insistence that a sustainable future requires inequalities to be addressed in synergy. The resolution does not call simply for the numerical presence of women in climate decision-making, but for the inclusion at all levels of decision-making of 'gender equality and gender justice objectives in policies, action plans and other measures', for systematic gender analyses, and for the inclusion of gender equality principles at all stages of climate change negotiation.

The European Parliament motion for a resolution on the European Green Deal (2019/2956(RSP)), put forward by Bas Eickhout on behalf of the Greens–European Free Alliance group, 'Deplores the lack of gender perspective, actions and goals in the European Green Deal Communication and urges the European Commission to include gender mainstreaming and gender-responsive climate and environmental action at all levels; calls on the Commission to deliver on the commitment made by President von der Leyen to promote gender equality in all policy making and on the proposals made by Vice-President Timmermans to pursue a "twin-track approach on gender and climate change" and "take measures to redress gender and climate issues into all aspects of European development policy" (para. 12). It also 'calls on the European Commission to implement systematic gender impact assessments and allocate specific funds for gender equality in relevant climate actions and policies of the European Green Deal' (para. 120).

The text that was finally adopted by the European Parliament as its resolution of 15 January 2020 on the European Green Deal (2019/2956(RSP)) lost some of this wording, but still 'emphasises the need for a gender perspective on actions and goals in the Green Deal, including gender mainstreaming and gender-responsive actions' (para. 6). The adopted text also included the following paragraph from the original motion: '113. Calls on the Commission in its efforts to promote the EU as leader of international climate and biodiversity negotiations to design a concrete action plan to deliver on the commitments of the renewed five-year Gender Action Plan agreed at COP25 (Enhanced Lima work programme), to promote gender equality in the UNFCCC process, and to appoint a permanent EU gender and climate change focal point, with sufficient budget resources, to implement and monitor gender-responsible climate action in the EU and globally', perhaps confirming Woodward and Van der Vleuten's (2014) argument that gender equality is less contentious when it applies outside the EU.

In summary, there is no evidence of systematic gender mainstreaming of EU climate change policy. Climate change is framed as a technical and market problem, or as one that is deeply entwined with foreign and security strategic priorities. These frames do not invite obvious links to people-centred solutions, which could favour a gendered approach (Allwood, 2014, p. 9). The European Parliament's efforts to integrate gender into climate change make an important contribution to policy debates, but climate decision-making has remained largely within the remit of the Council, which articulates a gender-sensitive approach to climate change only on the rare occasions when a Danish or Swedish presidency is able to exert influence.

An important additional obstacle to the mainstreaming of gender throughout climate policy is that climate change is constructed as a cross-cutting issue in itself and is situated in a series of nexuses with strategic priorities, such as migration and security. This contributes to the exclusion of gender equality from climate policy. The gender mainstreaming and policy coordination literature shows that overcoming this obstacle requires focusing on the objective of gender equality, rather than the process of gender mainstreaming, and recognizing that the goals of gender equality and climate justice are inseparable.

IV. A Just Transition to a Climate-neutral Future

EU institutions have adopted the rhetoric of a 'just transition' which 'leaves no-one behind'. The European Green Deal (2019) states that the transition to a climate-neutral future 'must be just and inclusive. It must put people first'. The idea of a just transition comes from North American trade unions concerned with protecting workers in carbon-intensive sectors. Trade unions and environmental organizations lobbied hard to insert a reference to the just transition in the Paris Agreement, which now acknowledges 'the imperatives of a just transition of the workforce and the creation of decent work and quality jobs in accordance with nationally defined priorities'. The European Parliament resolution on a climate and environmental emergency states that 'action [...] must be accompanied by strong social and inclusive measures to ensure a fair and equitable transition'. References to a just transition do not always provide any detail about what this means, however, and in EU climate policy documents the term often refers to addressing regional disparities, for example, between areas that produce coal and those that do not. Combined with the SDG rhetoric of 'leaving no-one behind', the notion of a just transition

© 2020 The Authors. JCMS: Journal of Common Market Studies published by University Association for Contemporary European Studies and John Wiley & Sons Ltd

is being used by civil society actors and by the European Parliament to build an inclusive approach to the creation of a sustainable future. This marks a change from the approach to climate action which focused on market and technological solutions to one that also recognizes some of the social implications of climate change and of climate action.

EU policy documents call for climate change to be mainstreamed throughout all EU activities. The European Parliament resolution of 14 March 2019 'stresses the need to mainstream climate ambition into all EU policies, including trade policy'. The Council conclusions of 4 October 2019 '[u]nderline the systemic nature of Europe's climate and environmental challenges' and stress 'the need to prioritise actions for the green transition that is just and is better integrating environment and climate aspects into the design of the EU's social, economic, and financial policies'.

This growing call for climate mainstreaming contributes to the increase in references to cross-cutting issues, nexuses and policy integration, coherence and coordination in EU policy documents. Policy integration is at the core of the SDGs, which recognize the important connections between policy sectors and objectives. Agenda 2030 states that gender equality is a prerequisite for sustainable development. The SDGs have an overarching pledge to the 'systematic mainstreaming of a gender perspective in the implementation of the Agenda' (2015, para. 20). However, at the same time, the SDGs separate gender (SDG 5) and climate change (SDG 13). EU reports on SDG progress show this split, with the reports on progress on SDG 13 remaining gender blind. The potential for the successful integration of climate change and gender equality has therefore not yet been realized.

Conclusion

What can a gender perspective bring to the analysis of EU climate policy? The effects of climate change are not the same for everyone. Existing inequalities affect the impact of climate change and the ability to respond to it. Measures introduced to reduce climate change or to adapt to it also have different effects on people, according to their gender, class, wealth, ethnicity, physical ability and other structural inequalities. There are gender differences in the production of climate change, in attitudes towards it, and in access to climate decision-making.

Feminist studies of gender mainstreaming have investigated the gaps between rhetoric and reality. They have shown how gender evaporates before it reaches the ground and have argued that a stated commitment to gender equality is often no more than symbolic (Longwe, 1997). In a crisis, gender issues are always pushed to the bottom of the agenda (Allwood, 2019; Muehlenhoff et al., 2020). But gender equality – and justice more broadly – cannot be left until after the crisis is resolved. It is not an add-on or an afterthought, but essential to creating a sustainable future for all (Cavaghan and O'Dwyer, 2018, pp. 104–5).

EU climate policy is edging away from an exclusive focus on technological solutions towards a recognition that climate change affects people, and that people are part of the solution. However, integrating diversity and intersectionality into the analysis of climate change and proposed responses to it is still a marginal concern. Efforts to address gender inequality and efforts to address climate change continue to exist in parallel, rather than being fully integrated into each other. Gender equality is not integrated into all aspects of decision-making and at all stages. Instead, it is tagged on or mentioned in separate documents and debates, in what Acosta *et al.* (2019, p. 15) refer to as a 'stale reproduction of set pieces of text [pointing to] significant levels of inertia in thinking and practice around gender mainstreaming issues'.

The Council conclusions 6153/19 on climate diplomacy describe 2019 as the year of pushing further convergence between the SDGs and climate agendas (2019). A successful integration of these two agendas would make a substantial contribution to a gender-and climate-just future, but again, this requires strong political will and effective policy coherence.

References

Acker, J. (1990) 'Hierarchies, Jobs, Bodies: A Theory of Gendered Organisations'. *Gender and Society*, Vol. 4, No. 2, pp. 139–58.

Acosta, M., van Bommel, S., van Wessel, M. *et al.* (2019) 'Discursive Translations of Gender Mainstreaming Norms: the Case of Agricultural and Climate Change Policies in Uganda'. *Women's Studies International Forum*, Vol. 74, pp. 9–19.

Agrawala, S. and Crick, F. (2009) 'Climate Change and Development: Time to Adapt'. In Palasuo, E. (ed.) *Rethinking Development in a Carbon-Constrained World: Development Cooperation and Climate Change* (Ministry for Foreign Affairs of Finland), pp. 26–40.

Allwood, G. (2013) 'Gender Mainstreaming and Policy Coherence for Development: Unintended Gender Consequences and EU Policy'. *Women's Studies International Forum*, Vol. 39, pp. 42–52.

Allwood, G. (2014) Gender Mainstreaming and EU Climate Change Policy. *European Integration online Papers (EIoP), Special issue 1* 18.

Allwood, G. (2019) 'Gender Equality in European Union Development Policy in Times of Crisis'. *Political Studies Review*. https://doi.org/10.1177/1478929919863224.

Alston, M. (2013) 'Women and Adaptation'. *WIRES Climate Change*, Vol. 4, No. 5, pp. 351–8.

Arora-Jonsson, S. and Sijapati, B.B. (2018) 'Disciplining Gender in Environmental Organisations: The Texts and Practices of Gender Mainstreaming'. *Gender, Work & Organization*, Vol. 25, No. 3, pp. 309–25.

BBC News. (2012) *EU Climate Change "worse for women" claim row.* 19 April, bbc.co.uk, accessed 10 August 2020.

Biedenkopf, K. and Dupont, C. (2013) 'A Toolbox Approach to the EU's External Climate Governance'. In Boening, A., Kremer, J.-F. and van Loon, A. (eds) *Global Power Europe* (Vol. 1) (Berlin: Springer), pp. 181–99.

Brody, A., Demetriades, J. and Esplen, E. (2008) Gender and Climate Change: Mapping the Linkages. BRIDGE, Institute of Development Studies, Brighton.

Buckingham, S. and Le Masson, V. (2017) 'Introduction'. In Buckingham, S. and Le Masson, V. (eds) *Understanding Climate Change through Gender Relations* (London: Routledge), pp. 1–12.

Carbone, M. (2013) 'International Development and the European Union's External Policies: Changing Contexts, Problematic Nexuses, Contested Partnerships'. *Cambridge Review of International Affairs*, Vol. 26, No. 3, pp. 483–96.

Cavaghan, R. and O'Dwyer, M. (2018) 'European Economic Governance in 2017: A Recovery for Whom?' *JCMS*, Vol. 56, pp. 97–108.

Chappell, L. and Guerrina, R. (2020) Understanding the Gender Regime in the European External Action Service. *Cooperation and Conflict* Vol. 55, No 2, pp. 261–80.

Collins, P.H. and Bilge, S. (2016) *Intersectionality* (Cambridge: Polity Press).

Connell, R. (2006) 'The Experience of Gender Change in Public Sector Organisations'. *Gender, Work & Organization*, Vol. 13, No. 5, pp. 435–52.

Copernicus Climate Change Service (2019). *European State of the Climate 2019. Full report: climate.copernicus.eu/ESOTC/2019*.

Council of the European Union. (2019) *Climate Diplomacy - Council Conclusions 6153/19*. 18 February.

Daly, M. (2005) 'Gender Mainstreaming in Theory and Practice'. *Social Politics*, Vol. 12, No. 3, pp. 433–4.

Dankelman, I. (ed.) (2010) *Gender and Climate Change: An Introduction* (London: Earthscan).

De Roeck, F., Orbie, J. and Delputte, S. (2018) 'Mainstreaming Climate Change Adaptation into the European Union's Development Assistance'. *Environmental Science & Policy*, Vol. 81, pp. 36–45. https://doi.org/10.1016/j.envsci.2017.12.005.

Djoudi, H., Locatelli, B., Vaast, C., Asher, K., Brockhaus, M. and Sijapati, B.B. (2016) 'Beyond Dichotomies: Gender and Intersecting Inequalities in Climate Change Studies'. *Ambio*, Vol. 45, No. 3, pp. 248–62.

Dupont, C. (2016) *Climate Policy Integration into EU Energy Policy. Progress and Prospects* (London and New York: Routledge).

Dupont, C. (2019) 'The EU's Collective Securitisation of Climate Change'. *West European Politics*, Vol. 42, No. 2. Available at https://doi.org/10.1080/01402382.2018.1510199.

Dupont, C. and Oberthür, S. (2015) 'The European Union'. In Bäckstrand, K. and Lövbrand, E. (eds) *Research Handbook on Climate Governance* (Cheltenham: Edward Elgar), pp. 224–36.

EIGE (2017) Gender Impact Assessment Guide. Vilnius.

Enloe, C. (2004) *The Curious Feminist: Searching for Women in a New Age of Empire* (Berkeley: University of California Press).

European Commission. (2003) *Climate change in the context of development cooperation*. COM (2003)85 final, 11 March.

European Commission. (2013) *An EU Strategy on adaptation to climate change*. COM(2013)216 final, 16 April.

European Commission. (2014) *A policy framework for climate and energy in the period from 2020 to 2030*. COM(2014)15 final, 22 January.

European Commission. (2014) *General Union Environment Action Programme to 2020: Living well, within the limits of our planet*. Luxembourg: EU Publications.

European Commission. (2018) *A Clean Planet for All: A European strategic long-term vision for a prosperous, modern, competitive and climate neutral economy*. COM(2018)773 final, 28 November.

European Commission. (2018) *In-depth analysis in support of the COM(2018)773: A Clean Planet for All*. 28 November.

European Commission. (2019) *The European Green Deal*. COM(2019)640 final, 11 December.

European Commission. (2020) *A Union of Equality: Gender Equality Strategy 2020-2025*. COM (2020)152 final, March.

European Council. (2007) *Treaty of Lisbon*. OJ C 306, 17 December.

European Parliament. (2019) *Motion for a Resolution on a European strategic long-term vision for a prosperous, modern, competitive and climate-neutral economy*. 11 March.

European Parliament. (2019) Resolution of 28 November 2019 on the climate and environmental emergency. 2019/2930(RSP)

European Parliament. (2012) *Resolution on women and climate change*. 2011/2197(INI), 20 April.

European Parliament. (2018) *Resolution on women, gender equality and climate justice 2017/2086 (INI)*. 16 January.

European Parliament. (2019) *Motion for a Resolution on the European Green Deal*. 2019/2956 (RSP), 15 January.

European Union. (2016) *Shared Vision, Common Action: A Stronger Europe. A Global Strategy for the European Union's Foreign and Security Policy*. June.

Franceschet, S., Krook, M.L. and Piscopo, J. (2012) *The Impact of Gender Quotas* (Oxford: Oxford University Press).

Furness, M. and Gänzle, S. (2017) 'The Security-Development Nexus in EU Foreign Relations after Lisbon: Policy Coherence at Last?' *Development and Policy Review*, Vol. 35, No. 4, pp. 475–92.

Guerrina, R. and Wright, K. (2016) 'Gendering Normative Power Europe: Lessons of the Women, Peace and Security Agenda'. *International Affairs*, Vol. 92, No. 2, pp. 293–312.

Gupta, J. and van der Grijp, N. (2010) In Gupta, J. and van der Grijp, N. (eds) *Mainstreaming Climate Change in Development Cooperation: Theory, Practice and Implications for the European Union* (Cambridge: Cambridge University Press).

Intergovernmental Panel on Climate Change (2018). Global warming of 1.5°C. Special Report, Geneva: World Meteorological Organization https://www.ipcc.ch/sr15/.

Jordan, A., Huitema, D., Van Asselt, H., Rayner, T. and Berkhout, F. (2010) *Climate Change Policy in the European Union* (Cambridge: Cambridge University Press).

Kaijser, A. and Kronsell, A. (2014) 'Climate Change through the Lens of Intersectionality'. *Environmental Politics*, Vol. 23, No. 3. https://doi.org/10.1080/09644016.2013.835203.

Kok, M.T.J. and de Coninck, H.C. (2007) 'Widening the Scope of Policies to Address Climate Change: Directions for Mainstreaming'. *Environmental Science and Policy*, Vol. 10, No. 7–8, pp. 587–99.

Kronsell, A. (2013) 'Gender and Transition in Climate Governance'. *Environmental Innovation and Societal Transitions*, Vol. 7, pp. 1–15.

Kronsell, A. (2015) 'Feminism'. In Bäckstrand, K. and Lövbrand, E. (eds) *Research Handbook on Climate Governance* (Cheltenham: Edward Elgar), pp. 73–83.

Lavenex, S. and Kunz, R. (2009) 'The Migration–Development Nexus in EU External Rleations'. In Carbone, M. (ed.) *European Integration* Policy Coherence and EU Development Policy (Abingdon: Routledge), pp. 439–57.

Longwe, S.H. (1997) 'The Evaporation of Gender Policies in the Patriarchal Cooking Pot'. *Development in Practice*, Vol. 7, No. 2, pp. 148–56.

MacGregor, S. (2014) 'Only Resist: Feminist Ecological Citizenship and the Post-politics of Climate Change'. *Hypatia*, Vol. 29, No. 3, pp. 617–33.

MacGregor, S. (2017) 'Moving beyond Impacts: More Answers to the "Gender and Climate Change" Question'. In Buckingham, S. and Le Masson, V. (eds) *Understanding Climate Change through Gender Relations* (London: Routledge), pp. 15–30.

Magnusdottir, G.L. and Kronsell, A. (2015) 'The (In)visibility of Gender in Scandinavian Climate Policy-making'. *International Feminist Journal of Politics*, Vol. 17, No. 2, pp. 308–26.

Magnusdottir, G.L. and Kronsell, A. (2016) 'The Double Democratic Deficit in Climate Policy-making by the EU Commission'. *Femina Politica*, Vol. 2, pp. 64–76.

Meier, P. and Celis, K. (2011) 'Sowing the Seeds of its Own Failure: Implementing the Concept of Gender Mainstreaming'. *Social Politics*, Vol. 18, No. 4, pp. 469–89.

Morrow, K. (2017) 'Integrating Gender Issues into the Global Climate Change Régime'. In Buckingham, S. and Le Masson, V. (eds) *Understanding Climate Change through Gender Relations* (London: Routledge), pp. 31–44.

Muehlenhoff, H.L., van der Vleuten, A. and Welfens, N. (2020) 'Slipping off or Turning the Tide? Gender Equality in European Union's External Relations in Times of Crisis'. *Political Studies Review*, Vol. 18, No. 3, pp. 332–28.

Nagel, J. (2012) 'Intersecting Identities and Global Climate Change'. *Identities*, Vol. 19, No. 4, pp. 467–76.

Nagel, J. (2016) *Gender and Climate Change: Impacts, Science, Policy* (New York: Routledge).

Oberthür, S. and Groen, L. (2018) 'Explaining Goal Achievement in International Negotiations: the EU and the Paris Agreement on Climate Change'. *Journal of European Public Policy*, Vol. 25, No. 5, pp. 708–27.

Porter, F. and Sweetman, C. (2005) 'Editorial'. In Portman, F. and Sweetman, C. (eds) *Mainstreaming Gender in Development: A Critical Review*. (Oxford: Oxfam) pp. 2–10.

Rao, A., Sandler, J., Kelleher, D. and Miller, C. (2016) *Gender at Work. Theory and Practice for 21st Century Organisations* (Abingdon: Routledge).

Rayner, T. and Jordan, A. (2010) 'Adapting to a Changing Climate: An Emerging EU Policy?' In Jordan, A., Huitema, D., Van Asselt, H. *et al.* (eds) *Climate Change Policy in the European Union* (Cambridge: Cambridge University Press), pp. 145–66.

Skinner, E. (2011) 'Gender and Climate Change: Overview Report'. Institute of Development Studies, Brighton

Stratigaki, M. (2005) 'Gender Mainstreaming vs Positive Action: An Ongoing Conflict in EU Gender Equality Policy'. *European Journal of Women's Studies*, Vol. 12, No. 2, pp. 165–86.

Sultana, F. (2014) 'Gendering Climate Change: Geographical Insights'. *Professional Geographer*, Vol. 66, No. 3, pp. 372–81.

Tschakert, P. and Machado, M. (2012) 'Gender Justice and Rights in Climate Change Adaptation: Opportunities and Pitfalls'. *Ethics and Social Welfare*, Vol. 6, No. 3, pp. 275–89.

United Nations Framework Convention on Climate Change. (2019) *Enhanced Lima work programme on gender and its gender action plan, Madrid*. Madrid, 2–13 December.

United Nations Gender Assembly. (2015) *Transforming our world: the 2030 Agenda for Sustainable Development*. A/RES/7011, 21 October.

Wahlström, M., Kocyba, P., De Vydt, M. and de Moor, J. (2019) Protest for a Future: Composition, Mobilisation and Motives of the Participants in Fridays for Future Climate Protests on 15 March 2019 in 13 European Cities.Available online at: https://www.researchgate.net/publication/334745801_Protest_for_a_future_Composition_mobilization_and_motives_of_the_participants_in_Fridays_For_Future_climate_protests_on_15_March_2019_in_13_European_cities. Last accessed 23 July 2020.

Women's Environment and Development Organization (2018) *Pocket Guide to Gender Equality under the UNFCCC* (Brussels: European Capacity Building Initiative).

Woodward, A. (2008) 'Too Late for Gender Mainstreaming? Taking Stock in Brussels'. *Journal of European Social Policy*, Vol. 18, No. 3, pp. 289–302.

Woodward, A. and van der Vleuten, A. (2014) 'EU and the Export of Gender Equality Norms: Myth and Facts'. In van der Vleuten, A., van Eerdewijk, A. and Roggeband, C. (eds) *Gender Equality Norms in Regional Governance: Transnational Dynamics in Europe, South America and Southern Africa* (Basingstoke: Palgrave Macmillan), pp. 67–92.

Youngs, R. (2014) Climate Change and EU Security Policy: An Unmet Challenge. Brussels. Availavble online at https://carnegieeurope.eu/2014/05/21/climate-change-and-eu-security-policy-unmet-challenge-pub-55658. Last accessed 23 July 2020.

Zalewski, M. (2010) '"I Don't Even Know what Gender Is": A Discussion of the Connections between Gender, Gender Mainstreaming and Feminist Theory'. *Review of International Studies*, Vol. 36, No. 1, pp. 3–27.

JCMS 2020 Volume 58. Annual Review. pp. 187–201   DOI: 10.1111/jcms.13076

The EU and its Neighbourhood: The Politics of Muddling Through

TOBIAS SCHUMACHER
European Neighbourhood Policy Chair, College of Europe, Natolin Campus, Warsaw, Poland

Introduction

Virtually all JCMS Annual Review articles on the EU's engagement in and towards its eastern and southern neighbourhoods published in recent years share almost identical assessments of EU influence: depictions range from 'stasis' (Whitman and Juncos, 2013), 'meagre' (Whitman and Juncos, 2014, p. 157) and 'marginal' (Juncos and Whitman, 2015, p. 212) to 'waning' (Pomorska and Noutcheva, 2017) and, thus, echo the critique that has been voiced elsewhere (Howorth, 2016; Schumacher *et al.*, 2018; Gstöhl, 2019). The year 2019 is no exception in this regard. EU relations with its 16 neighbouring countries have been marked by similar dynamics and trends as in previous years and continue to suffer from ambiguity, coherence problems and 'inherent design faults and political misjudgements' (Leigh, 2019, p. 386).

The EU's eastern and southern neighbourhoods in 2019 were characterized by multi-layered security crises, territorial conflicts and wars, slowly advancing or stagnating reform processes, or the consolidation of the so-called authoritarian turn, in conjunction with an unprecedented exposure of many neighbours to seemingly incessant inflows of irregular migrants. Conversely, the EU itself remained exposed to disintegration dynamics, as exemplified by Brexit – tipping the EU's internal power balance even further in favour of Germany – and the advancement of the illiberal script in several Member States. These phenomena are poised to affect negatively perceptions of the EU's credibility, influence and leverage in the neighbourhood and contribute further to an erosion of the already decreasing public support for European integration and the EU's supposedly normative appeal in several neighbouring societies (Lavrelashvili, 2016; Pomorska and Noutcheva, 2017, p. 168).

2019 witnessed a renewed search for alternative and attractive integration offers below the level of EU membership. On one hand, this was demonstrated by the European Commission's public consultation process on the future of the Eastern Partnership (EaP). This was initiated on 14 May 2019 by Commission President Jean-Claude Juncker and Commissioner for Neighbourhood and Enlargement Negotiations Johannes Hahn at the Brussels high-level conference on the tenth anniversary of the EaP and ended on 31 October 2019. Replicating the 2014–15 public review process of the European Neighbourhood Policy (ENP) (Furness *et al.*, 2019), this consultation process revolved around the idea of providing stakeholders from EU Member States and neighbouring regions with an opportunity to submit their propositions on the future strategic direction of the EaP and a new generation of post-2020 deliverables. As in 2014–15, the decision to turn the review process into a public exercise was motivated by the notion to increase inclusiveness and counter neighbours' long held views that 'co-ownership' – propagated for years by the EU – does 'not extend to defining the policy objectives, instruments and the scope of differentiation' (Wolzcuk, 2017, pp. 7). On the other hand, the EU's renewed efforts to not lose even more of the little influence it is left with in most parts of its 'near abroad' was exemplified by attempts on the part of the Commission to transpose instruments to southern neighbours, such as the Deep and Comprehensive Free Trade Area (DCFTA), that are being utilized in parts of the eastern neighbourhood already since mid-2014 (Georgia and Moldova) and 2016 respectively (Ukraine). This transposition was attempted in spite of deep-rooted opposition among societies and entrepreneurs in the southern neighbourhood and legitimate concerns as regards the utility of DCFTAs (Rudloff and Werenfels, 2018).

These factors were compounded by continuous go-alone practices of individual Member States and their open disregard for the ENP, contradicting the call – articulated in the 2015 Review of the ENP – for 'greater ownership', 'deeper involvement' and a 'more coherent effort' of Member States (European Commission and HR/VP, 2015). Further aggravating the already tenuous pursuit of coherence, EU institutions were marked by new mandates commencing over the course of 2019: the arrival of a new and more fragmented European Parliament in the first half of 2019, the belated coming into power of a self-proclaimed geopolitical Commission in December 2019, and the appointments of a new High Representative for Foreign and Security Policy and a new President of the European Council, respectively.

As will be discussed by this article, these dynamics affected EU-neighbourhood relations in 2019 and contributed not just to the continuation and deepening of transactional practices – at the expense of the promotion of democratic norms and values – in the framework of the ENP. They also reinforced the EU's image in its neighbourhoods of an actor that maintains its reliance on muddling through practices and that, more often than not, looks the other way when neighbourhood regimes are in violation of human rights and political and civil liberties. The article is divided into three main sections. The next section briefly analyses the EU's new strategic agenda 2019–24 and its relevance for EU-neighbourhood relations. The subsequent section discusses EaP-related dynamics and debates, as well as EU responses to challenges in its eastern neighbourhood, taking into account local and regional scope conditions. Mirroring this structure, the third section touches upon Union for the Mediterranean (UfM)-related developments before it analyses EU action towards southern neighbours and challenges they are faced with.

I. The New Strategic Agenda 2019–24 and EU-Neighbourhood Relations

The EU's pursuit of relations with its eastern and southern neighbours in 2019 remained embedded in the revised ENP of 2015 and the 2016 Global Strategy. This implies that it continued to draw on their subdued normative language and their security-driven foci on pragmatic transactionalism and the stabilization of, and resilience-building in, a neighbourhood that continues to be perceived by European decision-makers as a 'ring of fire' (The Economist, 2014). At the European Council of 20/21 June 2019, EU heads of states and governments decided to complement these two documents by adopting the new strategic agenda 2019–24, prepared at the May Sibiu Future for Europe Summit and replacing the strategic agenda 2014–19. The strategy hardly deserves to be labelled 'strategy', given that it merely enumerates often disjointed aspirations and does not have either a legally binding character or an exclusive focus on the ENP or the neighbourhood for that matter. Yet, it is noteworthy on at least two accounts.

Firstly, it declares rather pompously that the EU 'will pursue an ambitious neighbourhood policy', [...] 'promote its own unique model of cooperation as inspiration for others' and [...] 'promote democracy and human rights' (European Council, 2019). This is remarkable as it suggests yet another U-turn in EU foreign policy discourse and a return to the normative power Europe narrative that at least rhetorically underpinned the ENP until late 2015. This occurs in conjunction with a renewed, supposedly more pro-active focus on external norms and values support in the EU's neighbourhood, though the revised ENP of 2015 had relegated this objective to a second order status. That the need 'to pursue a strategic course of action and increase its capacity to act autonomously to safeguard its interests' and the need 'to uphold its values and way of life' are regarded as two sides of the same coin is also reflected in the title of the agenda's section dealing with EU external relations. Unlike the 2014–19 agenda, which spoke only of 'The Union as a strong global actor' and of the EU as a 'strong partner in our neighbourhood', the 2019 agenda subordinates all external relations-related objectives to the aim of 'promoting Europe's interests and values in the world'. The extent to which these resurfacing lofty announcements stand a chance of implementation, however, is rather limited. They would require not just all Member States to be 'more united in the stances we take', [...] 'making more resources available' – a qualification made by the new agenda itself. They would also presuppose the adoption of a hitherto missing common EU grand strategy that defines hierarchized policy goals and interests and that links them with available mechanisms, instruments and resources, while taking into account existing and potentially altering scope conditions in the neighbourhood.

Secondly, the new agenda pledges to 'uphold the European perspective for European States able and willing to join'. This promise could serve as a powerful reference point not just for candidate and potential candidate countries in the Western Balkans, but also those EU neighbours, such as Ukraine, Georgia and Moldova, that for years have been seeking to obtain a membership perspective and, therefore, a credible acknowledgement by the EU of their 'European aspiration' and 'European choice', as is stipulated in their respective Association Agreements. The French-inspired decision by the European Council of 17–18 October 2019 to not provide the Republic of North Macedonia and Albania with a date for the start of accession negotiations,[1] in spite of past promises and the Commission's positive recommendations of 17 April 2018 (European Commission, 2018), has however rendered this unlikely. Not only is the Council's refusal to uphold the 'European perspective' likely to damage the EU's image in its neighbourhoods even further. What is more, the decision was a major blow to those actors in the EU's 'near abroad' whose legitimacy is much reliant on their pro-European credentials, as it is torpedoing their efforts and leverage of integrating their societies closer into EU structures.

---

[1] *Politico*, 18 October 2019.

II. The EU and its Eastern Neighbours: In Search for New Forms of Association

The central event in 2019 in the framework of the EU's relations with its eastern neighbours was the tenth anniversary of the EaP which was marked at the EaP foreign ministers meeting on 13 May 2019 and the Brussels high-level conference held the next day. The conference was successful in bringing together EaP countries' heads of state and government (Ukraine, Georgia, Moldova) and foreign ministers (Armenia, Azerbaijan and Belarus), Jean-Claude Juncker, Federica Mogherini, Johannes Hahn and some 200 governmental and non-governmental stakeholders from EU Member States and EaP countries. It took place against the backdrop of a decision to discontinue the practice of holding every two years, and thus also in 2019, an EaP Summit, as it was deemed that presidential elections in Ukraine and European Parliament elections in May, as well as the process leading to the appointment of a new Commission and corresponding leadership positions in EU institutions, would paralyse such a summit from the outset. The majority of Member States saw the two events merely as an opportunity to demonstrate their on-going commitment to help EaP regimes transform and modernize their political systems and economies also in the future. According to this logic, the two events were mainly destined to transmit one message, notably that the EaP was still alive and operational, and that focusing on the '20 deliverables for 2020' does generate tangible transformation dividends. In contrast, the EaP-6, drawing on a recommendation by the outgoing European Parliament (2017), had hoped to extract from the EU new cooperation offers and, as far as Ukraine, Georgia and Moldova were concerned, even new integration perspectives and the prospect of EU membership negotiations.[2] Neither the high-level conference nor the previously held EaP foreign ministers' meeting resulted in the charting of a path that would help reconcile these diverging interests and reduce prevailing divisions inside the EU and within and among EaP countries over the future course of the framework and relations with Russia. This failure blatantly underlined that the EaP, ten years after its establishment, continues to be rooted in muddling through practices on the part of the EU and suffers from the absence of a meaningful *raison d'être*. Furthermore, it stills lacks a long-term strategy that provides all target countries and societies with a clarification as to whether the framework is a means to an (undefined) end or the end itself. Almost inevitably, this situation motivated neighbours' pro-European elites – at the two EaP events in May and also, for example, in the framework of the EU–Ukraine Summit of 8 July or the EU–Moldova Association Council of 30 September – to maintain their long-held demands and push for an upgrade of relations. For them, such an upgrade would result in a shift from a supposedly narrow Association Agreement-centred approach to an 'Association+', revolving around integration also into at least the EU's Energy and Digital Unions and the Schengen area, as well as the creation of bilateral customs unions. Neither the Commission and the European External Action Service (EEAS) nor a majority of Member States were ready to commit themselves to these demands, let alone address and clarify the future nature of relations with the EU's 'near abroad'. Instead, the compromise found was the initiation of yet another review of EU-neighbourhood relations – in fact, the third within the last ten years – the results of

[2]*Union Information Agency*, 13 July 2017; *Pravda*, 24 November 2017; *EUobserver*, 24 November 2017; *Anadolu Agency*, 27 May 2015.

which were not publicized in 2019 due to the temporary intra-institutional stasis in both the Commission and the EEAS.

Muddling through practices on the part of the EU were also the central feature of EU bilateral relations with most EaP countries. Once more, the EU shied away from holding incumbent eastern neighbourhood regimes fully accountable for half-hearted, sluggish or even entirely absent political and judicial reforms, state capture and misuse of state resources, intimidation or persecution of political opponents, indiscriminate use of force, or recurring non-compliance with universal human rights standards as well as political and civil liberties.

As far as Georgia is concerned, that according to Mogherini is the 'most advanced Eastern partner',[3] the Association Implementation Report on Georgia, issued on 30 January 2019, pointed to a number of serious problems. These relate to the rule of law, political interference in the judiciary, high-level corruption, and ineffective implementation of human rights and anti-discrimination legislation (European Commission and HR/VP, 2019). This was compounded by other reports (Human Rights Watch, 2020), citing the continuous abuses by law enforcement officials with impunity as well as the lack of compliance of the Law on Common Courts with all recommendations of the Venice Commission. In spite of these shortcomings, the EU, in a press statement of 5 March 2019, jointly issued with the Georgian government, praised the latter and 'welcomed the excellent state of EU–Georgia relations' (Council of the EU, 2019a). Also throughout the year, anxious to not undermine the image of Georgia as a 'success story',[4] the EU abstained from criticizing the Georgian authorities openly. Instead, it left it to its delegation in Tbilisi to join in mid-May muted calls on 'Georgian leaders'[5] to end violence and discrimination against LGBTQI+ persons and to merely recognize in November, together with the Tbilisi-based US Embassy, the 'deep disappointment of a wide segment of Georgian society'[6] at the parliament's failed electoral reform. Furthermore, it stayed suspiciously silent when Georgian police forces in late June engaged in a brutal crackdown of anti-government protests.[7] Also with regards to the unresolved conflicts over South Ossetia and Abkhazia the EU displayed a rather low profile. Instead of the Council or Mogherini, it was the EU's local delegation together with EU heads of mission that called for – but did not condemn – an end of the borderization activities by Russia-supported South Ossetian forces which had flared up in late August in the Chorchana–Tsnelisi area close to the Administrative Border Line (ABL).[8] Subsequently, the EU also refrained from working pro-actively towards the resumption of the Ergneti Incident Prevention and Response Mechanism (IPRM) which remains suspended.[9] At the same time, it pledged to provide assistance to Abkhazia (European Commission and HR/VP, 2019), even though it is not clear how this might mend widely held perceptions of the EU as a biased, pro-Georgia actor (Dobrescu and Schumacher, 2020).

[3]*OpenMediaHub*, 6 February 2018.
[4]*GeorgiaToday*, 8 April 2019.
[5]*EEAS*, 17 May 2019.
[6]*US Embassy in Georgia*, 17 November 2019.
[7]*Euractiv*, 25 June 2019.
[8]*Euractiv*, 30 August 2019.
[9]*Civil.ge*, 30 August 2019.

As regards the resolution of the Nagorno-Karabakh conflict between Azerbaijan and Armenia, the EU in 2019 did not play an influential role either, though through occasional declarations, such as the one issued at the November meeting of the OSCE Permanent Council (Delegation of the EU, 2019), it tried to evoke the notion of geopolitical relevance. Not being part of the OSCE Minsk Group, its actions were limited to reiterating its support for the latter. While holding on to its flawed and supposedly mismanaged civil society-oriented European Partnership for the Peaceful Settlement of the Conflict over Nagorno-Karabakh (EPNK),[10] it repeatedly expressed its hope that the Vienna meeting of late March by Azerbaijani President Aliyev and Armenian Prime Minister Pashinyan will result in the concrete 'preparation of populations for peace'.[11] Notwithstanding these declarations, it did not react to Pashinyan's provocative visit of Stepanakert in early August and reject his confrontational public announcement that 'Artsakh [Nagorno-Karabakh] is Armenia, the end',[12] thus giving the impression of tacitly agreeing with it. This happened against the backdrop of a deepening of EU–Armenia diplomatic relations in 2019, following the Velvet Revolution of early 2018 in Armenia and the December 2018 snap parliamentary elections. This is reflected by the large number of sector-specific meetings, the holding of the second EU–Armenia Partnership Council and the smooth adoption of the roadmap for the implementation of the Comprehensive and Enhanced Partnership Agreement (CEPA) in November. The provisional application since June 2018 of the CEPA, which by late December was still not ratified by nine EU Member States, did, however, generate asymmetric trade effects: It enabled the EU to increase its trade surplus and consolidate its market power while contributing initially to a worsening of Armenia's current account balance deficit.[13]

Though Azerbaijan's president Aliyev pardoned more than 50 political prisoners and perceived critics in March 2019, the regime maintained its totalitarian practices, severely violating human rights and political and civil liberties. According to credible reports,[14] it kept more than 100 opposition activists imprisoned and exposed them to torture and other ill-treatment while, at the same time, it continued to resort to arbitrary detentions, harassment and intimidation. These practices, in conjunction with the continuous abuse of state resources and the cementing of corrupt patronage networks, neither led to noteworthy condemnations by EU leaders nor did they preclude the EU from advancing negotiations on a new partnership agreement. The EU–Azerbaijan Cooperation Council of 4 April cynically declared 'that it was important to use the current momentum' (Council of the EU 2019) and even praised Azerbaijan for its 'valuable contribution to the development of the Eastern Partnership' (ibid.). While this rhetoric dealt yet another blow to reform actors in Azerbaijan, it followed the pattern – visible already for years and particularly salient since the intensification of relations in 2018 and the corresponding adoption of Partnership Priorities – of consolidating the transactional nature of relations and Azerbaijan's status as a strategic energy partner.

---

[10]See *NGO Monitor*, October 2018.
[11]This phrase has been coined by the foreign ministers of Azerbaijan and Armenia at their Paris meeting in January 2019. *Conciliation Resources*, July 2019.
[12]*OC-Media*, 7 August 2019.
[13]*IMF Country Report, No. 19/397*, December 2019.
[14]*SMDT*, 21 February 2019.

In contrast, the EU's approach towards Belarus, based on the Council conclusions of 15 February 2016, continued to oscillate between condemning the regime of President Lukashenko for its authoritarian practices and penalizing it by renewing restrictive measures (Council of the EU, 2019b). At the same time, it engaged the regime in the framework of the bilateral Coordination Group, the EU–Belarus human rights dialogue, financial cooperation with the EIB and the EBRD, and carefully chosen technical, sector-specific cooperation. Accordingly, in 2019, human rights, the rule of law and democratic governance featured more saliently in diplomatic exchanges with Belarus than with Azerbaijan. The numerous bilateral meetings held throughout the year and the decision by the EU in October to grant Belarus a Visa Facilitation Plan[15] signal that once Lithuania has given up its opposition to the construction of the Astravyets Power Plant and, therefore, no longer blocks the adoption of Partnership Priorities,[16] the recent trend towards a gradual normalization of relations – and a less normative EU approach to the human rights situation in Belarus – is poised to continue. This normalization is all the more likely if the rift between Lukashenko and Russian President Putin deepens and if the new Commission is serious about its ambitions of acting geopolitically.

Ukraine and Moldova have in common that in 2019 they witnessed the coming-to-power of new regimes. In the case of Moldova, though, a rather unlikely coalition composed of the pro-Russian Moldovan Socialist Party (PSRM), led by President Dodon, and the pro-Western ACUM block of Maia Sandu, already fell just five months later due to an orchestrated no-confidence vote by the PSRM and the previously ousted Democratic Party (DP).[17] Initially, EU leaders were quick in congratulating Sandu as prime minister of Moldova and Volodymyr Zelensky on his election as president of Ukraine.[18] But, at the same time, they cautioned that wide-ranging reforms needed to continue and, as far as Moldova is concerned, that 'calm and restraint' had to prevail.[19] Almost immediately after the nominally reformist and pro-European government of Sandu had been installed, the EU pledged its full support and subsequently unlocked much-needed financial assistance,[20] but refrained from making this support conditional on a concrete reform plan, let alone demonstrable achievements. This stood in sharp contrast to the EU's ex-ante and ex-post conditionality applied towards both the preceding oligarchic DP-led government that was in power until June and the pro-Russian PSRM/DP government that has been ruling Moldova since mid-November – even though they shared a similar reform-oriented discourse. Likewise, mainly as a result of the initial uncertainty that revolved around the new Ukrainian president's foreign and domestic policy agenda, the EU displayed a less stringent attitude towards Zelensky and the new Ukrainian authorities than it had showed towards their predecessors. In practice, this advance, in conjunction with significant legislative progress and Ukraine's more pro-active agenda-shaping, resulted in a more conciliatory atmosphere at the July Ukraine Summit, the simultaneously held Association Council and other joint body meetings.[21] It also led the EEAS and the

---

[15]*Radio Free Europe/Radio Liberty*, 9 October 2020.
[16]*Baltic Times*, 20 May 2019.
[17]*Euractiv*, 12 November 2019.
[18]*Politico*, 22 April 2019.
[19]*Unian*, 9 June 2019.
[20]*Radio Free Europe/Radio Liberty*, 15 July 2019.
[21]I owe this observation to Andriy Tyushka, College of Europe, Natolin.

Commission to display a more responsive and less paternalistic attitude than in the past. Member States in the summer of 2019 displayed even some notion of unity as they succeeded yet again to agree on the renewal of restrictive measures against Russia in response to its annexation of Crimea and Sevastopol and its non-compliance with the Minsk agreements.[22] However, French President Macron's remarks that the 'European continent will never be stable or secure if we don't pacify and clarify our relations with Russia',[23] and his subsequent *offensive de charme* towards Russian President Putin, have raised fears in Ukraine and other EaP countries, as well as among Member States, that France might be intent on undermining the fragile consensus within the European Council that Russia needs to be held accountable for its unlawful actions. In addition, this episode also demonstrates the extent to which, in 2019, it remained a formidable challenge for the EU to agree on an unequivocal position that named – and shamed – explicitly the parties to the Ukraine conflict. By the same token, this rendered impossible any attempt on the part of the EU or other Member States to help Ukraine and Germany establish a more consolidated and stronger stance in the Normandy Format talks from which the EU remained excluded.

III. The EU and its Southern Neighbours: Looking the Other Way

EU action vis-à-vis its troubled southern neighbourhood in 2019 was equally characterized by regular recourse to muddling through practices. As in previous years, this was the result of the EU's inability, and EU Member States' unwillingness, to agree on and subsequently adhere to a united stance that would allow them to pursue pragmatic, transactional as well as security-oriented interests without violating the self-imposed objective, as defined by Article 21 TEU, to advance in particular democracy, the rule of law, human rights and fundamental freedoms and respect for the principles of the United Nations Charter and international law. In multilateral settings this came to the fore during the League of Arab States (LAS) –EU Summit and the operations of the UfM. In the framework of bilateral relations with individual southern neighbours, the EU and EU Member States simply turned a blind eye, once more, to the on-going consolidation of autocratic rule and the systematic violations of human rights in most parts of North Africa and the Levant. This occurred mainly out of fear that putting these at the centre of bilateral interactions would endanger Member States' profitable trade relations and impact negatively on joint counter-terrorism efforts and the containment of irregular migration flows.

EU heads of state and government, together with the Presidents of the Commission and the European Council, met with their Arab counterparts in Sharm-El-Sheikh for the first time ever in late February to discuss exclusively security- and migration-related challenges as well as ways to intensify sectoral cooperation.[24] EU leaders displayed collective reluctance to mention the dire human rights situation in the southern neighbourhood and, by focusing on issues that did not even remotely touch upon Arab' regimes' autocratic rule, they bestowed, more openly than ever, international legitimacy upon them. In so doing, they ignored the poignant warning, voiced during the early stages of the 2011 Arab uprisings by then Commissioner Füle, that it is, 'at best, short-termism [to assume] that

---

[22] *Radio Free Europe/Radio Liberty*, 20 June 2019.
[23] *Financial Times*, 11 September 2019.
[24] *Euractiv*, 27 February 2019.

authoritarian regimes were a guarantee of stability in the region' (European Commission, 2011). As a result, they contributed to 'normalising totalitarianism in the Middle East' (Badarin, 2019).

This normalization has also been a long-standing feature of the UfM which is supposed to be for the Mediterranean what the EaP is for the EU's eastern neighbourhood, though its focus on predominantly ad-hoc technical and project-based cooperation, drawing on voluntary contributions by its 43 members, is even narrower than the EaP. This structural architecture, deliberately put in place in 2008 to deflect the stark differences that exist among EU Member States and Mediterranean interlocutors as regards the nature of their political systems and their regional policies, precluded the UfM in 2019 from yielding any significant results and made it impossible for the EU to exert influence even in politically non-sensitive areas. Against this backdrop, it is unsurprising that even the UfM's annual foreign ministers meeting, held in Barcelona on 10 October, was, by and large, absent from the public discourse in both Europe and the southern neighbourhood.

In contrast, the continuation of the migration crisis in the central Mediterranean remained in the spotlight, but generated controversial decisions by the EU. In 2019, Member States renewed twice the mandate of Operation EUNAVFOR-MED Sophia – the EU's maritime operation aimed at the neutralisation of human trafficking in the Mediterranean. But they failed to agree on a collective deployment of rescue vessels as a result of Italy's intransigent position to no longer allow for disembarkation of rescued migrants in Italian ports and its claim that providing vessels would represent a pull-factor and contribute to a worsening of the crisis.[25] Instead, and in spite of openly displayed critique by Mogherini that the sole use of air assets will prevent the mission from effectively implementing its mandate,[26] the EU, drawing also on the previously changed mandate of its Border Assistance Mission in Libya (EUBAM Libya), decided to enhance its support for the Libyan coastguard and their efforts to intercept smuggling vessels and return migrants to Libya. This decision was taken in blunt disregard of the fact that the coastguard itself comprises former traffickers and places migrants upon their forced return in Libyan detention camps where they are exposed to inhumane treatment, ranging from enslavement, rape and torture to death.[27] As a consequence of this approach and the EU's toleration of individual Member States' criminalization of independent search-and-rescue operations, the EU was indicted in June for crimes against humanity in the framework of a criminal complaint submitted to the International Criminal Court.[28]

In particular the high degree of intra-Council fragmentation over how best to deal with the territorial conflict in Libya, as well as the influential role played by actors such as the United Arab Emirates, Egypt, Saudi Arabia and Russia on one hand and Qatar and Turkey on the other (Mezran and Varvelli, 2017), have laid bare yet again the absence of a coherent and unambiguous EU policy towards Libya. Following the renewed outbreak of hostilities in April between the Libyan National Army, led by Khalifa Haftar, and militias supporting the internationally recognized Government of National Accord of Prime Minister Fayez al-Serraj, Mogherini repeatedly called for a ceasefire and a return to the UN-facilitated political process. These declarations and reassurances that 'member states

[25] *Euractiv*, 27 March 2019.
[26] *Politico*, 12 September 2019.
[27] *The Guardian*, 3 November 2019.
[28] *The Guardian*, 3 June 2019.

realise the need for a united European voice',[29] issued against the backdrop of the Commission's holding on to unfeasible capacity building programmes, could not disguise that neither France nor Italy had abandoned their respective go-alone practices or were willing to end their diplomatic feud over competing energy and security interests. This emerged most openly on 10 April when France vetoed the adoption of a text by the European Council, destined to condemn Haftar and urge his forces to end their military offensive. Furthermore, it came to the fore two months later, when French missiles – supposedly undercutting the UN arms embargo – were found in a military camp formerly used by Haftar forces.[30] It also resurfaced in mid-December when Italian Foreign Minister Di Maio engaged in bilateral talks with Haftar and al-Serraj without having coordinated these either with the Council or the EEAS.[31] Signs of disunity were accentuated even further in September 2019 when Germany, rather than the EU, announced the launching of the so-called 'Berlin process' – a series of consultations aimed at the launching of a peace conference and the return to the UN-led process – which was based on the misguided assumption that Haftar and the external actors supporting him would be willing to cease hostilities and start negotiations (Lacher, 2019).

Similarly, in its relations with Algeria, Morocco and Tunisia, the EU in 2019 opted for a muddling through approach, though with considerable variation. In the case of Tunisia, this meant that the EU continued to rely on the provision of rather unconditional generous technical and financial assistance (Debuysere, 2019) and attempts to revive the stagnating talks on a DCFTA, while ignoring growing signs of authoritarian backsliding (Günay and Sommavilla, 2019). As regards Algeria, EU bodies, with the exception of the European Parliament (2019), did not comment on domestic developments, as they worried of being accused of infringing on Algeria's sovereignty and that the existing strategic energy partnership might be negatively affected. This silence is particularly noteworthy as Algeria's so-called 'Revolution of Smiles' was marked by the largest anti-regime protests since 1962 and had already led to the peaceful ousting of President Bouteflika in early April.[32] Silence characterized also the EU's response to the on-going violation of political rights and civil liberties by the Moroccan regime. As in previous years, the EU abstained from voicing any critique of the *Makhzen* – the Moroccan Royal Palace – for its pervasive political and economic rule and reliance on patronage networks. In spite of the continuous absence of meaningful democratic reforms and Morocco's status as a country that is still classified as 'partly free',[33] the EU has initiated a 'Euro-Moroccan Partnership for Shared Prosperity' (Council of the EU, 2019c). This indulgence on democratic standards and rule of law can be explained by Morocco's strategic role in the fight against migration, in Member States joint-terrorism cooperation and their dependency on access to the fish-rich, Morocco-controlled waters of Western Sahara. Announced at the end of the Association Council meeting on 27 June, the 'model partnership, rich and mutual' – as EU and Moroccan representatives described relations already in 2017 (EEAS, 2017) – is another attempt by the EU to fill with life the 2008 Advanced Status, but demonstrates once more the regime's successful co-optation of the EU into an unjustified pro-Morocco discourse.

[29] *Euronews*, 4 September 2019.
[30] *The New York Times*, 9 July 2019.
[31] *Aljazeera*, 17 December 2019.
[32] *The New York Times*, 2 April 2019.
[33] *Freedom House*, Freedom in the World 2019.

Unlike in previous years, this co-optation did not stop short of the Western Sahara conflict, as the Moroccan regime succeeded in convincing the EU, pressured by France and Spain, to praise Morocco for its allegedly 'serious and credible efforts' (EEAS, 2017) to resolve the conflict. This changed rhetoric is a break with past declarations and indicates that the EU is now also officially endorsing Morocco's position regarding Western Sahara. This interpretation is substantiated by the decision of the Council of 4 March and the European Parliament of 12 February to adopt a new Sustainable Fisheries Partnership Agreement (SFPA) with Morocco (Council of the EU, 2019d), granting EU Member States' vessels fishing rights in Western Sahara waters. These decisions were taken against previous rulings of the European Court of Justice on 21 December 2016 and on 27 February 2018 that prescribed that any agreement with Morocco 'is valid in so far as it is not applicable to Western Sahara and to its adjacent waters'.[34]

As far as Egypt and other southern neighbours in the Levant are concerned, EU action, or rather inaction, was once again a reflection of previous years. In Egypt, the massive human rights violations by the regime of President al-Sisi, repeated crackdowns of anti-regime protests, frequent executions of political opponents, and the constitutional amendments, destined to increase al-Sisi's powers and his term of office,[35] have triggered only muted responses by the EU. As became apparent at the LAS–EU Summit, the Egyptian regime's autocratic practices did neither impact on diplomatic relations and on-going talks on the intensification of counter-terrorism cooperation,[36] nor did they motivate the EU to make financial aid conditional on tangible reforms, thus provoking some observers to speak of EU leaders as 'Sisi's useful idiots' (Hearst, 2019). Faced with limited opportunity structures in Syria, the EU was once again unable to utilize its Syria strategy of 2017 and, therefore, failed to generate tangible peace dividends or contribute to the implementation of United Nations Security Council Resolution 2254 of 18 December 2015 and the Geneva Communiqué of 30 June 2012. Instead, it continued to focus on the provision of humanitarian aid for Syrian refugees in conjunction with resilience-building in Jordan and Lebanon, which together host some 1.7 million Syrian refugees. The EU, together with the United Nations, organized the third donor conference 'Supporting the future of Syria and the region' on 12–14 March in Brussels and generated aid commitments of approximately 6.2 billion EUR. This achievement could, however, not conceal the tensions that still existed among Member States over whether and when the EU should start providing reconstruction aid to the Syrian regime of President Assad and begin with the repatriation of Europe-based Syrian refugees.[37] As far as Jordan and Lebanon are concerned, Anholt and Sinatti demonstrated aptly the extent to which EU resilience-building in both countries was first and foremost a 'strategy to contain refugees in the region and prevent migration to Europe' (2019, p. 326), fostering, rather than reducing, 'perplexity and distrust at the receiving end' (Badarin and Schumacher, 2020, p. 74). As a matter of fact, this is a sobering assessment that counters other voices who have come to view EU resilience-building in the Levant and beyond as the expression of a 'more modest and cooperative approach to EU intervention abroad' (Bargués-Pedreny, 2019, p. 1) and as a new panacea in EU neighbourhood policies.

[34] *Euractiv*, 27 February 2018.
[35] *Aljazeera*, 28 April 2019.
[36] *Asharq/Al-Awsat*, 4 September 2019.
[37] *Euractiv*, 14 March 2019.

After the EU had criticized the United States' recognition of Jerusalem as the capital of Israel in December 2017 and the subsequent relocation of the US Embassy from Tel Aviv to Jerusalem in May 2018, regional developments catapulted the unresolved Israeli–Palestinian conflict once more onto the agenda of the Foreign Affairs Council in late March 2019. In response to the announcement by US President Trump on 25 March to recognize also the Golan Heights, occupied and administered by Israel since 1967, the EU-28 on 27 March referred to UN Security Council Resolutions 242 and 497 and unanimously rejected both the US recognition and Israel's territorial claims.[38] Thus, the EU engaged swiftly with the issue and overcame potential conflicts of interests among Member States. This is remarkable in light of both the increasing convergence of positions of the Visegrád-4 – Hungary, Poland, Slovakia and the Czech Republic – with those of Israel (Dyduch, 2018) and the announcement by Romanian Prime Minister Dăncilă on 24 March to follow the example set by the US and also recognize Jerusalem as Israel's capital and, accordingly, move Romania's embassy to Jerusalem.[39] Mogherini was quick in pointing to the EU's position with respect to the Golan Heights and the West Bank and the illegality of Israeli settlement activities only three weeks later.[40] This, as well as subsequently made condemnations by the EU of demolitions of Palestinian houses through the Israeli Defence Forces could not preclude Jordanian King Abdullah II to cancel his state visit to Bucharest out of protest over Dăncilă's unabated intentions.[41] Also, and more important, the rare display of unanimity in the Council and Mogherini's public remarks contributed neither to a pacification on the ground nor to a rethink of the Israeli government.

Conclusions

Four years after the adoption of the revised ENP, EU policies towards the neighbourhoods are still suffering from the same, and in some cases even worsening, constraints as before. These have negatively affected once more the extent to which the EU was capable of exerting tangible influence and engage with mounting (geo-) political complexity, as well as local stakeholders' perceptions of the EU as a credible force for good. Initiatives, such as the public consultation process on the future of the EaP or the decision to transform Morocco's Advanced Status into a Partnership for Prosperity were thus nothing more than renewed attempts to disguise the notorious absence of a strategic vision for the vast and heterogeneous space beyond EU borders and the fact that the ENP continues to be a mere muddling through exercise.

In this light, the declared goal of the European Council, formulated by the new Strategic Agenda 2019–2024, to pursue an ambitious neighbourhood policy, does not represent the much needed shot in the arm. It was Member States that, due to their prioritization of national interests and corresponding recourse to go-alone practices and veto-playing, de facto have already rendered the Agenda null and void, ensuring that also this statement, like similar ones made in the past, has a short half-life period. That the EU will 'have

---

[38] *Times of Israel*, 27 March 2019.
[39] *Euractiv*, 25 March 2019.
[40] *Haaretz*, 17 April 2019.
[41] *IsraelHayom*, 16 May 2019.

to factor in power politics and become tougher and more responsive to changing circumstances' (Lehne 2020) is a message that in recent years seems to have reached both Brussels and Member States' capitals. Whether this message will not just be heard but eventually also understood and lead to substantive policy change remains questionable. What is clear, though, given the assertiveness of other external actors and their unabated determination to penetrate the EU's neighbourhoods politically, economically and militarily to the detriment of both their and the EU's stability, is that the EU cannot afford to continue indulging in muddling through practices.

References

Anholt, R. and Sinatti, G. (2019) 'Under the Guise of Resilience: The EU Approach to Migration and Forced Displacement in Jordan and Lebanon'. *Contemporary Security Policy*, Vol. 41, No. 2, pp. 311–35.

Badarin, E. (2019) 'EU Foreign Policy Normalises Totalitarianism in the Middle East'. *Middle East Eye*, 22 March. Available at: https://www.middleeasteye.net/opinion/eu-foreign-policy-normalises-totalitarianism-middle-east. Last accessed: 5 March 2020.

Badarin, E. and Schumacher, T. (2020) 'The EU, Resilience and the Southern Neighbourhood After the Arab Uprisings'. In Cusumano, E. (ed.) *Building Resilience Across the Mediterranean* (London: Routledge), pp. 83–6.

Bargués-Pedreny, P. (2019) 'Mogherini, the Queen of Resilience Reaches the End of her Mandate'. *CIDOB Opinion*, November.

Council of the EU (2019a) Joint Press Statement Following the 5th Association Council Meeting between the EU and Georgia. 5 March. Available at: https://www.consilium.europa.eu/en/press/press-releases/2019/03/05/joint-press-statement-following-the-5th-association-council-meeting-between-the-eu-and-georgia/. Last accessed: 2 March 2020.

Council of the EU (2019b) 'Belarus: EU Prolongs Arms Embargo and Sanctions against 4 Individuals for One Year'. Press release, 25 February. Available at: https://www.consilium.europa.eu/en/press/press-releases/2019/02/25/belarus-eu-prolongs-arms-embargo-and-sanctions-against-4-individuals-for-one-year/. Last accessed: 4 March 2020.

Council of the EU (2019c) Joint Declaration by the European Union and Morocco for the Fourteenth Meeting of the Association Council. Press release, 27 June. Available at: https://www.consilium.europa.eu/en/press/press-releases/2019/06/27/joint-declaration-by-the-european-union-and-the-kingdom-of-morocco-for-the-fourteenth-meeting-of-the-association-council/. Last accessed: 9 March 2020.

Council of the EU (2019d) 'EU–Morocco: Council Adopts Sustainable Fisheries Partnership Agreement'. Press release, 4 March. Available at: https://www.consilium.europa.eu/en/press/press-releases/2019/03/04/eu-morocco-council-adopts-sustainable-fisheries-partnership-agreement/. Last accessed: 9 March 2020.

Delegation of the EU (2019) Statement by the EU at the 1246th Meeting of the OSCE Permanent Council 7 November 2019 in Response to the Co-chairs of the Minsk Group, the Personal Representative of the Chairperson-in-Office on the Conflict Dealt with by the OSCE Minsk Conference, and the Head of the High-Level Planning Group. PC.DEL/1267/19/Rev.1, 12 November. Available at: https://www.osce.org/permanent-council/438725?download=true. Last accessed: 4 March 2020.

Dobrescu, M. and Schumacher, T. (2020) 'The Politics of Flexibility: Exploring the Contested Statehood–Actorness Nexus in Georgia'. *Geopolitics*, Vol. 25, No. 2, pp. 407–27.

Dyduch, J. (2018) 'The Visegrád Group's Policy towards Israel. Common Values and Interests as a Catalyst for Cooperation'. *SWP Comment*, C 54, December.

EEAS (2017) Déclaration conjointe de Federica Mogherini et le Ministre délégué aux Affaires étrangères du Royaume de Maroc, Nasser Bourita suite à leur rencontre. Joint Statement. 7 February. Available at: file:///C:/Users/User/Downloads/eeas_-_european_external_action_service_-_declaration_conjointe_de_federica_mogherini_et_le_ministre_delegue_aux_affaires_etrangeres_du_royaume_de_maroc_nasser_bourita_suite_a_leur_rencontre_-_2017-02-07.pdf. Last accessed: 9 March 2020.

European Commission (2011) Štefan Füle. European Commissioner for Enlargement and Neighbourhood Policy. Speech on the recent events in North Africa. Speech 11/130, 28 February. Available at: https://ec.europa.eu/commission/presscorner/detail/en/SPEECH_11_130. Last accessed on 5 March 2020.

European Commission (2018) 2018 Communication on EU Enlargement Policy. COM(2018) 450 final, 17 April. Available online at: https://ec.europa.eu/neighbourhood-enlargement/sites/near/files/20180417_strategy_paper_en.pdf. Last accessed: 1 March 2020.

European Commission and HR/VP (2015) Review of the European Neighbourhood Policy. JOIN (2015) 50 final, 18 November. Available online at: http://eeas.europa.eu/archives/docs/enp/documents/2015/151118_joint-communication_review-of-the-enp_en.pdf. Last accessed: 27 February 2020.

European Commission and HR/VP (2019) Association Implementation Report on Georgia. SWD (2019) 16 6 final, 30 January. Available online at: https://eeas.europa.eu/sites/eeas/files/2019_association_implementation_report_georgia_en.pdf. Last accessed: 2 March 2020.

European Council (2019) A New Strategic Agenda for the EU 2019–2024. 20 June. Available at: https://www.consilium.europa.eu/en/eu-strategic-agenda-2019-2024/. Last accessed: 3 March 2020.

European Parliament (2017) Eastern Partnership: November 2017 Summit. P8_TA(2017)0440, 15 November. Available online at: https://www.europarl.europa.eu/doceo/document/TA-8-2017-0440_EN.pdf. Last accessed: 02 March 2020.

Furness, M., Henökl, T. and Schumacher, T. (2019) 'Crisis, Coordination and Coherence: European Decision-Making and the 2015 European Neighbourhood Policy Review'. *European Foreign Affairs Review*, Vol. 24, No. 4, pp. 447–68.

Gstöhl, S. (2019) *The European Neighbourhood Policy in a Comparative Perspective* (London: Routledge).

Günay, C. and Sommavilla, F. (2019) 'Tunisia's Democratization at Risk'. *Mediterranean Politics*. https://doi.org/10.1080/13629395.2019.1631980

Hearst, D. (2019) 'Sisi's Useful Idiots: How Europe Endorses Egypt's Tyrant Leader'. *Middle East Eye*, 21 February. Available at: https://www.middleeasteye.net/opinion/sisis-useful-idiots-how-europe-endorses-egypts-tyrant-leader. Last accessed: 9 March 2019.

Howorth, J. (2016) '"Stability on the Borders": The Ukraine Crisis and the EU's Constrained Policy towards the Eastern Neighbourhood'. *JCMS*, Vol. 55, No. 1, pp. 121–36.

Human Right Watch (2020) 'Georgia. Events of 2019'. Available at: https://www.hrw.org/world-report/2020/country-chapters/georgia#5b498e. Last accessed: 2 March 2020.

Juncos, A. and Whitman, R. (2015) 'Europe as a Regional Actor: Neighbourhood Lost?' *JCMS*, Vol. 53 Annual Review, pp. 200–15.

Lacher, W. (2019) 'International Schemes. Libyan Realities'. *SWP Comment*, No. 45, November.

Lavrelashvili, T. (2016) 'Brexit: Five Ways It Might Affect the Eastern Partnership Countries'. *Wilfried Martens Centre for European Studies,* Blog, 12 July. Available at: https://www.martenscentre.eu/blog/brexit-five-ways-it-might-affect-eastern-partnership-countries. Last accessed: 27 February 2020.

Leigh, M. (2019) 'A View from the Policy Community: A New Strategic Narrative for Europe?' *European Security*, Vol. 28, No. 3, pp. 382–91.

Mezran, K. and Varvelli, A. (eds) (2017) *Foreign Actors in Libya's Crisis* (Milan: Atlantic Council and ISPI).

Pomorska, K. and Noutcheva, G. (2017) 'Europe as a Regional Actor: Waning Influence in an Unstable and Authoritarian Neighbourhood'. *JCMS*, Vol. 55, Annual Review, pp. 165–76.

Rudloff, B. and Werenfels, I. (2018) 'EU–Tunisia DCFTA: Good Intentions Not Enough'. *SWP Comment*, No. 49, November.

Schumacher, T., Marchetti, A. and Demmelhuber, T. (2018) *The Routledge Handbook on the European Neighbourhood Policy* (London: Routledge).

The Economist (2014) 'Europe's Ring of Fire', 20 September.

Whitman, R. and Juncos, A.E. (2013) 'Stasis in Status: Relations with the Wider Europe'. *JCMS*, Vol. 51 Annual Review, pp. 155–67.

Whitman, R. and Juncos, A.E. (2014) 'Challenging Events, Diminishing Influence? Relations with the Wider Europe'. *JCMS*, Vol. 52 Annual Review, pp. 157–69.

Wolzcuk, K. (2017) 'Perceptions of, and Attitudes towards, the Eastern Partnership amongst the Partner Countries' Political Elites'. *Eastern Partnership Review*, No. 11, December.

JCMS 2020 Volume 58. Annual Review. pp. 202–212   DOI: 10.1111/jcms.13120

Index

Note: Italicised page references indicate information contained in tables.